Centralia

A modern fable

by

Michael Saunders

ISBN 978-0-6151-6744-2

September 2007

For Bill Foy, Howard Shapiro and in Memory of Kent Brown

Chapter One

Klara woke up. How hot it was in her room! It was, indeed, very hot. She thought it might be a hundred degrees or more. It was so hot, it made her feel sick at her stomach. The window shades were up so that all the light came in. The light was blinding, just blinding! It was the blistering glare of summer afternoon. It was too much for her. She could barely see a thing in the frightful glare. She could see enough to tell the windows were all closed. There was no air conditioning on; there couldn't be. Why is it so hot?, she asked herself. I can't breathe in this heat, she thought. All she could do was lie there, pant, try to shield her eyes and not notice how sick she felt.

She called out for her daughter: "Doris!" she cried. "Doris!" she called again. It was all she could do to raise her voice even a bit. She knew Doris was there, knew her daughter hadn't left her. She could hear the TV. Doris and her shows; if she was in the house, the TV was on, that was for sure and certain. She never went off and left it turned on, so she must be there. But where, and why was it so hot?

Klara could barely move, she was so weak. The heat made her weak. She felt sick from it, and she had a headache, one of the bad ones, it was going to be, if she stayed awake long enough. Pray to go back to sleep, only it isn't really sleep, not really rest, is it? Oblivion, *Ohnmächtigkeit*.

It was so hard to do anything. Even moving just a little in the bed to get a bit more comfortable, even that was difficult, painful, even that made her scared to try. Even that made her think, *I suppose I'm going to die now; I'll try this and not be able to do it, and then I'll die; ja, ich wollte, ich könnte einfach sterben.* And then Doris would come in, eventually, and find her there, dead, and maybe she would cry a while, but honestly, finally, feel relieved.

Klara had to depend on Doris for everything, and the slightest thing she needed, the smallest want, took so much to communicate, took so much to accomplish, that she was constantly asking herself, How can I do this? Why is everything so difficult? Klara asked herself, How long have I been this way? How long has it been since I could wipe my own bottom? *Seit wie lange habe ich mein eigenes Arschloch nicht finden können, verdammtnochmal!** She wasn't sure; she couldn't remember how long she'd been lying flat on her back in her bed, unable to do much at all except call for help. Like with papa, she said to herself, when I came home, in 'twenty-nine; only he couldn't speak; at least I can talk.

One thing was for sure: Klara was not crazy. Her mind was clear. She understood what was happening to her. This made the whole business that much more horrible, of course. She might not remember how long it had been since she could get about on her own, but she could tell, from day to day, how parts of her were failing. She felt her body slowly disintegrating. One day she could move her right leg, the next day she couldn't. Things didn't fall apart in any particularly neat order, either, which was somehow annoying. It seemed a shabby way to have this happen: Why not

---

* "How long has it been since I've been able to find my own asshole?"

have both legs go at the same time, why would one eye not open the same way as the other, why did it hurt here on one shoulder and not on the same place on the other shoulder? A neater disintegration would have, perhaps, been easier to bear, but this sloppiness, this stealthy eruption all over the place, here and there, it was really so entirely unnecessary. *Das ist ja ganz gemein, dieses Todwerden*[†] she thought to herself.

She was, indeed, dying; of cancer, of old age, take your pick. Awful business, and after spending so much time taking care of other people as they had died; what a perverse way for things to end up. And if it weren't enough that she could see her disintegration happening, if it weren't clear to her from the agonies she endured every day in full consciousness, or at least in the fullness of the consciousness left to her at the end of each day's falling apart, she could take a hint from what she heard Doris saying: talking on the phone to her brother Walter, arguing with him constantly over the fact that there he sat in San Diego and hadn't bothered to come home since she couldn't remember when while Doris sat there, taking care of everything by herself, with no help from anyone, and how Doris was at the point where she saw no alternative but to call the Hospice in Deerfield Beach and get some help dealing with mama, because goodness only knew how much longer it would be, but no matter how long it would take, and it could be weeks, months, even, as sick as mama was, but no matter what, when it got down to the end it wasn't going to be pretty, and Doris wasn't going to face that by herself, it just wasn't fair.

[†] "This business of dying is so vulgar."

You're right it's not fair, thought Klara to herself, and that's the one thing that ties everything together: at every turn, at every major juncture, at every point where you stop and take a breath, all you can conclude is, This just isn't fair. Jan, God rest his soul, and then mama and then papa and Mark and William, *ach Gott hüte sie!*†, good god in heaven, and how many more she couldn't remember, and now she was at the end of it herself, why couldn't she just go pop? Like a lightbulb, just go out all of a sudden, and then be taken away and that would be that? What sort of god would allow this? *Qwatsch*, that's what they say in German, perfect word for it, *lauter Qwatsch!*††

Oh, so many German words today, today I'm full of German, thought Klara, I promised mama I'd never say another German word, not after all that business with the Nazis, so terrible, she thought, what a terrible shame, what an evil thing, so much evil, poor Jan, she thought, poor Jan, *der war der einziger Mann den ich wahrlich liebte, mein ganzes Leben lang, der einzige.** And mama never knew she had promised not to use German ever again, but she knew it would have been what her mama would have wanted, she would have been so ashamed of what they did, unspeakable, those dreadful things, said Klara, such horror. *Wieso bin ich heute wieder deutsch geworden?***

As Klara's body fell apart, as it simply stopped working, she became more aware of how much more intensely active her mind

---

† "May God protect them!"

†† "Balderdash....pure balderdash!"

* "He was the only man I really ever loved, my whole life, the only one."

** "How is it that I've become German again today?"

became. As the world outside was growing smaller, the world inside was getting much, much bigger. What a surprising development, as if the death of her body was forcing her inner self to grow by great leaps. A growing spurt at ninety-seven, she thought, how ridiculous! *Das is ja gar nicht konzequent, mit sieben-und-neunzig im Sterbebett mit diesem komischen Wiederwachsen anzufangen[†]*, she thought.

The enlargement of her inner life came as a result of a confluence between her memories and her experience of present moments. She found that her experience of the present and the past had begun to intermingle. This made everything seem much larger, everything about her world inside: it all seemed much busier, much fuller than she could remember, and when for brief moments she found herself thinking objectively about the fact that she was trying to remember how she had remembered things at earlier stages of her life, she found the convolutions somewhat dizzying, like finding oneself suddenly thrown onto a busy street by some odd bit of magic. Sometimes she would think about the past as past, and that was fairly normal; other times she would imagine sitting and talking with mama or Jan or papa, and it would be as if it were happening now, until she would awake from the seeming and know what she had just seen and heard could not have been real, even though everything was clear, solid, as true as anything else had seemed. She found this confusion annoying. It was as if someone were playing a trick on her, a joke, a practical joke. What makes a joke practical?, she asked.

[†] "It's not at all dignified, to begin again at ninety-seven with this comical resumption of growth."

What an odd thing that was, to be here in this hot room where nothing was ever happening, except that she was always lying there staring at the walls or out the window, because she wouldn't have the TV in there with her, she could but she wouldn't, to be here and then to see someone, Mark or papa or, once in a long long while it would be Jan, yes it would be he and they would be together and she would be talking with him and it would be just as it had been in Berlin, all that time ago, and she would think nothing about it until she realized she was thinking about the past, she was seeing the past as if it were right now, but it wasn't, it was just a memory, just seemed more real than most memories, but how real, as real as the green of the wall or the trees through the window, the palmettos waving in the wind. She didn't tell Doris that, if she could avoid it, didn't say any more than she had to about seeing people from the past, she tried to keep that sort of thing to herself, because she didn't want Doris to think she was losing her mind. Dying she could think, but crazy, no.

Her body's weakness preyed upon her heavily. Sometimes it took so much to overcome the weakness, the failure of her arms and legs, her voice, her bowels, her eyes, that she doubted sometimes whether all this was really happening to her. Did she really struggle for what seemed like hours just to move a pillow half as much as she wanted so her neck wouldn't hurt? Could it possibly take that long, take that much effort, just to nudge a bed pillow no more than an inch or so? Did she really hurt as much as she seemed to? Could the pains in her abdomen, the trembling, could that be real? How could it be that seeing Jan, tall, handsome, dear Jan, was false, and the pain in her gut was not? Reality is pain, she thought. The secret of life. *Das lohnt sich nicht, zu lernen.*[†]

It would have been a wonder to Klara if she could have known how tough she really was. The cancer had spread so far throughout her body that there was barely a part of her that hadn't been attacked by it. It was a very greedy cancer: how furious it was when it found places in her it couldn't get to! If the pain it caused her had been visited suddenly on a person half her age, a fifth her age, a strong, well-fed young person, that person would have quickly died of shock; that person would have burned up on the very outer edges of her pain, never having gotten to the core of the bright, shrieking demon that was her constant companion. She bore it because her body simply wouldn't give up. Her life had prepared her for it, and she met it without knowing how well.

The doctors were stingy with pain medicine, fearful she would become addicted. They warned of the prospect of her becoming drug-dependent, and Doris asked them, What difference does it make, can't you see she's dying? Who cares if she gets hooked on the stuff? But Klara had been mortified at the prospect of being given morphine. She had known of people who were addicts, in her youth she had seen such people, and now that she was offered drugs to kill the pain, she felt ashamed, implicated in something common, something low, so she readily acquiesced as the wise doctors told her she would be better with less medicine.

She could not see how tiny she was against the bigness of her fading from life, and she could not convey the great fullness, the overwhelming busyness of her dying, to anyone. Not to Doris, cer-

---

[†] "That isn't worth learning."

tainly. Klara could tell how much it hurt Doris to have to be the one to sit there with her, day after day, managing the awful, dirty business of keeping her mother's old, unlovely body clean and ready for each new day's creeping decay. She could tell that Doris knew she was suffering, and she knew her daughter felt helpless to do much except wait with her.

"Doris!" Klara called out again. "Doris!" She could hear the TV blaring in the background. She supposed Doris was probably asleep on the couch. Klara could barely think, it was so hot. If she could only pull the window shades down, that would help. Why were they all up? Whose idea was that? She tried closing her eyes. Maybe that would help. She closed her eyes, but she could still see light through the illuminated red of her eyelids. She needed it to be dark. She felt a little perspiration on her face—her lip, her forehead, her neck—and she felt thirsty, parched. The nausea from the heat was still there, but she was beginning to feel a chill, too. How odd, she thought. I'm hot and chilled at the same time. How very odd all this is, she thought. *Merkwürdig.*

Klara woke up again, not knowing she'd ever fallen asleep. The room was dark now, and it was cooler, much cooler. The bed felt as if it had been changed, but how could it have been changed without her having noticed that? How had Doris managed to change the sheets without her realizing it? The bed felt different, too. It seemed too small somehow. There was no TV noise in the background, but there were other sounds, ones she didn't recognize. Gradually she began to hear voices, and she opened her eyes a little, strained to focus. There was something very different about everything.

She was not in pain, for one thing. She felt as if her body had been laundered, somehow, on the inside. It was amazing to consider, but she was no longer in pain. Astonishing! Everything was different now. She was no longer thirsty, and she no longer felt weak, though she wasn't really aware of being able to move all that well, either. But the difference was that it didn't bother her now, she was quite comfortable, couldn't remember when she'd been this comfortable, in fact. Perhaps she was wrong, perhaps she wasn't dying, after all? When had she felt this good? What a relief it was! How good it felt, just from no longer hurting! How good it felt!

Klara found herself feeling a kind of giddiness that was new to her. She would try to look at something across the room, do something as simple as look about her to see who was in the room, and find that no matter how hard she tried, she couldn't see all that clearly who was in the room with her. Sometimes it appeared there was more than one person there, but she couldn't see clearly who it was. As she considered this fact, it occurred to her that it really didn't bother her all that much that she couldn't tell who she was looking at. So what if there was someone new in the room? So what if she couldn't see their faces? She felt a kind of delight in this new-found calm, this newly acquired state of grace with the uncertainty of things, and since, thank God, there was no more pain, all in the world she had to do was lie there in her bed and feel good. What a delightful turn of events, and how silly of her to think she was sick, was dying, for heaven's sake!

Klara dreamt about Jan, and she could see him, young and blond and handsome. She saw him as she had first seen him, coming into the Konditorei in the Friedrichstraße, the one she went to when she had a few coins in her pocket and could treat herself to *ein Kännchen Kaffee und ein Stück Linzertorte*. Klara remembered that day, when Jan came into the shop, the ladies behind the counter stopped what they were doing to look. He was so handsome, everyone stopped what they were doing and looked at him a minute or so. He seemed a bit shy, as if he were used to being stared at, as if he were uncomfortable with the fact that people were staring at him. He wore a grey suit that day, a hat with a broad brim, and when he took it off, his hair was perfectly in place, and Klara noticed that one detail almost as quickly as she noticed how handsome he was, with his blue, blue eyes and his pale skin. He was almost too beautiful to be a man, she thought.

And he had looked right at her and smiled slightly, bowing as he went to the counter and ordered a coffee, just a cup, which he sat and drank, at a small table across the other side of the sweetshop. And Klara had watched him, while pretending to eat her Linzertorte and reading her book, and he had just sat there looking out the window, politely minding his own business and not speaking to anyone. Both of them were alone. They were the only two clients in the sweetshop. Because she was alone, and because he was the only other person in the shop, and because he was so handsome, Klara studied him. He minded his own business, and gave the appearance of not noticing he was being studied. He took out a little book, a journal of some kind, wrote a few words in it, studied what he had written, then wrote a little more, carefully picking up his coffee cup and drinking without making sipping sounds, and sitting up very erect. His sitting posture seemed formal to Klara; it seemed to require more effort than normal sitting, and that made Klara notice her own posture which, by comparison with his, was very poor and probably unhealthy. She thought to herself, He's an aristocrat, he sits like someone who has been taught how to sit, or maybe he's a teacher, but no, his clothes are too expensive. Yes, he's an aristo-

crat, maybe a civil servant, a bureaucrat? But no, probably not the
government, he's too young, isn't he, and too good-looking? An
aristocrat *sans métier*, then? And she noticed that he was even more
handsome than she had first thought. The more she looked at him,
in profile, the more handsome he became, and she thought again
that he didn't quite look like most men, that he was almost beautiful, not handsome but actually beautiful, and she wondered to herself if that caused him trouble, for he looked like someone whose
good looks would have done just that, brought him grief, not gifts
and rewards, but grief.

■■■

When he finished drinking his coffee he paid his bill and then
he left. On his way out, he looked at Klara again and smiled. She
remembered looking up at him as he was leaving. She saw again
how handsome he was, and she felt a flutter, a blush, as she found
herself caught at looking at him. Then he was gone.

So their first meeting was hardly a meeting at all. Jan later said
it didn't count, the day in the sweetshop, because they never really
had a conversation. Klara could never get him to admit it outright,
but she was sure he had no recollection of having seen her. She
clearly recalled seeing him, however, and even now, on her
deathbed, she could see him as she'd seen him then, sixty years or
so earlier. Klara told Jan it did count, the first sighting, if not a
meeting then it was a sighting, because it was when she fell in love
with him. Jan said that was absurd, that it was impossible for her to
fall in love with him under the circumstances, since she had no idea
what sort of person he was, only that he was about this tall and wore
a grey suit that day and had made himself relatively presentable
before putting the grey suit on. Klara listened when he said such
things and said there was always a betrayal of his vanity in the in-

clusion of these totally unnecessary, self-deprecating remarks about what his appearance had been like on such-and-such an occasion, and it was part of what made her fall in love with him, the fact, which she claimed to have discerned at the very first meeting--at least, at the meeting which she counted as being first—that he was the sort of man who dressed and presented himself in the most fastidious way and who, come the end of the world complete with all four Horsemen, trumpets blaring and mountains crumbling and oceans boiling, would have nonetheless dressed just as fastidiously and would have managed to work into the conversation, as the heavenly host were dividing the good from the bad, some offhand remark about how ragged and impoverished he looked when, in fact, he looked as if he had just stepped out of a movie, a musical where everyone is young, sings like an angel and dances like Fred Astaire.

It was later at that they actually exchanged words. There was an exhibition of art by several artists working in the woodcut medium at the Oberstdorfer Gallerie, and Klara was interested in virtually all the artists being represented: Emil Nolde, Karl Schmitt-Rottluf, Käthe Kollwitz, how could she not be interested? The exhibition was called "Einfahrt in die Neue Kunst," and everyone in Berlin was talking about it.

Klara had come to Berlin in 1924 to study art history and to improve her German. Born Klara Westover in Savannah, Georgia, she was encouraged to take up art historical studies by her parents. Her father, Hans-Dietrich Westhofer, had emigrated from Germany to the United States in the 1890s with his wife, Elisabeth, and their son Rolf. Once settled in the United States, Hans-Dietrich and his wife followed relatives who had emigrated earlier, moving to Savannah, where there was a well-established settlement of Austrian immigrants. Away from the pressures of immigrant conflicts in New York and Chicago, the Westhofers found in the South a more relaxed attitude towards the exoticism of their names and accents. Working diligently to become assimilated into their new country's culture, the little family found that, aside from the utterly brutal summer, the marshland of coastal Georgia offered them a welcoming, odd new home. Hans-Dietrich's only accommodation to the new country was to drop the "Dietrich" change his first name to John and anglicize his last name, so that he became John Westover.

Westover was an accomplished musician: he played the piano, the violin, the cello and the organ with great distinction. He also had great talent at writing choral arrangements. His musical gifts enabled him to support the family by giving lessons and, eventually, by becoming a church organist, very much in demand throughout Savannah. Such were his gifts that churches fought over him, sending him bribes of baked goods and flowers, and sending spies to the other churches to find out what he was being paid so that a better offer could be made. John thus found a life in his new home made difficult principally by the necessity of continually resisting the various advances made by the various vestries in the area. His organ playing was powerful and accomplished, and he was a handsome man, tall and blonde, with blue eyes that startled with their beauty and clarity. Yes, thought Klara, Jan and papa were so much like each other, I wonder if I would have thought the same thing if I had ever seen them side by side? He also had a perfect baritone singing voice, and so was the cause of many a lingering glance among the ladies of Savannah.

Klara was the first person in the Westover family to be born a real, bona fide American, a fact of which the Westovers were very proud. She resembled her mother Elisabeth, a small, delicate woman with light brown hair and dark brown eyes. Klara was born with blonde hair, but as she grew older, her hair darkened, so that by the time she became a young woman people often mistook her mother for her older sister. As Elisabeth was only twenty when she gave birth to Klara, it was not unreasonable that people mistook them for sisters. Elisabeth was a housewife, managing well the home that John was able to provide for with his musical talents. Elisabeth took pride in her children, working to strike a balance between showing her affection to them (she loved them fiercely) and urging them to become strong and independent. In Klara she found a girl of limited artistic talents but considerable intellectual ones, and so Elisabeth resolved to turn her daughter into a great scholar, hoping she would eventually become a university professor.

In every particular regarding their children, John and Elisabeth researched diligently, discreetly, and thoughtfully to find and exploit the resources they believed would produce the best upbringing. As parents they were decidedly single-minded in working to make the wisest judgments they could to shape their children into remarkable, fully developed people. Working together in a singularly effective partnership, John and Elisabeth lived their lives around helping their children to grow up well. The son, Rolf, showed early promise as a musician, and so was given everything he needed to develop his gift. He eventually became a concert violinist, and made a career of playing for the major symphony orchestras in the country.

The Westovers, unlike many families of their day, made no distinction between the care of their older son and their younger daughter. They were extraordinary in the way they never failed to give as much care and attention to one child as to the other. As a result, Klara advanced through her primary school education with great distinction. She spoke English with a slight Southern accent, and practiced her German at home with mother and father and brother. As Elisabeth was an educated woman herself, she also saw to it that she schooled her children in French.

Early on in life, Klara showed some talent for drawing, but relatively little interest in playing musical instruments. Undaunted by her lack of interest in music, her parents encouraged her to develop her considerable gifts in reading and writing. She performed so well in primary school that it was suggested that she might skip the fifth grade. Elisabeth considered the suggestion, and finally decided that it would be best to allow the girl to follow the children of her own age at least until the sixth grade, so as to assure that Klara would develop in a way that balanced the social and the intellectual. In their private moments the Westovers confessed to each other that they were both agnostic, a fact that they never shared with their children, thinking it was enough that they chose to raise them as Methodists.

Upon Klara's finishing the sixth grade, it was decided she would be placed in a boarding school for girls. This was a difficult decision for the Westovers, as they loved their daughter as dearly as they loved anything or anyone in the world. They feared, however, that if she were left in the public school system to complete her education, because she was a girl she would be left stunted by a system that clearly meant only to prepare women for housework and child-rearing. Though Elisabeth had no regrets about being a housewife herself, she was determined that her daughter would at least be given the resources to choose what Elisabeth herself called a "real career, as good as any man's."

Because Elisabeth had been raised to be independent and curious about the world, she greeted the prospect of going to boarding school as a new adventure. She was sent to Lindhurst Academy for Ladies in Richmond, Virginia, where she received an excellent education. At Lindhurst it became clear that Klara was no painter, but that she did have considerable talents at writing and debating. As she approached graduation, she thought over what she thought should be the direction of her adult life, and she decided that a career as an art historian, possibly as a restorer of old art or perhaps as an art-archeologist, would be the right direction for her. Happy with her decision, Klara's parents determined that the perfect thing for her was to embark on a tour of the great cities Europe to continue her studies at some of the continent's great academies and museums, the hope being that she would find her niche in the world of art. As John was very successful with his work as church organist and choral director, the family was blessed with plenty of money, and the Westovers could think of no better use to put it to than making sure that Rolf and Klara were afforded every opportunity available to study and work wherever it seemed best for them. Klara thus spent a year traveling alone to London, Paris, and finally Berlin to study and to observe. In this way Klara was able to see much more of the world than most young American ladies of far greater means would have imagined for themselves.

Klara was, as I have said, a small, delicate woman, much like her mother. She had an exquisite complexion, a round face and large brown eyes. She was beautiful in the way that was fashionable in the 'twenties. Her mother taught her the secret of appearing to be a woman of the world, and it was simply this: to dress simply, but with elegance, and to avoid excessive ornamentation in her appearance. The result of her mother's counseling on appearance was that, as a young woman, Klara was generally thought to be wealthier and older than she was. She was the kind of girl whose intelligence shone through in her face in a way that enhanced her beauty. Nothing about her appearance gave the impression of an ingénue from the provinces.

Klara became accustomed to traveling with a her parents while she was a girl. This came about when her father was asked to teach or to play in a city other than Savannah. Her habituation to train travel exposed her to contact with all sorts of people, as her parents insisted on traveling second class, even though they could have afforded to travel more expensively. This meant that Klara was given the opportunity to meet and to talk with people from all over, an opportunity she met with eagerness and charm. She could hold her own in conversation with adults, and she could endure an encounter with a big-city snob or grandee without experiencing the slightest anxiety or discomfort. In general she did not think much of her sex. Her education had left her chiefly to wonder why women were so complicit in their own subjugation. She had yet to meet a man who could intimidate her. She knew how to use a shotgun for she was, after all, a Southerner.

Klara's powers of observation were very keen, so she took in the world opened to her by her travels with great understanding. Having spent the early years of her womanhood at a boarding school, she was not used to being around boys other than her brother and father, but her family's care in raising her had been such that she was completely sure of herself, without being arrogant, and thus she was able, by the time she set out on her *Wandungsjahre*, to move among strangers in public without fear or awkwardness. Observing people in public, it became clear to her that there was a whole world of adventure in the dance that was done between men and women in courtship. She was curious about that world, and she looked forward to learning her way around it.

Inquiries were made for Klara such that she was able to obtain an internship with the office of the Curator of Paintings at the Kieffer-Reinhardt Stiftung in Berlin. The internship actually carried with it a small stipend, so that she was able to feel that she was actually entering the fullness of professional life when she took up her work there. She worked three days a week helping to catalog old documents dealing with the acquisition of properties at the museum, and there she met other interns, many of whom were artists in their own right. The other interns were all native Germans, and they regarded her with a certain disdain at first. When it became clear that her German was good and that she was friendly, well-read, and very down-to-earth, her fellows warmed up to her, gradually showing their affection her "Klari," transforming the final "a" of her name into an "I" in a demonstration of familiarity. Klara preferred her name to be left unchanged, but she was happy enough with the sign of affection that she never let on it bothered her a bit to be so addressed.

Though her German was very good when she came to Berlin, Klara quickly found that the German her parents spoke at home was old-fashioned and provincial. In fact, her parents' German bore very little similarity to the dialect spoken by Berliners. Berlin was a huge, modern city, worldly and fast-moving, pressed full of all manner of cultural influences and expressions, and the local dialect reflected this. Berlin German was comparable to Brooklyn English in its most inflected form, except perhaps that Berlin German was even more far-removed from the standard language than any American dialect is from standard speech. Little by little, Klara began to acquire the Berlin accent, under the tutelage of her young German friends, and her gift for languages made it possible for her to advance so quickly in her development that soon her friends were forgetting to make any accommodations at all for the fact that she was a "foreigner." In effect, she was becoming a Berliner.

It was thus after spending the morning cataloging documents concerning a recent acquisition of a set of sketches by Titian that Klara came to be in the Konditorei Messner in the Friedrichstraße one afternoon. This was the day she first saw Jan, born Jan Mieslewski, in Krakow. Klara wondered how many times in her life she had remembered that first sighting and had thought again how many questions she had asked herself about the sort of person he must be. There were so many beautiful—that was, indeed, the word she had to use, as handsome really didn't quite suit—so many beautiful young, elegant men in Berlin, many of them having come from somewhere else to make a career in the great city. With such an abundance of elegant specimens of the male sex milling about, the occasion of seeing yet another one was hardly worth noting. When she first saw him, however, Klara noted not only that Jan was as beautiful a young man as she had seen, but that he had an aura about him that made him stand apart from the crowd. Klara wondered what he did for a living. She remembered thinking, in the sweetshop, I wonder what sort of person he is? As beautiful as he was, could he be a gigolo? Wasn't it silly to have thought that? There were so many of them slinking about the city, one had to be careful. Was he from a wealthy family? She thought not, she remembered thinking. Rich young men, she thought, probably don't go around by themselves and stop into sweetshops for a cup of coffee. A rich young man would go to a proper café for his coffee, and he would probably sit outside, and he would almost certainly meet someone he knew and spend a leisurely bit of time with them. Perhaps the beautiful young blond man was a confidence man, though he didn't give the impression of being that sort, either—he wasn't slick-looking, and he didn't look hungry, ready to ingratiate himself, the way such men tended to look. He actually had a kind of vacant look, a sort of unknowing innocence. Maybe, then, he was a scholar? Or someone who had just run away from home or from someone, she thought. She found, in any case, that it was difficult to figure out just what the handsome young man's story was, and the mere fact that, based on the scant evidence she had from her first sighting, she wasn't at all sure what sort of person he really was. It did not escape her notice, however, that this tall, very blond, very handsome young man made her think about her father, also blond and tall and handsome.

She did not figure out the young man's story, for he left the sweetshop before it occurred to her to simply say hello to him and get him to reveal something about himself. She did think, it would be nice to meet such a fellow, assuming that his well-wrought exterior wasn't hiding something equally nasty inside. And that was that.

But things, of course, didn't end there, did they? No, thank goodness, no. A week or so later Klara went with a few friends to the exhibition "Die Neue Kunst" at the Oberstdorfer Gallerie. How much a part of life it was in Berlin then to find a room full of shocking, new art and extraordinary people talking about ideas! It was a time when people rioted over what they saw at the theatre, when men got into fights over what someone had done on a stage, over what someone had hung on a wall. On this particular evening, the primary subject of conversation was how what was being called the new Expressionism was an attack on the utopian fantasies of the earlier generation of modern artists. Down with the sentimentalists!, everyone was saying, *lauter Schwärmerei!*, hey were all saying, like a gaggle of magpies, really, very comical, looking back on it! *Give us an art that shows the truth!* Oh! My goodness, how naïve everyone was, with their slogans and their foot-stamping and their fists! How full of sincerity they all were, how ridiculous and wonderful, how daring. Is it possible to be that daring, still, or is it impossible to be brave now that everything is allowed? The gallery was full of the buzz and hum of people witnessing what seemed to them to be a rebirthing of art, how exciting it was to be there!

Klara found herself not engaging in much talk in this charged environment, even though her perspective as an outsider was of some interest to her companions. Moving from group to group, Klara found herself a bit bored by the discussions that all seemed to center not on what was presented on the canvases but what was implied by them outside the realm of art. So it was not only a delightful surprise but also a real relief when Klara saw the beautiful young man whom she had seen in the Konditorei.

As it was a Friday evening, people were elegantly dressed, and the young man stood out among them. For a second time, then, Klara noticed how the young man stood out in his surroundings.

Klara watched him as she moved about the gallery, being dragged here and there by her friends, who noticed that she was distracted. She found herself watching the young man as her friends urged her to look at the art. She determined that he was somehow well-placed here, but she couldn't figure out what he was actually doing at the gallery. At first it seemed to her that he might be somehow connected to the gallery; perhaps he was an art dealer who worked for the gallery and who was somehow involved with mounting the exhibition. He moved about the place with ease, speaking now and then with various people in the gathering. The people he spoke with looked very wealthy; they looked like buyers, perhaps customers of his, and he spoke with them at length, giving the impression he was familiar and comfortable with them.

Klara listened as carefully as she could through the din of the crowd for a sample of his voice: it was a pleasant man's voice, not deep, not high, thank goodness, not shrill or harsh, rather soft, and overall, an attractive man's voice, the kind of voice that Klara would enjoy hearing in conversation. He spoke German with an accent, but she couldn't place it; maybe it was Russian, she thought, definitely not English or French. He also spoke other languages, too: she caught him speaking rapidly in something that sounded Slavic, and she heard a few French and English words here and there. His English was spoken with the accent of a European, and she concluded that he might be either from Scandinavia or from one of the eastern countries. She was certain, however, that he was not German.

Klara was fascinated by this young man; he had fallen twice into her line of vision, and she thought that must mean something. She decided she had to meet him, to learn more about him. She

went up to him, when she found him alone for a moment, and introduced herself, extending her hand to the astonished young man:

"Hello, I'm Klara Westover," she said in German.

Jan looked at her hand a moment, blushed and took it, bowing
in the German manner and almost, but not quite, touching his lips to
the extended hand. "I am Jan Mieslewski," he answered. Standing
next to him now, listening to him and watching him face-to-face,
Klara was all but certain he was Polish. She looked intently at him,
noticing how handsome he was. His skin was the most beautiful
skin she had ever seen.

"I've been trying to figure out what your role here is," said
Klara.

Again astonished, blushing and obviously uncomfortable with
such a direct statement, Jan looked at her with open astonishment
and stammered, "My role? I don't know what you mean, I'm afraid,
mademoiselle."

"What brings you to the exhibition, then?" asked Klara. She
was aware that the young man was all but thunderstruck by her di-
rectness. It seemed to immobilize him. She felt worldly, knowing
that she had reduced a handsome young man to stuttering, herself a
girl from the tropics.

Jan answered, "I am here to buy some things, if I see something
that I like. And you?" He seemed to be looking for a way to escape
the conversation without seeming rude.

"Oh, some friends brought me here," Klara said. "We're"—and
here she thought for the right word, hoping not to give herself away
as what she was, which was little more than a file clerk—"*attached*
to the Kieffer-Reinhardt Stiftung, so naturally we knew about the

exhibition. There is so much interesting new work to see in Berlin, it's very exciting," she said, looking about the room.

Jan seemed to recognize something in the last statement. He smiled and asked, "So, you are not from Berlin?"

Klara looked up at him—he was such a great deal taller than she, the difference in their heights was comical. As she looked up at him, it occurred to her that someone looking at the two of them together might think she was a normal-sized person looking up at a monument. She was also aware that there was a hint of irony in his voice—of course, it was obvious she wasn't from Berlin. So then, he was having a bit of fun at her expense. She decided to answer by assuming an air of worldly self-confidence, as if it were common for her to have to correct someone's assumption that she was a native Berliner. She sucked in her cheeks a bit and answered: "No, actually, I'm not from here. I'm from America."

Jan smiled at her response. "You German is excellent, mademoiselle," he said. "You are enjoying your stay in Berlin?"

"Thank you, Herr Mieslewski. *Your* German is also very good," said Klara, noticing Jan's being taken aback by her comment. "I think I could easily stay in Berlin forever," she said. "That is, assuming I can find a permanent position here." She blushed instantly at having given away the insignificance of her *attachment* to the Kieffer-Reinhardt Stiftung.

"You aren't here with family or a chaperone, then?" asked Jan.

Klara bristled at the image implied by Herr Mieslewski's question. No doubt he saw her as a tourist, one of the hordes that had come to gawk at all the 'culture,' as her own country was so utterly bereft of anything resembling it. "No, I'm alone," said Klara. "I work at the Kieffer-Reinhardt Stiftung, and I am enrolled in art history courses at the Freie Universität," she said. Then, realizing she had no reason to try to impress this young man, she recovered her composure a bit, resolved to stop trying so hard. She said: "I am a cataloguist, handling documents relating to acquisitions for the Stiftung. And I am studying art history, in the hope that I shall gain a position as an art historian."

Her account of herself did what it needed to do: it told Jan that she was not a tourist, and that she had serious aspirations of having a career. Hearing this, he changed his tone with her. He seemed no longer interested in extricating himself from talking with her. He seemed, as far as she could tell, genuinely interested in having an honest conversation. He said, "You must come with interesting credentials, a foreigner, if you will forgive me, securing a position at the Kieffer-Reinhardt. It's hard to find a place there for a German. I'm impressed."

Hearing him say the word *impressed*, Klara felt ashamed of herself for hehaving like a *Streber*, a grasping social climber. She felt herself chastised, but did her best to make use of the experience by simply being herself, without affectation.

"It's only an internship," she said. "It runs out in another year."

"And then you will go back to America?" asked Jan.

"I don't know," said Klara. "My parents sent me here to find out if I could cultivate a career." Immediately Klara regretted having mentioned her parents: it made her sound like a schoolgirl. She blushed at the thought of appearing callow to this fellow. She tried to move past her embarrassment. She continued: "I think they would like to see me find my place in life, and if that means remaining in Europe, they wouldn't be opposed."

"But is it not better for you to go back to America?" asked Jan.

"My family came from Germany and ended up in Savannah, in Georgia," said Klara. "If I go back to Savannah, I might get married and have a family, but I could hardly expect to have a career."

"Is that not the right thing for a young woman to do?" asked Jan.

"Is there only one right thing for a young woman to do?" asked Klara.

"Ah," said Jan. "You are a modern woman."

"Yes," said Klara, "I am. That is what I was raised to be, and that is what I have become."

"That is very good," said Jan.

Klara asked, "So you said you're here to buy something, if you see the right piece?"

"Yes," said Jan. "It's at this kind of exhibition that you see the sort of thing, sometimes, that sparks some interest."

"So, then, are you buying to sell, or are you a collector?" asked Klara.

"I have a modest collection," said Jan.

Klara believed she had misjudged Jan. It occurred to her that she might tell him she had suspected he was a gigolo, but then she thought she would simply look foolish. So, he was a rich Polish art collector. How interesting, she thought. She asked, "so have you found anything you find worthy of your collection?"

"I came here to see the works by Käthe Kollwitz," said Jan. "But ever since I arrived I have been intercepted by acquaintances, and so far have not had the opportunity to look at what is here very much. Do you mind if we go to look at her work, then? I fear some-one might already have bought the pieces I'm most likely to want."

"That would be very nice," said Klara.

They walked towards a space along the gallery wall where there were several images placed side-by-side, all of them in black-and-white, all of them depicting what looked like refugees, mostly mothers and children, fleeing some catastrophe. The images were stark and sad, but also very beautiful. Klara could see that they must be woodcuts, judging by the look of the images on the paper. She had never seen any of Kollwitz' work before, though she had heard the name mentioned here and there. The scenes depicted in the images were obviously intended to warn about the horrors of war and famine.

"It's very brave of Frau Kollwitz to make such images," said Klara.

"Well, yes," said Jan. "But now that you have said exactly that, I would be interested in hearing what you mean."

"Everybody wants to forget the great war," said Klara. "It's bad enough to see the survivors scuttling around, with their horrible faces. People have stopped treating the war veterans like people. There are so many of them, it is a great horror. I think the gaiety of the times is something of an attempt to drown out the memory of all that misery," she said. "I love Berlin, love the audacity of the city, the fierceness of all these modern wonders—the art, the music, the theatre, the extraordinary people rushing by in all directions, at all hours. The most famous minds of the world are here, right now, in Berlin. Here is where the modern world is coming forth, is making itself. I don't think there is a more alive place on earth right now. I think for now, Berlin is the center of the world. But so much contrast here: for every modern wonder there's a horror to match it. The poor are very bad off here. Hardly the sort of thing a great modern city, *the* great modern city, can afford to be true about itself. And this is what Frau Kollwitz sees—not the worldly whores of Picasso or the beautiful machines of Marinetti, but the poorest of the poor, the people who are being left behind, because they always get left behind. These people in her woodcuts could be living now, or they could be depictions of people a hundred years ago, five hundred years ago. I think, perhaps, for her the idea of modernity is rather absurd. I would suppose Frau Kollwitz doesn't appeal to a very wide audience."

Jan was clearly interested in what Klara was seeing, what she was saying as she looked at the pieces on the wall. "She is more admired by other artists than by the public," he said. "Her technique as a draughtsman is remarkable. She is highly skilled, and she controls her skill with great humility. There is no bombast in her work, but plenty of feeling. And perhaps it is the absence of bombast, after all, that makes her relatively unappealing to a wider audience. That makes her work more affordable to people like me. So, as so often happens with art, those of us who profess to be her greatest admirers rush forth at every opportunity to profit from her exclusivity. I must say, as a devoté of Frau Kollwitz, I'm quite taken by your assessment. I agree with you when you say she is a brave artist. The fact is she has been doing the same kind of work for some time now. She has been working as an artist for many years—since the eighties. She must be in her fifties by now. And she still sees the same things she's always seen, throughout the past several decades: destitution, the survivors of the worst misfortunes, and the horrors the weakest among us must endure. She has accomplished something that few artists can claim: she has managed to make people angry for almost thirty years. Unlike most of her generation, she has been embraced by the younger generation of artists. Now she is one of the heroines of the new movements."

Klara looked at the woodcuts on the wall, scanning them to see how they related thematically. They all depicted women huddling around their children. It struck her that, though the images depicted sorrow and despair, there was something beautifully decorative about them. They suggested something of the character of the *Jugendstil*, with their fluid shapes, the mingling of the flowing lines of clothing with the suggestion of a kind of almost dance-like movement in the figures of the people, who were invariably rendered in a tightly clustered group. This clustering of the groups of people suggested to Klara that the artist was seeing them as more than intimately connected—she clearly intended to represent them as being not a collection of individual figures but rather as being nodes of a single figure. It occurred to Klara that what was being rendered was the notion of a family—the figures tightly organized weren't meant to suggest individual, lone people. They were meant to suggest human identity in the aggregate. Of course, noticeable by its absence was the father. Nowhere in these images did Klara see the rendering of an adult man. There were boys, surely, in some of the images; in others there were old men, dried up, battered, little more than skeletons. In one of the pieces she noticed that there was a boy who seemed dead or dying, draped across his mother's arms. Klara looked at the title: *Pièta*. So where were the adult men in these images, Klara asked herself? Of course, they were off at war, or already dead from fighting. The more she looked at the images, the more Klara felt their emotional impact. The woman who made these pictures was a person of great skill and of great emotion. She was clearly a moral artist, in the best sense of the word.

Jan interrupted her thoughts, saying: "You appear to be affected by the work of Frau Kollwitz."

Klara answered, "I've not been aware of her work except for the posters. I am ashamed to say it. She is as good an artist as any of the rest of the ones here."

Jan answered, "She is quite a master of the print arts. One wonders why she does not apply her skill to painting, and one tries to imagine what the results would be if she were to do so."

Klara thought about what Jan was saying, trying to picture in her mind's eye what sorts of paintings would come from a woman who could make woodcuts such as these. Klara had not seen many modern woodcuts, and the ones she had seen at the Kieffer-Reinhardt Stiftung were all much smaller than what she was seeing here before her. She had seen a few images by Dürer, masterworks, of course, but they were much smaller than the images she was looking at now, and very different emotionally. Dürer was full of allegory—his images were full of visual puzzles. Kollwitz, however, was entirely direct. There was no ambiguity about what she was portraying. Even so, her images were powerful, they suggested real flesh and blood in a way that Klara could not see in an artist like Dürer.

Klara thought to herself that it seemed as if Kollwitz had understood the emotional power of the woodcut in ways that hadn't occurred to artists before. Klara's admiration for the artist grew as she considered the skill and the imagination behind the choices that had been made to produce what she was seeing. She thought to ask Jan, "What do you make of the blending of decorative elements with such intense comment?"

Jan asked her, "What do you mean by comment?"

Klara answered, "She is telling stories with these images, stories about the plight of the poor and the victims of war. Is that not comment, observing something critical about the nature of the social fabric, and how it seems these days to be unraveling?"

Jan nodded. "Ah," he said, "you see she makes politics with her pictures. Yes, that is true. You must know, for example, that she lost a son, Peter, in the great war. He was just old enough to fight as a soldier, and he was killed. I understand he was her darling, training to be an artist, like his mother. She suffered personally in the great war, and it continues to show in her work."

"You seem to know a good deal about her," said Klara. "Have you met her?"

"No," said Jan, smiling and shaking his head, "in fact, I haven't. But she is very well-known in Berlin. Her husband is a doctor, and she is active in many groups devoted to social justice. So, one hears about her if one knows where to listen. The officials hate her, of course. She makes them nervous, reminding everyone how much misery there is in our beautiful, modern German republic."

"I was just a girl during the war, so all I remember is the parades," said Klara. "It was very exciting, seeing all the handsome men in their uniforms. They would march through town, and people would line up and cheer them. What can a child know about such things? We were so far removed from what was happening, we didn't have to see the real horror until the wounded men started coming home. There were no bombs, no gas, just survivors after the fighting had been done. So for us, in my country, the war didn't really begin until it had ended for you, I suppose. But not everybody continues now—Is it eight years now since the war ended?—to talk about the war's effects. The city is full of people living like children. It's a wonderful place, but also very foolish. A city full of young people, probably many of them were children during the war, like me. That's what brings people to Berlin, laughter and forgetting everything and gaiety, all the things that young people do."

"Is that what brought *you* to Berlin?" asked Jan.

"No," said Klara, "my family are German, and they hope I shall have gotten my education by the time I leave here." She thought to herself how odd it felt to say out loud that one day she might leave the city. She hadn't thought about it consciously, but she was already finding herself at home here, perhaps never more that at this moment, when she stood beside this young man who defied her expectations, looking at art by a woman she'd never thought much about, finding the artist's work affected her and made her want to live a better life. But it still puzzled her, as she tried to collect her thoughts, that there was this blending of decorative and strongly moral elements in the images of mothers and children she was seeing before her. She asked, "Do you not see something odd about the mixture of decorative elements with all this suggestion of emotion?"

Jan considered what she was saying, and searched in the images for an understanding. He could see what she meant: the figures in the images, their details, their shapes, their groupings, all displayed a kind of decorative quality. The faces were not realistic: they were suggested by strong segments of black line, rendering the shapes in a slightly deformed manner that recalled the Gothic style of illustration. The deformation of figures wasn't ugly so much as simply stylized, heightening the viewer's sense that the execution of the shapes depended on a method, a deliberate set of choices, a kind of artifice. Jan thought through what he was seeing, and then he said: "Perhaps what you see as decoration is an expression of humility on the artist's part. Perhaps she is saying, 'Look, this is not real suffering you are looking at, but only a representation of it.' No artist can really capture the suffering of people, and to admit that by deliberately rendering the representation in such a clearly artificial way is to show respect for these people and perhaps, to invite the viewer to look further, beyond the image, to see the reality that the image is pointing to."

Klara looked up at him as he spoke, watching as his eyes darted back and forth between the woodcuts, and she thought about what he was saying. It was a very competent explanation, and it made her see the images in a new way. She thought again what it would be like to see a painting by this woman artist, and she thought that the artist, Frau Kollwitz, had chosen fragile paper and a printing process, not unlike that used to produce posters and newspapers, to suggest a kind of closeness with her subjects, common people, workers, people beset by impermanence, the people most affected by the uncertainty and want that were the products of recent human history. She said, "So, it is clear she could paint beautiful paintings if she wanted to. But instead she chooses to remind the viewer of her solidarity with the poor, choosing ink and paper, the cheap, everyday tools of communication between simple people. She is a person of great seriousness, Frau Kollwitz."

"Yes," said Jan, "I believe you are right. She increases her art by showing her dominion over it. She is a true master."

"Well, then," said Klara, "Do you think you will buy any of these for your collection?"

Jan answered, "It seems a foolish question to ask, doesn't it? She is very much the Prussian, the best kind, making this art that obliges you to ask, 'What on earth are you doing here thinking about pretty pictures when there are legions of people suffering in the world?' Perhaps I shall buy them all and then make a contribution to the milk fund, if I am to follow their example properly. I must also have a look at a few pieces in the next room, though. Otto Dix and Max Pechstein, some other favorites of mine. Not like Frau Kollwitz—quite decadent, according to some people."

With that Jan excused himself, bowing slightly and disappearing into the crowd. Klara was left with her impressions of him and of the art on the wall before her. She was grateful for the encounter; she thought to herself that if it hadn't been for this young Polish man, she probably wouldn't have stopped to linger any longer before Kollwitz's work than before that of the other artists. In fact, Jan had obliged her to stop and look, and to consider what was right in front of her. She hoped they might meet again.

Klara found her friends and left the exhibition. They went to a *Lokal*, drank and talked art and politics late into the night. All the while she was with her friends, Klara thought about Jan and about the work of Käthe Kollwitz. Jan was a grown-up; Kollwitz was a master, an elder. Her friends were still children, callow, trying to find their own substance by pouring themselves into various poses, various affectations. Having spent the evening looking at and talking about images, she found herself ill at ease with so much seeming. She felt she didn't belong with them, but she wondered if she belonged anywhere else.

The following day Klara went back to the Oberstdorfer Gallerie and, using birthday money she had received from her mother earlier that year, bought one of Kollwitz's woodcuts. It was entitled "Der Verlorene," the *Lost One*. It depicted a grieving mother cradling her dead son. She had been saving her money for a trip to Italy during the summer, but she decided she would make better use of the money by securing a piece of Kollwitz's work, to inspire her and to remind her to think about art in ways more serious than she was sometimes inclined to do. She also found that, when she looked at the woodcut, she thought about Jan.

A month or so passed for Klara in the usual manner: work and study and evenings with her circle of friends. It was June and Berlin was full of tourists, which meant that Klara's friends often sought ways to leave the city. For Klara the hustle and bustle and the presence of so many foreigners were simply additional things to love about Berlin. Having grown up in Savannah, with its formal English architecture juxtaposed against the unruliness of the semi-tropical marshland, with its smallness and its perpetual quiet, she came to feel that Berlin was a real city. Savannah, she came to believe, was nothing more than a deliberate copy of a city, a peculiarly American attempt to perfect what had been attempted in the older cities of Europe—like Berlin—but never achieved. Klara came to see this as indicating something about the American ethos—that it is based on a firm belief in the perfectibility of human character, the supposition behind this belief being that all human beings are not only capable of but *destined* to be perfected, and that the evidence of that perfection, of complete obedience to God, is prosperity.

Berlin revealed itself to be a completely different sort of city. First, its scale—it dwarfed most American cities, and this fact alone made one realize how young, if not how infantile, American culture was. Second, it was a city built through so many ages that one could read the city, in a very real sense, in its architecture, its public monuments, and in the other ways that the passage of so much time—over a thousand years—of continual habitation imprinted themselves on the place and the people. Where a city like Savannah spoke to beliefs about the individual, Klara found herself thinking that a city like Berlin spoke about human beings on a grander scale, speaking of history itself, and concluding that the history of people is the story of the acquisition and exercise of power. Klara found something honest in this, that everywhere she looked in Berlin she found a discourse on power, on the power of human beings to shape the world and to control each other. This, she concluded, is what a mature city says about itself; a big, great city speaks with a great, big voice.

She understood now that she was becoming a true Berliner. She felt herself getting taller, somehow, taking up more space intellectually. She could hold her own in a political discussion with her German friends, and she shared their view that the Treaty of Versailles had crippled Germany, and that it was up to Germany to pull itself out of the state of servitude imposed on it at the end of the Great War.

Late in June Klara received an unexpected letter in the morning post. It was from Jan Mieslewski. It read as follows:

My Dear Miss Westover:

You will please excuse the intrusion of the present letter. We met about two months ago at an exhibition of art in the Oberstdorfer Gallerie. We had a very edifying discussion on the work of Frau Kollwitz. I learned a few days after the exhibition that you had bought the very piece I had settled on obtaining for myself. If it will not be too odious a prospect to consider, I would be interested in meeting with you to discuss the possibility of my making you an offer for the piece. I assure you my terms will be suitably generous, and am hopeful you will receive this news with only the most agreeable sentiments. I hope I may call upon you this coming Wednesday, at five o'clock, at your residence to discuss the results of your reflection upon my offer.

Sincerely,

Jan Mieslewski

Klara was delighted to be receiving a letter from Jan. She had wanted to cultivate a friendship with him, but had no idea how to go about it, since at their last meeting they hadn't exchanged contact information. Reading the letter over, she immediately felt excited at the prospect of meeting him again. He was such an extraordinary creature, at once almost foppishly well-kept, at the same time possessed of an intellect, and an esthetic sensibility, that a mere dandy would never cultivate. She thought at once about how she might entertain him, offering him tea and cakes and showing herself to be a woman of the world.

Then it occurred to her that he must have used some kind of subterfuge to find her. How, after all, had he gotten her address? It must have been from the gallery. Klara found herself immediately becoming angry at the thought that this young man had been able to get personal information about her from people whom she'd treated no worse than to have paid them full price for a piece of art. What sort of people were there at this gallery? Reflecting a bit further, Klara thought, If he is what he says he is, then he will have many intimate contacts with the people who own this and probably many other galleries in the city. I'm just an American woman, a mere tourist. I've never done business with these people before. He, on the other hand, being a regular customer, probably knows whom he must bribe, if bribes are even necessary, to get what he wants. Klara concluded that Herr Mieslewski must indeed be a man of substance, or else he wouldn't have been able to importune upon the gallery to risk alienating her affections in favor of his.

Thinking further, Klara realized that his letter was really not so much an offer as an order. He had stopped just short of informing her that he would be appearing at her home—*her* home, after all—the following Wednesday to conclude the business (meaning, to collect *his* artwork). This struck Klara as being odder still: so delicately beautiful a creature as he (there was no other way of saying it) didn't give the impression of being, to put it honestly, man enough to assume such a forceful position concerning this or any other transaction. When she first saw him, sipping coffee at the sweetshop, she had seen nothing more than a fascinatingly pretty boy. Now here he was, practically forcing his way into her apartment. She had every reason for being outraged. She decided she would return his letter together with a note she would write, thanking him for communicating his interest, but telling him she had no intention of either meeting with him or of discussing the sale of an object she had no intention of parting with.

Klara Smith, née Westover, now laid in her bed in her small house in Deerfield Beach, Florida and thought about Jan. She had not seen him in more than sixty years. She thought about how they had fallen in love over a fight over a picture she'd bought. She had bought a woodcut he had wanted. He tried to convince her to sell it to him. She had no interest in selling. It wasn't that valuable a piece of art, to begin with. And anyway, he had made her want it, so what business did he have trying to get it back from her? She thought it was interesting, endearing, actually, that a man such as he should find the picture—a mother holding a child, possibly a dead one—so appealing. She could never get him to explain satisfactorily what the image meant to him. Klara remembered he found it irresistible to wonder what sorts of works the artist might have made if she had worked in a medium other than print art, what sorts of colors she would have chosen, what manner of execution, how beautiful the paintings would have been, the ones she never painted. He said she reminded him of Van Gogh, in her appreciation of the small details of the lives of the poor, of the insignificant, in her mastery of the emotional expressiveness of lines, all kinds of lines. Unlike Van Gogh (Jan said, all those years ago), Kollwitz didn't end up using them—her subjects, her many skills—to play out her own madness. There was no trace of madness in her work, only a deep reservoir of empathy. It was good to remember what Jan said all those years ago; remembering was almost all she had left of him.

And as she heard him talk about the woodcut, about his response to the artist, Klara fell ever more deeply in love with him, and so she protracted the fight over the woodcut by "agreeing" to meet Jan to discuss the matter. It was a ruse; she never intended to sell the woodcut. She asked herself sometimes, how long did Jan believe he was negotiating for a piece of art? When did he know it was about something else?

For his part, Jan was a gentleman, patient and attentive, never giving the impression that he felt himself sullied by giving of his time to this mere nobody of an American woman. True, she was born of good German stock, but after all was said and done, she was a person of no importance, none at all. Occasionally Klara would refuse his invitations to meet, pleading some prior engagement where there was none, simply to give him the impression that her social life was full enough so that the matter of dealing with him was of relatively little urgency. Not a week went by without her hearing from him, a greeting card left with her *Zimmerwirtin*, a telephone call, or an unannounced appearance on his part, inviting her to go for a walk along Unter den Linden or an impromptu dinner out somewhere.

A month or so passed in this fashion, until finally, meeting Jan "by chance" outside the Stadtsbibliothek one afternoon, Klara told him, "You must know by now that I have no intention of selling the woodcut. It is not to spite you that I mean to keep it, you must understand and believe that. It was you, yourself who taught me to look at Frau Kollwitz's work, and now that you ask me to part with it, I find the suggestion intolerable. Of all people, you must understand this if, as you repeatedly remind me, you admire her work. What does it matter to you if I have one small piece of her work, when you have an entire collection?" she asked.

He could only stand there and blink and look for an answer, but none came to him. Later Jan would say that he remembered not so much what she said as how she looked and sounded as she stood before him, and he thought to himself, this young woman has really, fully made herself at home here, she is almost no longer an American. She loves Berlin, he thought, she is making a claim upon the place, and that is why she wants to keep the woodcut. When they would talk about this later, he would say this: "It was realizing that you were the sort of person who could fall in love with a place, that you could really, genuinely fill yourself with the spirit of a city, not a man or a religion or a politics, but a city, that made me begin to feel something for you."

"Did you know what you were feeling?" Klara would ask.

"Not for awhile," he would say. "For some time, all I knew was how beautiful you looked to me, tiny, intent, calm, dignified, perfectly lovely in your new grey suit and your arms full of books."

"Were they always full of books?" she would ask.

"That's what I remember," he would say.

So it was that through an imperceptible process of change the matter of the woodcut receded into the background. Klara and Jan began their courtship in the late summer of 1925. By fall they were lovers.

For the next two years Klara and Jan were happy with each other. Klara made it clear, first of all, that she had no interest in marrying Jan, and second that she was as interested in her career as she was in him. This both hurt him and made him more keenly interested. He admired her intelligence and her wit, and he thought of her as exotic: a girl from America, from the South, with its savages, its swamps and alligators. Though he knew she came from a family of German immigrants, he always imagined she was half-Indian. On her deathbed sixty years later, remembering Jan, Klara remembered what he would say to her, what he would whisper, when they made love: "My little Indian girl," he would say, and she would say, "My big Cossack."

In 1927 Klara's internship ran out. By the time it expired, however, she had proven herself to be such a skilled librarian that the chief of her section petitioned to have a permanent position created for her. This was something of a scandal, as she was not merely a foreigner, but an American. Klara's parents were openly distressed when she wrote them to tell her good news. They had wanted her to stay in Europe long enough to become a supremely educated lady and a scholar who would find a career anywhere she wanted—in

America. The thought that she might end up wanting to stay in Germany—with its ever more ominous signs of growing social unrest—left the Westovers thinking they had made a terrible blunder in allowing their daughter so much freedom. By this point, however, Klara had become her own person. Sixty years later, at the end, she thought to herself, *I had no idea how far away I'd gone. They sent me off to become a modern lady, and that's just what happened*, she said to herself aloud.

"Mama?" said Doris. She was sitting beside Klara now, sitting right next to her. Klara had been thinking about Jan, thinking about the best of their time together. Coming back to the present was a shock, it felt harsh, she though she might be sick at her stomach.

"How you feelin', mama?" asked Doris. Klara felt very angry at being interrupted in her conversation. She had just been talking with Jan, they had simply been talking, that's all, and remembering everything so well, so clearly, and it had been so nice, he was so beautiful, and now this, now she was hearing this awful woman's voice, and it made her angry. This woman who had the nerve to interrupt Jan and her: who was she? She was so old and ugly, Her daughter was old and ugly, and Jan was so handsome, so tender and so handsome.

"Can you sit up, mama?" asked the strange woman. So stupid, so phony, Klara thought. *Sie, meine Tochter? Das ist aber lächer-lich*, she thought, half out loud. She wanted to be left in peace, she wanted to see Jan again, to see him again, to continue the conversation. Klara turned her head and saw the strange old woman sitting on the bed next to her. She was shocked at the intrusion. She just wanted to be left alone. "Would you please go away now, miss?," she asked the old woman in her room. *"Es ist hier privat, wissen Sie? Könnten Sie mich nicht in Ruhe lassen, um Gottes willen!"*[†]

The stranger looked befuddled as Klara spoke. "What, mama?" she asked. "What is lächerlich today, mama? You have a joke to tell, then? Can you sit up and eat?" she asked.

Klara sank back in her bed, allowing her eyes to close. Anyway, they burned when she kept them open; it was a relief to close them. She didn't have the strength to fight anymore, and she couldn't think about what she was fighting over. So much fussing about, she thought. *Quatsch!*

She loved Berlin. She loved walking about, listening to people, to the traffic, to the accumulated hum of all that was happening everywhere around her. She loved the city so much it hardly ever occurred to her to leave it, to travel as a tourist and see the rest of the world. Jan invited her to travel with him, just for pleasure, but she often made excuses, fearful that she might miss some new wonder in the city, a new play or a concert or even a new story in the newspaper. Jan told her she was more attached to Berlin than to him. She stammered and blinked and said it wasn't true. He laughed and said there was no way he could ever win against the charms of an entire city, especially not when the city was Berlin. She could tell he was actually a bit hurt by the realization of how strong her connection, in fact, really was, her feeling of affinity for Berlin. *Did I never tell him how much I loved him? That can't be true. I told him all the time. Every time we made love, every time I looked at him. He must have known.*

[†] "This is a private residence, you know? Couldn't you leave me in peace, for God's sake?"

Through much of 1928 Jan and Klara traveled as much as her work and temperament would allow. With Jan she saw places she might not have visited on her own: Prague and Budapest, Ankara and Cairo. Periodically her family wrote to her, passing on to her news of what was happening at home. If they ever intimated that her stay in Berlin had lasted longer than anyone would have hoped, she didn't notice. Jan made no demands on Klara; he treated her like a lover, and his passion never cooled. He understood her need to remain free of marriage, and he remained true to her, as far as she could tell. He worked at his life, collecting, studying, and traveling, and he attended to Klara. For her part, Klara worked diligently at her position in the acquisitions department of the Kieffer-Reinhardt Stiftung. Her competence and efficiency allowed her to work with a number of very prominent museum benefactors and art conservators. Along the way she began to learn the business of art conservation as it was being practiced at one of the most well-regarded art foundations in Europe. She was being groomed for a position of greater importance, an honor for a woman and a foreigner.

Everything changed in 1929. In February of that year Klara received bad news from home. Her father wrote her and told her that her mother had died of influenza. The news was a great shock. Klara had always known her mother to be a healthy, robust person. In fact, Elisabeth Westover was not quite fifty years old when she died. Klara could tell from her father's letter that he was in a state of shock. Of course, he must be beside himself with grief, for Elisabeth and he had been as close as a couple could be. Klara imagined how much her mother's death must have thrown her father into despair.

The news of her mother's death threw Klara into a state of con-fusion. On the one hand, she knew her father needed someone to console him. She knew her brother was close by, but Rolf and her father had always had a rather cool relationship. He would not be likely to be much comfort to his father. John Westover had always been closer to the women in his life than to men; losing his wife was a wound that could best be dressed by the touch of another woman to whom he felt close. That meant Klara. It meant it was her duty, first, to go to him and help him manage his way through his pain.

On the other hand, Klara felt herself well-settled in Berlin. She had been in Europe for a little over four years, and in all that time had never gone back home to America. For one thing, she had been obliged to live modestly, at least before she met Jan, and transatlan-tic travel was expensive. Her work permitted her to take short trips, but the time needed to go all the way from Berlin to Savannah would have been unmanageable for someone trying to build a pro-fessional work life in such an intensely competitive field as the one she had chosen.

The truth was that Klara had spent enough time in Berlin that she had begun to feel herself a completely different person from the young woman her parents had sent to Europe to become a lady and a scholar. She had become what she had set out to be, or at least, she was well on her way. In any case, even presented with the fact of her mother's death, she was protective enough of her new life so that she was not ready to leave it. After all, by the time she got home, the funeral would have been held and her mother would have been laid to rest. It had taken a few weeks for her to get her father's letter. Her mother had already been buried. Of that there could be no doubt. But still, her mother had died, and what was she thinking about doing to acknowledge it? Where was her grief, Klara asked herself? Wherever it was, it was far behind the voice telling her that she was in danger of losing the life she had found.

Full of guilt, fearful she would lose her carefully constructed life, Klara did not go home after her mother's death. She wrote to her father and lied to him about her reasons for not going to be with him. She knew it was horrible to lie under such circumstances, and she even wondered whether her father would be able to see through her concocted version of the truth. She said that she was in the middle of a great project at work and was told that if she were to leave to attend to her family matters, she would lose her job. Her superiors were very sympathetic, she said, but because attending to her family would mean a long ocean voyage to America and a stay of indefinite duration, she could not be guaranteed a position if she were to leave. So she left it to her father to decide for her: did he want her to come home and be with him, or should she stay in Europe and grieve on her own? She couldn't believe she was writing such things, but she could not bring herself to leave Jan, her work, and her new life. The thought of returning to Savannah horrified her.

A month went by before Klara received a response from her father. She didn't know what to make of the long pause between her letter and his. Naturally, she imagined the worst. When John Westover wrote to his daughter, however, it was to reassure her that it was better for her to stay where she was. He wrote that he could not bear to see her lose the position she had worked so hard to obtain. Her mother would want her to continue, he wrote. Perhaps, he continued, he could come to visit her in Berlin once a little time had passed, once he could see his way clear to traveling. Reading her father's letter, Klara felt as though a pall had lowered over her. She had no idea where she was able to find a part of herself that could so easily lie, with such *sang foid*, to the father who had loved her and had devoted his life to urging her to a place of prominence in the world. Just so, she told herself. Just so. He had worked, her mother had worked, to make it possible for Klara to live the life of a woman of the world. What sense did it make to drop everything now and go sit beside a cold, quiet grave?

So Klara continued with her life in Berlin. Even as she did so, she felt life darken around her, somehow. She went out less. She spent days away from Jan, and when she was with him, she was often in a foul mood. She concentrated more on her work. That, after all, was what she was supposed to be doing, working. Her friends left her to herself. She tried not to notice when they appeared to be talking about her. She tried to keep on at her work, and indeed, she was very good at it. That, at least, was continuing as it should, her work. One thing not to worry about. Jan didn't press her; he didn't talk at all about the matter. She told him her father had asked her to stay in Berlin rather than come home, and Jan never challenged her, never made an effort to encourage her to go home and be with her family.

In June of that year her brother Rolf wrote her. When she read the news he had to share, she doubled over in pain. The letter told her that her father had suffered a stroke, and that it was urgent she come home and be with him. She had no doubt that she was responsible for her father's stroke. The day after she received the news about her father, Klara told her superior that she needed to leave to care for her father. Her astonished department head, whom she had not told her mother had died, was very tender and responsive, and offered to help her make travel arrangements to get home to Savannah as speedily as possible. When she told Jan that she needed to go back home, he was a gentleman, treating her tenderly and quickly, efficiently making arrangements she was too upset to think about to get her ready to leave Berlin and make the long trip home. She left her apartment and most of her belongings behind, certain that she would be back in a few months.

When she got home Klara found her father near death. His stroke had been terribly severe. It had taken his speech. The right side of his face sagged horribly, and he was as helpless as a child. The stroke had aged him dramatically; not quite sixty at the time, he looked like a man in his eighties when Klara saw him. The transformation was incomprehensible. Seeing her father's reduced state, Klara found it difficult to speak. She was met by great numbers of people who offered to help her and her father. Some of them made comments about how unfortunate it had been that she had not been there when her mother died. She had no response. Being met by her father's many friends, by her brother, Klara thought to herself that she had awakened from a dream, the dream of her life in Berlin, into the wakeful ugliness of her real life. She couldn't help thinking that: Berlin was a dream, and this is my real life. She could not have been more torn between two notions: on the one hand, she felt deep guilt at the hesitation that had kept her from her father after her mother's death; on the other hand, Klara was sure the life she'd led in Berlin was her true life, and that coming back home was like a kind of dismemberment. Klara was certain that if she had come home earlier, her father would not have had the stroke. She was just as sure that leaving Berlin was placing herself in a kind of peril she could not describe, but sensed as clearly as she sensed the pain over her father's stroke. There was no doubt about it, any of it.

When she left Berlin, Klara told herself that it would only be for a month, maybe two, until she could see about her father and make sure he was in good hands. Some things she couldn't allow herself to think fully: that her father's career as a musician was, almost certainly, at its end; that he would need to find a way to continue to produce income to support himself; that he would, almost certainly, never be as he had been; and that it was quite possible that, having suffered a stroke, he might suffer another, and might soon die, in any case. The half-formed versions of these thoughts had to compete with the confusion of internal voices that raised themselves: wouldn't it be better for her to not go home at all, but to continue living the life her parents had urged her into? How could she think about leaving her position at the Kieffer-Reinhardt for any amount of time, knowing how many well-qualified Germans would rush in and take her place if given the opportunity? Berlin was the most important city in Europe, the center of innovation and progress for the entire continent, so it was full of ambitious, talented people. If she were to leave, a thousand people could and would quickly step forward to replace her, and the foundation would probably forget about her. If she left for any amount of time, she feared, it would be as if she had never been there in the first place, had never worked doggedly to learn what she had learned.

After all was said and all was considered, the simple fact was that Klara had come to belong in Berlin. She had traveled enough throughout Europe to have a sense of just how remarkable a place it was. The Great War had left a kind of lingering energy in Berlin, a peculiar combination of something like humility with an intense readiness for invention, a willingness to let go of the past, politically, socially, and most clearly of all, esthetically, and almost literally take flight on the possibility of the future. It was this, Klara thought, that made her fall in love with the city: her sense that the entire city was engaged in a kind of exuberant transport, a being borne aloft by the simple willingness to look forward into the future of humanity. With the exception of New York City, there was no more modern place on earth than Berlin in 1929, no place so fiercely alive with the optimism and dynamism of the Machine Age. Klara feared that if she left what she had found in Berlin, she would never find it again; returning from sleepy Savannah after wading through the muck of filial duties, she would return to find something had shifted in her absence, the rhythm of the city would have altered itself in a way that she, no longer present, would be unable to figure out and compensate for, leaving her out of step in the one place that mattered to her.

Her conscience had guided her back home, even though leaving Berlin, if only for awhile, felt like tearing herself in pieces. And so she came back to Savannah, and she met the accusing faces of the people around her father, the parishioners, the musicians, the doctors, the preachers and, perhaps worst of all, her own brother, Rolf, who looked as though he had aged unnaturally, too. Rolf was always closest to Mama, thought Klara. He's been grieving a while, and Papa's stroke has only made everything so much worse. And then, when she saw her father, Klara thought she might faint. He had shrunken, had withered into a man she could barely recognize. Thinking this, she realized how long it had been since she'd seen him: almost six years. She had gone to Europe to spend perhaps four years there, studying and working. Her industry and talent had won her a place as permanent as any life offered a young woman of her generation. She was so much the daughter her parents had hoped she would be that she had simply launched full-speed into the life of a professional scholar, a working woman. In the meantime her mother had died and her father had become a prematurely old man. Klara asked herself how much of his aging was due to the sacrifices he'd made so that her brother and she would have a good life, an American life. Her parents worked so that Rolf and she could become the people they already saw in their mind's eyes. Yes, thought Klara, in some way they always looked at her brother and her as being already famous, accomplished. For them it was just a matter of finding the proper outlet to allow the brilliance of their children to express itself. Such confidence, such single-minded determination to mold their children, thought Klara, was unlike anything she'd ever seen parents do with their children. There was, in her mother in father, absolutely no ego, no need to memorialize themselves in the lives of their children. It was, rather, their job to find the right doors and, opening them, reveal what was already there.

But now things were different; her father was severely ill; the man who had once had a full, crisp tenor voice could no longer speak. He was very weak, and appeared only dimly aware of his surroundings. Seeing her father so fully reduced was a great shock to Klara. She found herself trying to remember the way he looked when she last saw him, but she couldn't, and that shocked her, too. The man she now saw before her was someone she didn't really know. She felt more alone than she could ever remember having felt.

Rolf wandered around the house like a ghost. He never went out, and stayed mostly to himself in his room. In the course of one of their few long conversations, Klara learned that during her absence Rolf had never moved away from his parents' home. It seemed he was there for the entirety of his mother's illness, which had lasted about a month. During that time Rolf had fought with his father, the issue being whether or not Klara should be urged to come home. Mr. Westover had argued at the time that there was no need for Klara to return home, that his wife would be back on her feet in no time. Elisabeth, for her part, had also said she did not want her daughter to be summoned, not because she regarded her illness as insignificant, but because she wanted her daughter to forge ahead and continue working. Hearing this, Klara felt vindicated in her choice not to come home after her mother's death, but she also felt deeply chastened by the example of her mother's self-lessness. In the end it was humility that won out, and Klara resigned herself to becoming her father's caretaker.

So it was that Klara was obliged to leave one career, barely begun, behind. Barely comprehending how her life had turned upside down so quickly, she became her father's nurse. She tried not to think about Berlin, about Jan and about all she had left behind. Her father's health was so delicate that he needed full-time care. The Westovers had put aside money, though how they had managed it, with all they had spent on their children's care and education, Klara could not imagine. When gradually she learned how much money her father earned as a church organist, she was quite surprised. She had remembered his playing—which now she was almost certain she would never hear again—as simply a part of the formal nature of Sundays, and so it had never occurred to her that something as inconsiderable as his playing the organ might have been so fully responsible for the relative comfort with which the family lived. As much money as the Westovers had put aside, though, it was clear to Klara that care would have to be exercised to make sure, first of all, that her father would be cared for.

That clearly meant that she would have to spend more time in Savannah than she had planned. She wrote to Jan, telling him what she found at home, and explained that she would need, as a matter of family obligation, to plan to stay at home indefinitely to see to her father's needs. She saw no way to get back to Berlin, but she didn't have the heart to tell that to Jan. She thought again and again how selfish she had been not coming back home after her mother died, and she thought she would probably never pay her penance, no matter what she did.

Klara opened her eyes. It struck her, suddenly, for no reason at all, how odd it was that it seemed, when she opened her eyes, that nothing had happened, that she hadn't done anything at all, that nothing about her had moved or changed shape or gone anywhere. And yet, what a difference there was between eyes open and eyes shut! Eyes open: colors and surfaces, things happening of their own accord, the world flowing by or just sitting there, on its own terms. Eyes shut: she still saw, in a manner of speaking, but of course it was an internal seeing, the kind of seeing that was ordered by all that she had experienced or failed to experience, all she could re- member, all she could imagine. Two sides of a mirror? Two direc- tions? An *either* and its necessary *or*? If seeing with eyes open was looking at the surface of something, eyes closed was being sub- merged in seeing. Is it possible, thought Klara, not to see? Do blind people have nothing like images playing across their mind? Is it possible, really, to not see?

Klara looked across the room. The wall was still a pale green, a cheerful color, not too demanding, not too terribly present. There was very little in the room on that side, over there, as there had always been very little, very few objects to look at, and still, when she looked in that direction, there was a full field of vision, a full wall of green, and if she studied the wall she could see that the light played over it in minute ways, that the green was not a constant, even green, everywhere the same on the entire wall: it was, in fact, a teeming crowd of shades, areas of shadow and gradients of green and all the other colors of the spectrum, could that be right? Could the wall be covered with so and so many (how many? How could I possibly count them?) tiny dots, I don't know how big, pointillistically dappled onto the green of the wall by the interference of all the other objects in the room, the colors they shed and the ones they reflected, the shading of objects casting their shadows across each other's path of illumination and reflection, all these spaces of color and darkness hitting the green of the wall, covered over the imperfect color of the wallboard which, by its imperfection, creates an infinitely, minutely jagged landscape of light and dark, all of it together, all the different plays of light, of dark, making of the green of the wall an endlessly changing surface.

Jan taught her to see, to look and see deeply. She fell in love with him and took him for granted, took the time they had together for granted. They had their youth with each other, using it the way young people do, as if there were an endless supply of it, squandering it and not having the slightest idea that they, that she, would one day look back and say, I didn't get enough, I can't believe that's all I got, but I won't get what I want now, because I won't.

Klara stayed home and took care of her father. She was ashamed of the things she had thought after her mother died. Her brother never spoke of it, but then he didn't have to, because she, Klara, couldn't stop reminding herself of just how cold a choice it had been not to have come home after hearing of her mother's death. And so she became her father's custodian. He did not recover, except in small, small ways; he failed to regain his speech, and he remained bedridden. He did get to the point where he was able to communicate, only with Klara, using his eyes and a few small hand movements. In this way it became necessary that Klara stay close by. There could be no question of handing over her father's care to someone else. It fell to Klara to manage the house, and this she did as well as she could. Rolk gradually got a little better about going out into the world, making a meager living as a music teacher. His grief over his mother's death and his father's infirmity made him sullen and silent, and it was clear it was all he could do to keep from dissolving altogether into his own sadness, his own inertia.

Klara continued to correspond with Jan, though it was painful to do so. She thought about writing to Jan, telling him that it was foolish of them to continue to correspond, that it was impossible for her to think about coming back to Berlin and resuming her career. She could not quite manage to tell herself that her professional life was effectively ended, but neither could she permit herself to think of leaving her father.

When the stock market crashed in October, when the whole world went crazy with fear, when everything was, all of a sudden, worthless, and everyone was, all of a sudden, poorer than anyone could imagine ever being, when everything around her became colored by confusion, hunger, and uncertainty: what did she feel? She looked back over that terrible time many times, trying to remember what she had felt during those awful days after the crash. Not what she thought, but what she felt—that was important to hold onto. It was like being in a war, only there was no enemy, or rather, the enemy was everywhere and everything. It was like being tossed overboard, she thought, being tossed overboard into a storm, out in the middle of the ocean, and what does one feel then but fear and being very small against something so big it has no limits, something so strong its strength—the strength to destroy—can't be known?

Jan had taught her to see, and then she was obliged to leave her life with him. She wasn't even permitted really to say goodbye. She had just to leave and then go home to her father and her battered family, and then, after that, the Great Depression, and no possibility of finding her way back to her life in Berlin. Gradually she was able to find a colored woman who was reliable enough to manage the house and her father, and this permitted her to go out and look for work, to help keep the house in order. Through a series of contacts, owing mostly to her father's great popularity, Klara found a position eventually at the Telfair Museum, where she became the assistant to the director. So she took care of her father as best she could, she managed her brother and gave him a wide berth, and the three of them managed to hold on as best they could in the house where she had grown up.

Jan continued to write, even after Klara herself stopped writing. Some letters she read, others she didn't open. She saved them all, kept them in a desk drawer in her bedroom, next to her toiletries, neatly tied together. One day a package came and she didn't open it right away, seeing it was from Jan. It was 1933 and the news from Berlin was the worst she could imagine: the National Socialists had come to power, had actually taken over the entire country. She thought about her friends in Berlin, friends who, like Jan, wrote to her but whom she had long since left off answering. How horrified they must have been that that scum Hitler came to be Kanzler. The liberty-loving Berliners must have thought it was all a terrible, tasteless joke, seeing that filthy Austrian monkey and his baboons take power. It would be years before Klara would realize that the Berlin she had gotten to know was actually only a tiny little corner of the whole place. She had fallen in with artists, writers, art collectors, communists and pamphleteers. That was her Berlin.

The package turned out to be the woodcut Klara had bought, the one by the artist Käthe Kollwitz. Klara thought to herself what a gesture of magnanimity it was for Jan to parcel it up and send it to her, as he was so fond of it, himself. She read in his letter accompanying the woodcut that he was sending it to her because the way things were going in Germany, work such as that by Frau Kollwitz was beginning to be considered dangerous:

> ...This *Affenregierung* that has been installed in Berlin is now rounding up all sorts of people, denouncing them as enemies of the state, as pollutants. Grocers, tailors, bankers, even peasants are now revealed to be enemies of the German state. Of course the Jews are being treated with the utmost contempt, as are the Poles. I had not known my people were such criminals, such purveyors of perversity and disease, but now I have the Brown Shirts to thank for being corrected in my misunderstanding. Even books and pictures are now enemies of the state. Anything that is seen as being not native to this peculiar phenomenon, this Aryan folk as it is held to exist in some

core of pure Germanity that keeps getting harder and harder to locate, as its enemies appear to become more numerous, anything and everything, even the picture of a mother cradling her child, is seen as *entartet*. I fear we shall go a long time before we see an end to the darkness that is gathering around us.

Together with the Kollwitz I send you for safekeeping, I send you also an object from my collection I have not, until now, talked about. It is difficult to know how to begin speaking of it, precisely because of what it means. Namely, you will find in the back of the frame of the Kollwitz a small parcel which contains a musical manuscript. It is none other than a draft, left unfinished, of a Polonaise by the composer Fréderic Chopin. The manuscript is written in the composer's own hand, and was written within the last few months of his life. It was intended to be a gift for the daughter of his lover, then estranged, Madame Georges Sand. The daughter, Solange Clésinger, married badly and was disowned by her mother. Solange remained close to Chopin until the end, and as thanks for her steadfastness, he began to work on a piece of music which, it is said, he intended to give to her as a gift. His health failed and he never completed it. At the time of his death even Mme. Clésinger wasn't aware of the manuscript's existence. It passed through several hands, during the confusion that followed Chopin's death, and came at last to fall into the hands of a dealer in old documents here in Berlin. The details of its coming into my hands are so complex that I cannot relate all of them to you here, as I am pressed to take care of other things in the near future. Life here has grown so difficult that I fear, if I don't move the things that mean the most to me to places where I can be confident they will be protected from harm—but I cannot even finish articulating such a thought on paper, other than to ask you simply to keep the manuscript safely for me until I can meet you in person and ask you to return it to me. I know despite our separation you will not fail me in this, and I thank you for the constancy you have proven to me that lets me know I can count on you.

Jan

Chapter One

And so Klara kept the letters and the manuscript, not knowing what to do with it. Jan would come to collect it. They would resume their life together, and she would take care of papa. Rolf would resume his career, he would become a great musician, and she would marry Jan, perhaps, and they would have a couple of children, and she would find a position in a museum or a gallery, perhaps, in Berlin, if she were lucky, and they would live the lives they deserved to live.

But that's not what happened. Jan stopped writing in 1934. Klara wrote to him; she never got an answer. She tried to find out how to contact him in Berlin, and soon found he had disappeared. Time went on, and she continued to care for her father. John Westover died in 1939, on the day the news was announced that Poland had been invaded by Germany. On the day her father died, Klara thought about Jan. She thought she would die from despair.

But Klara didn't die. She met a nice man, Bob Smith, a widower, at church. She married him in 1942. She married him because there was no reason not to, and because he was a decent man. She didn't love him, but he never seemed to mind. He was kind and quiet, and he never asked much of her. She bore him a daughter, Doris, who was their only child. Bob lived until he was seventy-six. He died of cancer. Klara survived her husband's death a remarkably long time, living until she was ninety-three. She finally died in 1999 at her home in Deerfield Beach, Florida. She was survived by her daughter. After her death her house and belongings were liquidated in an estate sale. The woodcut she had bought when she was twenty-one was put in a yard sale. It was bought by a young man from out of town, and sold for seventy-five dollars.

Chapter Two

The big, ugly building squatted on the hilltop. Designed to suggest a Venetian palace, it looked more like a tire factory. All its ornamental details—the tall domed towers at each of the four corners, the cornice over the main entrance, the bas-relief of three oversized charioteers perched on what looked like Shetland ponies, the clumsily turned columns— conspired to make the structure look childish, but with no hint of whimsy. Built as an exhibition hall for the Cotton Exhibition of 1892, this structure sat at one corner of a quadrangle formed by three other similar—but not exactly identical—buildings. An observer arriving for the first time was tempted to think how it had come to pass that not just one but *four* thus so conspiratorially ugly structures could have survived.

The hilltop on which the four halls were located had been a pretty splendid one before it had been leveled off to make a building site. Situated almost at the exact point where the Georgia piedmont fell into the coastal plain, it had offered an expansive view of the surrounding area. From the hilltop, before it was altered, you could look north and see rolling hills covered in oak, sweet gum and poplar, then look south and see a gently flattening, vast expanse of oak, chestnut and poplar forest stretching towards the Atlantic ocean.

Until a few decades before the exhibition halls were built, Creek Indians had used the vantage point of the hilltop as a watch post. In their last years of residency, the Creek observed the camp-fires and marked the progress of the settlers who had come to build the railroad. They conferred among themselves about the newly arrived settlers. They agreed the newcomers were ugly, foul-smelling and full of disease. "These people won't last long," they said. "They're very stupid." "Yes, stupid. They don't ever listen to what you tell them." "It's always the same with them; they're like children—they think they know everything." "That's right—the other day I was talking with Yellow Dog and he told me about how they all think there's buried treasure all over the place." "Yes, it really is foolish, this talk about treasure. Treasure? What would they do if they found it? They lie in their own excrement, they're riddled with all sorts of ailment and pestilence. The only things they appreciate are what they haven't yet managed to steal from one another. They're all about to drop dead in their tracks from living such terrible lives, so what do they want with treasure?" "They seem to have to hold onto everything, as if nothing is real unless they have it in their hands." "It would be sad if they weren't so comical." "Yes, in that case it would be sad, wouldn't it?"

Having last been painted during the early 1980s in brown and beige, the four old exhibition halls were all that was left of what had been built as a 200-acre park. The park was situated a few miles to the south of what had grown to be the city of Centralia, so named because of its central location along the railroad lines. In its day—the first few decades of the 20th century—the park had been a lively place, a place where fashionable people came. Local boosters saw to it that park events were widely publicized in the regional press so that, on the basis of often somewhat embellished claims about the marvels that were to be beheld there, people made the bone-shaking journey down primitive roads that connected Centralia with the surrounding region just to come to the grand events that were held at the park. Having arrived, visitors were treated to an assortment of attractions that included the usual fairground entertainments, as well as a boating lake and a Japanese garden. The lake and the lovely garden had disappeared so long ago, however; only a few of the oldest ladies in town still occasionally dreamt of ever having been to such a place.

The park was originally intended only to accommodate the great 1892 Cotton Exhibition; the fair had been conceived to celebrate the South's emergence from the suffocating economic depression of the 1880s. All the buildings of the park were slated to be demolished after the exhibition was to end in September, 1892. The success of the exhibition, however, surprised virtually everyone involved in planning it. It drew far more people from much farther away than anyone could have foreseen. Thanks to this turn of events and unusually warm weather, the city leaders extended the exhibition's run until the middle of October. Looking further ahead, they planned a grand show to mark the turn of the century. The chamber of commerce enlisted publicity men from afar to make sure the next event would rival anything offered in New York or Chicago.

So it happened that the Centennial Exposition of 1900-1901 was indeed a much bigger sensation than the 1892 exhibition. Everyone throughout the South gossiped about it, and most everyone who could made the journey went to see it. It featured a much expanded park appointed with a carousel and pipe organ imported all the way from Brighton, England. People waited for hours just to buy a ticket to ride the carousel. On several occasions the police had to intercede to control unruly visitors who began to grow weary of waiting their turns at rides and attractions. Organized under the theme "The New South," the Exposition was organized around the theme of envisioning Centralia in the new century. The Centennial Exposition featured displays of all manner of newfangled gadgets and inventions. The undisputed hit of the show was a huge, walk-through diorama showing the Centralia of the year 1950. In this vision of the city's future, American engineering genius had harnessed the resources of the nearby Kennechopke river to create a vast network of canals. This fantastic system of waterways functioned in the imagined city as a system of thoroughfares. By means of these canals, the captains of industry as well as the prominent citizens of 1950 Centralia floated motorized crafts of all sizes to move their property and their persons to other similarly improved cities throughout the Southeast. Among these sister cities were Appalachicola in the Gulf of Mexico, grown to rival Chicago and a Charleston that had overtaken Savannah on the Atlantic, all of them arrayed like ladies in waiting around the grand train of development that had grown up to cradle the new Centralia: a monstrous city of astonishing scale, a marvel of human engineering that (according to various maps arranged as inserts throughout the exhibit) had grown to dwarf New York City as the country's and the world's principal metropolis. The feature of the diorama that caught many people's imaginations (and that caused more than a few—especially from rival Southern cities—to laugh derisively) was that of a fantastic transportation terminus that featured a kind of flying passenger craft: a motorized balloon outfitted with a large passenger gondola. A map of the world and accompanying legend showed how, in the world of 1950, Centralia would have become established as one of the central points of conveyance in a vast, endlessly bustling network of air travel craft.

As if all these wonders weren't enough, the Exhibition also featured a debate between the then sitting (and locally despised) President McKinley and the much beloved William Jennings Bryant. The date of the address was September 24, 1900, a beautiful, warm day with a cloudless sky. The debate started at five in the afternoon, and was to last until after sundown. The subject of the debate was the role of the South in the new century. Bryant went first, giving the sort of speech that was his specialty. He warned of the dangers of empire-building. He reminded his listeners of the bloodshed that attended Great Britain's then-recent adventures in Africa and the Orient. Bryant implied with masterful subtlety that England's violent adventures in Africa were bound to have the same disastrous effects as the occupation by the Union military that had kept the South in bondage since the end of the recent American war. He cited the laws enacted by the vengeful Reconstruction Congress which made it economically prohibitive for industry to operate in Southern states, while northern states were given the resources and support to develop truly modern industry. Bryant worked the crowd into a frenzy with his inspired rhetoric and passionate delivery, and was interrupted four times by long demonstrations of cheering and the repeated performance of a jingle that celebrated already his victory in the upcoming presidential election.

Emboldened and deeply moved by the crowd's show of affection, Bryant admonished the audience to "leave the rest of the world to Almighty God and chart instead the vast oceans of domestic possibility." Turning at one point to the President, Bryant actually pointed a finger as he admonished McKinley not to lead the country back into economic want. With great emotion he challenged the President "not to bankrupt the nation in the name of costly foreign adventures." The crowd was thrilled by Bryant's daring in addressing McKinley and the Republicans with such articulate frankness.

President McKinley listened patiently to his opponent's speech. He seemed unmoved by what he heard. When it was his turn to speak, he rose slowly and approached the front of the great platform. As McKinley walked to the podium, he passed a collection of city fathers who looked blankly over the crowd and fidgeted with their hats. The audience he faced numbered upwards of five thousand people. He looked out at the assembly before him and saw clearly how little they thought of him. Then he began to speak. At the first sounds of his comparatively high, flat, Midwestern voice, some people began to snicker. Undeterred by this show of contempt, the President continued, compensating for the slight rise in noise level by talking louder.

McKinley said that the Centennial Exposition marked a solemn ceremonial division between the past and the future. He said his administration would seize the opportunity of this unique point in time. It would mark the end of an America at war with itself. It would herald a new century of strong yet peaceful leadership among the great nations of the world.

With uncharacteristic eloquence, the President asked the crowd to remember the lessons of America's bloody conflict with itself. He said we were obliged to honor our own dead. He said we could do justice to the fallen by confronting tyranny wherever we found it. He said also that to fulfill its new role our young country would have to progress from youth to maturity. As America grew up, he said, it would have to take a place of prominence among other nations. As an example of this new maturity, he cited the rebirth of Centralia after the *War Between the States*, as he called it. He used Centralia's example to adjure the people of the South's next great city to look forward to a new century. It was our destiny, he said, to lead the world into a century defined by American greatness.

The audience was surprised by the President's speech. By reputation a taciturn, humorless Midwesterner, McKinley was not known as an eloquent speaker. In fact, as he spoke on that day in Centralia, he impressed not nearly so much by delivery as by the substance of what he said. Battered survivors of Reconstruction, the audience who'd come here looking forward to booing him off the stage found themselves touched deeply by the respect he showed for what the South had endured. They were poured full of pride over the suggestion that, as Centralians first and as Americans second, they possessed some kind of greatness. Certain as they were of their own righteousness—for what they had endured, for what they had survived—it was an emotionally charged event to have an outsider say it all out loud and in front of so many witnesses. In short, McKinley's words certified to the people of Centralia their unequaled excellence in all things before the rest of mankind, and by certifying this simple fact, the President made the crowd love him. When he finished speaking, the audience cheered him for the better part of an hour.

Bryant was stunned by the effect of the President's performance. He was perhaps the only man in the audience who realized what had actually happened—that the President had sized up this crowd, figuring out that all he needed to do to win them was to tell them, in so many words, how wonderful they were. Bryant sought to reclaim the stage to give his carefully rehearsed summation speech. It was one of his favorites, a speech he had already delivered to great effect to crowds in dozens of other cities over the past decade. He never got a chance to deliver it.

The following day the Centralia *Beacon* gushed with details of the President's triumph. The editors effused that, for the second time in less than fifty years, a Republican had set the *whole* state ablaze. Taking up the mood of the moment, a local retail establishment even advertised a "fire" sale. Over the next few days, the *Beacon* reported several concocted stories about Centralia's envisioned role in the new internationalist America of the twentieth century. Circulation rose sharply and, for a brief time, Centralia was puffed absolutely full of itself.

Less than a year after his triumph in Centralia, McKinley was dead by a murderer's hand. Mortally wounded in Albany, New York, McKinley died much as a soldier would have, bleeding to death from an assassin's wounds. To the people of the South's Next Great City, the President's death bore a special mark of importance. He had bravely appeared before a crowd of people he knew must hate him. He had won them over with a vision of vigor and greatness, only to go on to be silenced less than a year later on his own political turf. Stranger still, he was mortally wounded while attending another centennial exhibition: the one in Albany, New York. The country reeled from the monstrous event. The new century had barely been born before it was stained with the most ancient of crimes.

Chapter Three

Over the following two decades, the Centralia Exhibition Park was used widely for large, popular events. In the early nineteen-thirties, the park became the home of the annual Great Southland Fair. Held at the beginning of autumn, the fair was low-brow entertainment that was intended to cheer folks up. It featured freak shows, hoochie coochie dancers, watermelon-eating contests and other sideshow diversions. Aside from the Southland Fair, there were circuses, revival meetings, agricultural shows and livestock auctions. The park actually saw a good deal of traffic until after World War Two, when drive-in theatres began to appear, pulling the growing population away to the promise of more sophisticated entertainment. By the late fifties, entertainment had so completely transformed itself, even here in the largely rural South, that people went less and less to parks like this. A new generation of citizens was seeking new diversions, so that the park and neighborhood around it fell altogether out of fashion.

About five miles north of the Centennial Exhibition Park, a new civic center was built in the middle of the old central business district. The new civic center had two climate-controlled exhibition halls and a state-of-the art auditorium. What with the new civic center and the other tall buildings going up downtown, fewer and fewer shows were brought to the old exhibition grounds, and by the sixties, the park was closed and slated once again for demolition. Soon much of the park was parceled up and ploughed under. The lake was drained and a football stadium was erected in its place. The rest of the grounds were reshaped into low-cost housing, strip malls and highways. Around what had once been a monument to Centralia's hope for the coming century, a landscape of urban decay sprouted. A bumper crop of misery bred around the park. It came into full bloom during the white flight of the sixties and seventies.

What was now left was a quadrangle of ugly exhibition halls and a large, oddly shaped piece of what had once been a busy park. All that remained of the sixty or so other buildings of the Centennial Exposition were now visible as fragments of walls here and there. These fragments formed the boundaries for a parking lot. The large lot was enclosed by a high chain-link fence. Atop the fence was a crown of barbed wire tangled with trash. Tall grasses, weeds, mimosa and sweet gum trees broke through the pavement in mean, little clumps of growth. The weeds threatened to pull the whole wreck back into the ground.

As the park was falling into its decline, downtown Centralia had begun to change, as well. What had been a city had grown into a metropolitan area, a fact that left a good many Southerners uncertain as to how to act. A city was something most Southerners could live with, but a metropolitan area meant choosing sides: the old guard on the one side saw a metropolis as something dirty, tainted with Yankee vices and the prospect of large concentrations of roving bands of negroes and other undesirables; the younger generation, on the other side, saw the prospect of fabulous wealth and the opportunity to get back at the Yankees for oppressing the South for so long. In this conflict as in so many others, it was the real estate developers who won the day. In a few meeting rooms in various places throughout the region, it was decided that what Centralia needed most was a proper big-city skyline. Hence, along the city's main thoroughfare a clump of non-descript skyscrapers began to rise in the early sixties. One by one the old hotels, banks and department stores that had once lined the city's main avenue began to disappear. They were replaced by mirror-faced office silos and dour, scaled-down copies of buildings that had been built in larger, northern cities. The grand old train station on the edge of downtown was razed and replaced by a sports arena which, in turn, was pulled down and replaced by another sports arena barely twenty years later. The city's streetcars disappeared and were replaced by buses and automobiles. Streets were widened and the heart of the old city was carved into an elaborate, dangerous highway interchange. The old neighborhoods surrounding the city center were chopped up and walled in by faceless factories, warehouses and parking lots.

By the mid-seventies even the new development downtown had become irrelevant to the region's economy. Most of the money and power began a slow creep northward up the interstate. The city re-constituted itself into office parks, malls and subdivisions. Just as they grew and prospered from the presence of the monumental crossroads of interstate routes that met in downtown Centralia, the outlying counties asserted their independence from the inner city. Centralia was dividing and creeping away from itself, like an efflorescence of grass.

While Centralia continued to grow, the old exhibition grounds sat idle. The city announced several times its intention to raze the buildings left still standing and sell the property to an investor. None of these plans materialized, however. Finally, in the early 1980s Harold Farmer, a local slumlord, rented the old exhibition grounds for very little money. He opened the place one week-end a month to admit bands of gypsy traders. They arrived in mobile homes, trucks and vans to unload tons of wares of all kinds. This great pile of objects was brought to be sold at the Centralia Antiques Festival. The detritus left by countless spinsters, abandoned relatives and declining family fortunes was here assembled, priced and taken up by wily, cruising droves of an equally endless variety of housewives, queens, hipsters, retirees, militiamen and nostalgia buffs. Everybody, seller and buyer alike, came here for one of two reasons: to buy cheap or to sell dear. Everybody wanted either a bargain or a treasure.

What constituted a really good find varied from person to person, from moment to moment. For example, there was Mrs. Tuttle, a sixty-ish, self-styled "decorator" from South Carolina. We place the term *decorator* in double quotes because, though that's what Mrs. Tuttle called herself, no one could actually ever pin her down and describe any specific work she'd ever *done* as a decorator. Mrs. Tuttle had not always been a fan of the Antiques Festival. Some years back she came to the festival for the first time just to indulge her sister. The latter, an excellent lady who taught elementary school for forty years in one of Centralia's finest neighborhoods, lived in an old section of town not far from the exhibition grounds. She came to the Antiques Festival from time to time to hunt for porcelain bric-a-brac. As she grew older and less able to get about on her own, she tried to encourage her sister, the aforementioned Mrs. Tuttle, to take her to the show.

Prior to her visit to the Festival with her sister, Mrs. Tuttle had thought it was beneath her to mix with "pickers," as she called the dealers and visitors to shows like the Centralia Festival. During this first visit she barely got inside the first building before, while sniffing impatiently through a vendor's booth, she found, to her utter astonishment, a *genuine* treasure! It was three—not one, not two, but *three*—signed Lalique mantel clocks, and they were priced at $15 apiece. Having spotted the impossible find, she never gave herself away to the man who operated the booth, a sick-looking fellow who sat silently on his stool all the time, holding an unlit Pall Mall in his mouth. Beneath his feet hunched his dog, an ancient, nearly bald Pekingese-Beagle mix. Occasionally the dog got up, dithered and wagged its tail while it looked up through sparse lashes at Mrs. Tuttle. She grimaced and covered her mouth with her hand when she thought she was breathing the same air as the ugly beast. Meanwhile she surveyed the other wares in the booth. She was careful not to appear too interested in the three beauties.

Being by nature a predatory sort of person, Mrs. Tuttle immediately calculated in her mind what she should do to play out the deal she had just stumbled upon. She was determined to have the beautiful clocks she had found, and she was determined to have them at the best possible price. She left with a simple *thank you* and wandered down the aisle a bit. Pausing in several booths to paw absent-mindedly over a few things, she made her way back to the site of her discovery within a few minutes. Affecting a look of idle distraction, she asked the man if he could do any better on the clocks. He finally offered her thirty-five dollars for the lot. She worked inwardly to control her sensation of vertigo as she allowed him to wrap the three clocks in bags packed with newspaper. Then she left the show, half-believing she was about to have a stroke, almost leaving her sister behind.

Once she was able to recover a bit she paused to reflect a bit: her discovery gave her the best buzz she'd had in years. Imagine:

not one but *three* Lalique (which she pronounced "LA-LEE-CUE") clocks, lying around in a huge junk sale! She took her sister home without letting on what she had found. She made excuses that she had to get back to Columbia that same night. On the way back home, she called her contact with an appraising firm from her car phone and arranged to have the clocks examined. The following day she sent the three darlings (they were immaculate, and they were hand-signed) to New York. A month later she tottered out to her mailbox, where she found an envelope that contained a letter printed on heavy embossed paper and a check for $4500.

That was her great find at the Centralia Festival. It had kept her coming back every month since. She used her the money from the clocks to treat herself. She went to the bank and bought two certificates of deposit. She paid for a vacation trip to Jerusalem with her Bible study group (to their great dismay). She got a new paint job on her Town and Country. And she had herself custom-fitted the most beautiful thing she owned: a brand new, top-of-the-line, pale lavender blonde Eva Gabor signature wig. Wearing it added nearly a full foot to her height. Her good fortune had almost literally transformed Mrs. Tuttle into part of the landscape of the show.

There was no way to deny it: Mrs. Tuttle had joined the ranks of the pickers. Within a year of her debut she became one of the most notoriously niggling, ubiquitous visitors to the show. To accommodate the booty she hauled home from all the weekend shows she went to, she ordered a pre-fab outbuilding from Sears and had it erected in her back yard just behind the garage. At the Centralia show she even managed to bluff her way in nearly every month during set-up (she was certainly not alone among show visitors in doing this). She fought her way in so she could have a look at all the treasures before the rest of the public was admitted. On such occasions, she could often be seen poking her nose into the back of someone's van, trying to finagle a deal while they were unloading. The sight of her distinctively colored nimbus of hair became a signature image for the festival. You could tell when she was really excited because her wig would get a little crooked, so that she appeared to be looking askance at everything. When local drag queens started dressing as her at Halloween, no one had to explain the costume. Luckily one year the local gay newspaper published an op-ed piece imploring the community to "retire" the combination of big purple hair and too-colorful old lady attire. From that point forward Mrs. Tuttle returned to being a singularity, at least in appearance.

By the sharpest of contrasts, there was Mr. Duncan Fincham, a creature every bit of everything Mrs. Tuttle was not and could never dream of being. A regular visitor to the show, Fincham came for the first Centralia Festival in May, 1982 and hadn't missed more than a few week-ends since. In all that time, as far as anyone could tell, he never bought a single item: not a single funnel cake, nor a single coca-cola, nor a whirligig for his garden, nor a painting for his sofa, nor a single, simple stick of furniture, nor a lamp nor a lampshade nor a drawer pull nor a postcard. Every show he came, he came each day of the show, lingering from opening to closing time. He spent each day going slowly from one booth to another, carefully, delicately, respectfully inspecting certain items that managed to command his attention. There was no telling what would draw him into a state of introspection or wonderment. As he visited the dealers' booths and looked at their wares, he asked questions and told stories. He always knew never to get in the way of the paying customers, and when he spoke, he was so diffident, so sweet and careful, that only the most boorish of dealers were inclined to treat him with less than complete respect.

Even as he queried the dealers about their wares, he would sometimes tell something of himself, and it seemed to those who came to know him—in the way one comes to know such people on such occasions—that he came as much to display himself, somehow, among all the lost objects, as he came to see *them*. To those who met him, it became clear that he came there because he belonged there. He told of living in Hawaii, Alaska and New Zealand. He told of his wife and two daughters in South Africa, whom he hadn't seen or heard from in over thirty years. He told of his journeys to Brazil, his years in Thailand. No one believed any of these stories. His lack of credibility was owing, perhaps more than anything else, to the evidence presented by his appearance. Mr. Fincham looked like an ancient spider monkey that was about to die from something truly awful: he was a tiny, sere little man with a wizened, effeminate face and buck teeth, unkempt red-brown hair and tattered clothes. No one could imagine him fathering another human being, heading a household or finding his way out of his one small corner of familiarity in his own home town. He struck no one as the sort of man who would have lived the life he described for himself.

Of course, it didn't matter whether he was telling the truth about himself or making the whole story up, and despite his truly painful appearance, he wasn't unwelcome; he was interesting company, and the lives he chose to have lived were more intriguing than the usual diet of gossip that occupied much of the dealers' conversation. People at the show even found themselves comparing notes from the fragments of Mr. Fincham's purported history that each of them heard—not to uncover the fraud but to fill in the gaps so they could get as much of a whole narrative strung together as possible. Oddly, no one could discover any outright contradictions in the fantastic tales he told about himself.

Mr. Fincham was welcome, most of all, because of the great reverence he showed for the smallest, most inconsiderable objects someone had thought to save. He happened upon a trinket:

"Excuse me, please, but could you tell me what this is?" he asked.

"That's a box made of a lady's hair," said the dealer.

Hearing this account, Mr. Fincham looked astonished, as though nothing in his entire life had ever surprised him so much as learning there were such things as boxes woven from human hair. He asked, "Why would somebody make a box out of hair? What would you put in it?" He was more than deeply fascinated; he was alarmed.

"Look, open it up and see what's in it. See? Inside there's another box, also made of hair, but the hair is a different color." The vendor, knowing Fincham wouldn't buy the piece, knew nonetheless that watching Fincham discover what he was looking at was as good almost as good as making a sale.

Of course, Mr. Fincham was very thoughtful and quiet for a moment as he looked now at two finely woven boxes made of hair. He asked, "Why is it a different color? Is it someone else's hair? Why would you go around collecting people's hair to make boxes?"

An innocent question, thought the vendor. She said: "It's all hers—whoever the lady was who made the first one—only from when she was younger."

"Oh, a lady did this. Both of them? Well, I guess a man wouldn't do a thing like that, would he? So, the box inside was made before the box outside?"

"That's right."

"What's inside the second box, then?"

"Another box, another color. And again. And yet again. Five in all."

"Oh," Fincham remarked after a long silence, "how sad. She made the boxes herself from her own hair, you think? The last box, the one that holds all the others, she was fixin' to die. Oh, my, would you look at what she did? She boxed up her girlhood inside her death. What would make a person do such a thing?"

"Humility, maybe? A little remembrance she intended only for herself, maybe, or perhaps it was for her daughter or granddaughter, to mark the passing of things."

"But the way she did it," he said, "the end is what you see first. She did it so things pass backwards."

"Or do they?"

"Well, that really is a good question, isn't it?" he asked. "It's a simple thing, but it says a lot."

"Yes, it says a lot."

No one minded that he never bought anything, because in his wonder he sometimes helped people rediscover what they already had. Dealers sometimes quoted portions of his visionary disquisitions to one another. He marveled at the endless variety of objects at the show, and he listened with a child's eagerness as he was told what this or that thing was made for. It was as if he were discovering everything about human past—discovering every detail for the first time. Nothing failed to interest him. Knowing this made you not mind that he took up space and never spent a dime. He never came empty-handed, in his way, and so was always a welcome guest. A guest: other people were simply trade, but Fincham was someone you offered to share a sandwich or a drink, which he always accepted with the perfect, simple gratitude of someone who savored the slowness of things.

It was assumed widely that he was mildly, harmlessly crazy, that he lived in a group home someplace near downtown. It was just as often said that he was a rich eccentric, the last son of old Centralia money, probably an embarrassment to his family, who were probably hoping that enough neglect would lead him to an early and convenient death. Perhaps he was someone who didn't have to work and who, therefore, didn't really need to buy anything or to be anywhere any day of the week. No one knew how he got to the show, and few could imagine him operating something like an automobile. In short, his apparent lack of an occupation, his utter peculiarity, and his general shabbiness made it unclear to observant people whether he was destitute and crazy or just—old, and typically Southern, money.

If the people who came to shop were an odd lot, the dealers were odder still. Among the dealers there were drop-outs, losers, and misfits. There were hordes of failures: failed accountants, failed artists, failed parents and failed children. There were teams: husband and wife teams, teams of lovers, and parent/child teams. And there were legions of loners. There were refugees from small towns and large corporations. There were visionaries, scoundrels, and idiots. There were devout, loving craftspeople and soulless, invidious frauds. At any given moment, two careful observers might reasonably disagree as to which dealer fit best into which category.

As in any community there was a pecking order here. Establishing and affirming this order occupied the dealers during the long stretches of time that tended to span between sales. Most often the debate tended to distinguish between what constituted an antique, a collectible item, and a piece of junk. Most people agreed that Coke bottles and plaster of Paris ducks dressed in hand-made gingham outfits were junk. Beyond that there wasn't much agreement about anything.

The show was very popular, very well-attended. Because of this, new vendors had to get on a waiting list for a booth. Often a new arrival was obliged to set up in one of the open-air booths until an inside space became available. Some inside booths were even passed from one generation to another, a subject of some controversy. Setting up outside was risky and unpleasant. This was due to the fact that Centralia's weather was so changeable and, often, brutal. From May through August, it was generally hot and unbearably muggy. During this part of the year mosquitoes, flies, wasps, fleas and hosts of other pests ruled the outdoors. September was generally a pleasant month, though still rather buggy. From October through December it rained relentlessly, but there were relatively few bugs. In January and February it was either cold or cold and wet. During this season the ants, roaches and spiders went indoors, showing up in all kinds of unwanted places. From mid-March to the end of April, you could generally count on decent, moderate temperatures, though sometimes it would turn bitterly cold during this season. Though it was warm enough during this time, however, the pollen was so unbearable that most people had to stay indoors or end up in the emergency room. This meant that outdoor dealers and their customers were, more often than not, utterly miserable a good ten months a year—this in a part of the world some truly hellish booster had had the bright idea of calling the "sun belt."

Shielded from direct contact with the weather, indoor dealers were, nonetheless, more or less equally affected by it. If it was hot outside, it was hotter inside. If it was cold outside, it was just as cold inside. This meant that the only real advantage to having an inside booth was that you didn't get wet from the rain. From June through August, it was not uncommon to hear of an inside dealer keeling over with heatstroke. Once every couple of years or so, one or two even dropped dead from exposure to the elements.

Building Two was a favorite with many festival-goers. It was widely held to be populated by more than the usual assortment of characters. Typical among them was Nathan Greenwood, a dealer from Charleston. He was not the most successful dealer at the show, but he was very popular, both with buyers and other dealers. Nathan had a considerable talent for finding treasures and oddities ranging from high art to low humor. He had achieved something of a legendary status some time back when he had an altercation with a prospective buyer. The latter was a scruffy young man who noticed a pile of old post cards in Nathan's booth one day during the show. The young man pawed at a delightful hand-painted Japanese card from about 1900. The card depicted a fan emblazoned with peach blossoms, the paint still lovely and bright. The fellow had taken the card from a basket marked "All cards $1.00 apiece, FIRM." He held the card up for Nathan to see (a gesture much despised by vendors). Then he asked, "Can you do any better on this?" We should interject at this point that, as the encounter in question occurred on a Saturday, Nathan had already endured two days of abuse from bargain hunters, including a lengthy argument with Mrs. Tuttle over an under-priced Loetz vase. At any rate, Nathan responded to the young man's inquiry about the postcard by calmly walking over to where the fellow stood, lazily holding the card in one hand, the other hand on his hip. (*That does it!*, thought Nathan, looking in horror at the man's affected posture). Then Nathan looked the man straight in the eye and snatched the card from him. He tore it into pieces and hurled them at the fellow, saying, "There you go; now you can have it for free!"

The young man stared at Nathan for a moment, then left quickly, without a word. Nathan's neighbor, a porcelain dealer named Shauntavius Washington, suddenly let out a loud WHOOP! she said, "Ya'll get ready to call 911, 'cause Nathan fixin' to do *bidness*!" At that several other vendors rushed over to the lady. She continued to laugh and make a fuss while Nathan paced in his booth, arms folded across his chest, not talking to a soul. The story was transmitted down the aisle. As it traveled, little eruptions of laughter arose here and there. Finally, when the neighbors deemed it safe, some wag borrowed a blunderbuss from the scary gun collector down the way a bit, hung a white rag on it, and formed a procession of vendors who approached Nathan's booth with mock solemnity, waving the sign of truce. When the procession reached Nathan's booth he turned to them, scowling. Then he broke into a belly laugh and received their congratulations, a ridiculous display of silent kowtowing, saying, "I thought I was going to have a stroke, I was so mad at that boy! But enough is enough! Fuck 'em and feed 'em beans!"

That day the afternoon passed without much business activity, but no one seemed to care. Nathan found himself saying hello and having a pleasant conversation for the first time with several vendors he had seen but barely talked to for the past ten years or more. At length, the friendly banter subsided and a more familiar sense of dullness fell over the show.

That show turned out to be a particularly bad one, as a matter of fact. On the last day of the show, the two men in the corner booth, whom Nathan referred to as the dish queens, started to pack up at about three o'clock, two hours before the show was scheduled to end. It was August, a notoriously bad month for the show, and most everyone had done poorly. Some had not managed even a single sale for the four days of the show—not one single sale. At about four o'clock, a loud hoarse cry arose from the corner booth: "Motherfucking son of a BITCH!" With that a dish hit the floor and screeched into splinters. Then silence; then a sputter of laughter; then another dish. Then two or three. Then several. Then loud, whooping laughter mixed with breaking dish sounds, then cheers, until breaking sounds rose with laughter and hollering from places here and there throughout the building.

Generally, it took Nathan about two hours to pack up and get out of the building. This was because the other vendors scrambled like schoolchildren to get out. By seven o'clock on this second Sunday in August, Nathan was glazed with sweat and too hungry, dirty and tired to think about anything. He had packed up his unsold treasures and was entering the on-ramp to I-75 north, heading back home to Charleston. He dreaded the five-and-a-half hour drive. Each time he set out to go back home he thought about the fateful trip two years back. At that time sick with the flu, he had embarked on the return trip only to pass out at the wheel from fatigue near Covington. Soon after losing control of the van, he crashed into one of those plastic barrel guard rails. When he regained consciousness, he was met by the sight of the most delicious state trooper he had ever laid eyes on—a muscle-boy reeking suspiciously of Aramis with blue-black hair and pale skin and a wad of chewing tobacco in one cheek (oh, well)—who pulled him from the wreckage. In horror Nathan looked at the overturned van, vaguely thinking about the art deco dining room suit and the Venetian art glass inside, saying to himself, No way!

To his astonishment he wasn't charged with any offense. To his even greater astonishment, once the van was turned upright, he found that the only thing that was broken inside the van was the CD player on his boombox, which greeted him upside-down and open-faced, vomiting disks as he opened the driver-side door. Miraculously, the van was drivable. When he got back to Charleston and got his insurance agency to assess the damage, however, the adjuster totaled the van because of its age. This meant that, at the end of a show during which he had made virtually no money, Nathan was obliged to buy a nearly new van with the small, insufficient settlement his insurance had given him for the old one. "It's that nasty ole waterbug, God, messin' with me again," thought Nathan, thinking of what the neighborhood bag lady, Mae, said in one of her rants whenever she met with a series of misfortunes. Wonder where Mae is now, thought Nathan, catching a glimpse of the receding skyline in his rearview mirror. The last time he had seen Mae was just before Hurricane Hugo. That was over ten years ago.

Chapter Four

Grant Barker sat on a folding chair in the corner of his booth. It was another Saturday in another August, and another Centralia show was crawling through its course. Nobody was selling anything. Grant passed the time trying to ignore the stifling heat. He amused himself by thumbing through the yellow pages he had stolen some time back from the phone booth at the Waffle House in Buena Vista. He was going to use it to play a kind of word game he had invented for weekend shows. The game included what he called an appetizer and a main course. The appetizer consisted of looking up the names of all the nail salons in a city directory and transcribing the best ones in a little binder notebook. Today he was finding nothing of any real interest: Nail Madness, Nailed!, You've Got Nail!, House of Nails, NailStorm. The meager findings made him sigh as he thought, the South is disappearing; where will it all end?

After the appetizer had yielded its rewards, he could take up the main course. This part of the entertainment involved leafing through the directory to look up hair salon names and transcribe them. Today's catch: Crown of Glory, House of Hair, Hair Madness, Mane Event, Bubba's Beauty Mart, Hairanoia (is there a town of any size in this country that *doesn't* have its own *Hairanoia*?), Hair Today, HairPort 98—nothing, after all, but quotidian fare.

Grant had been inspired to invent the game a year or so previously. At that time he was driving though St. Augustine on a buying trip. He had driven the full length of US 1 through Florida more than once, so the trip held little novelty for him. In fact, whenever he made the trip down the old highway, he found himself thinking more and more how little of it was holding onto its original character: small motels with large, boastful signs, concrete-block Florida houses and little roadside shops were gradually being replaced by gated "communities" full of vast, metastasized pseudo-villas that looked like furniture outlets or theme eateries, and toney-looking shopping centers that catered to the tastes of snowbirds thinking they were fleeing the misery they'd created for themselves back up north. Sometimes he'd jump over from US 1 to A1A, scene of another, even more horrible decline. It seemed as though each time he drove down A1A, he saw another huge, ugly condo development had been crapped onto the beach, blocking the ocean view for several hundred yards in each direction, built to look like the Alhambra, or Versailles, or Blenheim, only *better*.

On this last trip, however, he happened to look up from the road, somewhere near St. Augustine, and notice, in large, happy, cursive letters, a sign that read, "Quick Snacks--Hair Styles!" What a combination, he thought, and he found himself filled with delight at the thought of someone stopping in the middle of doing a perm to fill a to-go order for a cheese dog, some slaw and a big gulp. When he got home he decided to create an homage to Quick Snacks, Hair Styles! He bought a brand-new binder notebook, and he used it to record anything, any word or phrase he came across, that conveyed some of the mad, shameless whimsy of Quick Snacks, Hair Styles! He had been collecting odd business names and recording them in his binder ever since that day. On luckier days he found among his found words a sense of giddiness and abandon that seemed to be lacking in the rest of life.

As the pickings today were proving slim, he grew tired of the game. He looked up at the sparse crowd passing by. Not much interest in antique prints today. Most folks here probably just too cheap or poor to spend four dollars at the movies. So: here we are. Grant thought about how much effort he had put into planning his display, setting things up for just the right moment, the right person to come and fall in love with the same things he'd fallen in love with, and for what?

Grant was a rarity at the Centralia Antiques Festival: a local dealer who had his own shop. He made a meager living running either a framing shop that also sold antique prints, or a print shop that offered framing, depending on whom he was talking to at any given time. To supplement his income he took to working the larger weekend antique shows within commuting distance. Now, for what seemed like the thousandth time, he looked about himself at the gawking passers-by and asked silently whether he was wasting his time. He had only been working the weekend show circuit for less than two years. Nonetheless, the time he'd spent at shows like this one had already begun to stretch out behind him like an unbelievably ugly desert. Time to start looking for a way out.

Breathing a long, deep sigh, he spotted a guy walking slowly down the aisle. Why notice this one in particular? Not the prettiest man in the pack, not a troll, either. Just striking, somehow. He just stood out among all the others, looking intently at all the things that filled the displays, working his way slowly from booth to booth. It occurred to Grant that the man who had caught his eye appeared to be noticing everything in every booth. Grant wondered for half a

minute whether this guy was another Duncan Fincham, the sweet
old crazy guy that hung around all the time, looking at every single
thing there was to see. That must be it, thought Grant: it was the
way this older guy looked so intently at everything, piles of crap
and small geegaws that other people weren't even noticing—the
fact that he seemed to see everything was what made him stand out.
He was either crazy or very, very interested in lots of things. An
older guy and, after all, not bad looking, the more Grant thought
about it, really not bad at all: slender body, dressed from a thrift
store (Italian lizardskin brogans with a pair of Levi's and an old
Hawaiian shirt); medium height; salt and pepper hair. Rather an odd
face, actually: large, intense babydoll eyes. As the guy got closer,
Grant could see more than a little pain in them, thought Grant, but
they were alive eyes, not the vacant snake eyes of most gay men;
boyish features that didn't decay as he got nearer, a few, barely noticeable lines belying his age. Graceful, deliberate walk. Gotta be a
poof, thought Grant, he just has to be, and blow me if he isn't a
dealer.

As the odd-looking guy approached Grant's booth, the latter
rose from his folding chair and walked towards the aisle. Grant positioned himself for contact. Then he began doing his version of the
dealer's booth dance. Through gestures alone it conveys a territorial
claim: I don't want to scare you away, but don't mess with my stuff.

Grant began his performance with a conventional opening. He
walked casually over to a rack of etchings that had been pawed by
earlier visitors; he rearranged them neatly. Then he looked around
the booth and gave the appearance of thinking seriously about
cleaning the place up. As he hadn't had a decent conversation all
day, he was interested in talking with the guy—more exactly, in

making *him* talk, to see what that would be like—but he knew he needed to let things happen. As he went through his paces, he noticed the funny-looking guy was now eyeing the black and white piece that hung on the wall. The stranger studied the print admiringly for awhile. His eyes moved slowly over the soft curves of the mother and child scene as he stood before it with his hands clasped behind his back. Grant waited a bit, then decided to take a chance on chumming the fellow up. He said softly, "If there's anything I can help you with, let me know." Then he turned away to busy himself, careful not to make eye contact, waiting to see if the hook had set.

Nathan Greenwood turned from the woodcut and smiled at Grant. "Thank you," he said. "That's quite a nice Kollwitz you've got."

Grant registered surprise at what the fellow said. He tossed out a joke: "Excuse me? Do I need to do a zipper check?" What on earth made me say that?, Grant thought to himself. That was the faggiest thing I have ever done.

Nathan Greenwood looked him up and down and up again. He looked Grant straight in the eye and said, "Not on my account. I meant the woodcut. The picture you have hanging on the wall." Nathan smiled slightly, then turned back to look at the artwork.

Grant felt his face change color. "Oh, that," he said. "I don't know much about it, actually. Saw it at an estate sale and liked it. It is nice, isn't it? And the frame, too. I'm pretty sure it's original."

Nathan turned back to him again and gave a look of surprise. "Yes," he said, "I would have to guess you're right about that," he said. "Quite a rarity, too. Not so much the image itself as the fact that you do have it in what looks very much like its original frame and mat. I'd say that it's all but impossible, as a matter of fact, that it should be here in this condition."

This guy appeared to know something about the piece, and it seemed he was enjoying having the advantage over Grant. This was hardly the first time Grant had found himself in such a situation. After all, he was a young man, still learning his way around. Most of the other dealers had been in the business much longer than he. Dealing with the usually unbidden advice of the older generation was part of his education as a dealer. Learning the trade was about judging the value of things; it was even more about developing what at least looked like patience. He studied his response for a moment, not wanting to say the wrong thing or urge the conversation too much in any particular direction. If things were going to happen, they would happen in their own time. He said, thoughtfully, "As a matter of fact, I really bought it for the frame. The image itself isn't my kind of thing, so much, but the frame is very nice. Arts and Crafts, very nice quality."

Nathan arched his eyebrows and smiled again, then walked around behind Grant to look back at the print from another angle. "Yes, very nice." Nathan said. "Let me make sure I understand this: you bought the image because you like the frame, but you don't know much about the image itself? I notice there's no price on it—what's up with that?" Nathan registered disbelief as he questioned Grant about the woodcut.

Grant's look indicated he actually hadn't thought much about the print analytically before now. Now feeling challenged by Nathan's questions, Grant began to look critically at the piece. "Well, my period is a bit earlier than this. I found it in an estate sale and it was, like I said, the frame that really got me. So intricate, the carv-

ing. I'm thinking the frame was hand-carved, possibly for this particular image. And the pieces are joined incredibly well. Look, you
almost can't tell where the edges come together. It is really fine
work, and look at how the matting picks up some of the tones of the
large figure. The whole thing is a composition. You look at how the
pieces are put together and it really isn't that much of a wonder that
it's survived. I do framing in my shop, so that's how I can see the
work is so good here."

"Yes, it's remarkable work," said Nathan. "It's a museum
piece, of course. So why no price? Is it not for sale?"

"Well, I'm not sure what to do with it, to be honest," said
Grant. "Like I said, it's not my area, the subject matter of the image,
but I knew when I found it there was something different about it,
so I thought it was a mistake not to buy it. I guess I'm really hoping
someone will help me learn something about it. So I don't know if
it's for sale or not. Sounds like you know something. Care to
share?"

Nathan looked back at Grant, noticed the pure green of his
eyes. He made a mental note of the handsome, pale face framed by
dark, nearly black, roughly cut hair. He scrambled to catalog
quickly the many details of the face before he looked away. He took
a deep breath, looked back up again and answered, "I think I can
give you some information," said Nathan. "And I think you should
proceed with caution on this." Nathan stood a little closer to look at
the image, and noticed the characteristic scrawl in the bottom right
corner of the image. It was a signature in pencil, one he had seen a
number of times before. Nathan continued: "Here in the right-hand
corner of the image you can see her signature: the first name is
scrawled so you can only make out the first letter, K, which is for

Käthe, and then the last name is rather abstractly scrawled out to the right of that: Kollwitz. Very masculine-looking signature, actually. I don't think she was masculine, though. She was something of an archetypal mother. If she were alive today I bet she'd have Birkenstocks and an old Volvo station wagon with lots of stickers on the back," said Nathan.

"Are you saying she'd be a lesbian?" asked Grant.

"No, but a straight woman with lots of dyke friends," said Nathan. "Maybe even active in the local Trotskyite cell. She was married and had several children, was Mrs. Kollwitz, née Schmidt, I do believe," he added. "She lived and worked most her life in Berlin, a pretty long life, actually, married to a good doctor who saw mostly poor patients. Most of Kollwitz's models were taken from her husband's clientele. Lots of depictions of poverty and suffering in her work, which eventually got her into trouble with the Nazis, who thought of her as degenerate. She was an active and very brave social activist, very anti-war, very much on the side of the people her husband tried to patch back together," said Nathan. "What you have here is a woodcut that looks like part of a series she did somewhere between 1921 and 1925, and the intricacy of the frame, which I do, indeed, believe is the original frame, supports that. She did several pieces called *pietàs*, like this one, with a woman holding and folded over a dead child. Sort of suggests Edvard Munch, this one. Munch was an inspiration for her, of course. Kollwitz was always connected with the Expressionists, but she really predated them, though her later work included woodcuts that were really clearly Expressionist. Anyway, the quality of the whole presentation you have here, I would think this piece was exhibited in a formal show at some point early in its life. It's definitely a showcase piece." Nathan paused a bit, then turned to look at Grant, blushing and then smiling. He remained quiet a moment.

Grant sensed that he was being studied. He didn't mind. He did wonder if the guy was simply flirting or flirting and telling the truth. Yep, he's a 'mo, Grant thought to himself, and a real smartypants, too. Grant felt another rush of surprise. He hadn't expected to be courted by an older man who showed up out of nowhere to provide an expert opinion. He hadn't expected to like the sensation of being looked at by a stranger. He said, "Sounds like you know your stuff, mister."

Nathan laughed at Grant's pronunciation and at being called "mister." In a crisp German accent he said the name: "Käthe Kollwitz." He continued: "Very well-regarded, of course. She is considered one of the most accomplished draughtsmen in all of Western art. She has a number of museums named after her, and her works are in the National Gallery of Art in D.C.. She died during the bombing of Berlin, close to the end of Word War Two. What you have here is a piece of her work in her prime. If it's an original pressing, I would think you have a really nice find on your hands."

Grant felt himself perk up as he talked with the stranger. So far that day his encounters with people had been hum-drum, and he was enjoying the chance to talk substance. He sensed that this guy was what some people would call a character. He liked the way that Nathan talked, the way he phrased his words, his mannerisms. He began to feel excited at the prospect of making a discovery. "No fooling?" he asked. "So, you think I have a real find on my hands?"

Nathan responded dryly, "Well, I'd think, yes, definitely, it's a real find. I don't know what the value of the image would be in exact dollars, but I would guess, especially since you have it with this incredible frame, possibly in the seventy-five hundred dollar range, maybe much more."

Grant's face opened up into a look of awe. He said, "Seventy-five hundred dollars? Are you kidding me?"

Nathan looked at him again, laughing softly, a gentle, genuine laugh of pleasure. He was enjoying watching a discovery unfold. He pointed to the image and said, "It's really hard to say. I think you should have it appraised by a real-live appraiser," said Nathan. "Her lithographs are fairly rare, but not impossible to find. Same with the woodcuts. The thing you have to be careful with is the fact that lithographs and woodcuts can be very easily copied, and the forgers are really very, very smart. They outsmarted the Ghetty with its kouros not all that long ago, and they aren't getting any dumber. You see Kollwitz's work on Ebay, and they run from around fifteen hundred dollars to upwards of ten thousand dollars or so. You could probably pay a lot more if you bought from a gallery or through a decorator. What complicates the matter for me is the frame. You can find a Kollwitz, but you never see one in its original frame. That changes everything. I just don't know what an appraiser would tell you in this case. Except no honest person would tell you it's worthless, of course."

Grant took a moment to take in Nathan's assessment. Why doesn't he just buy it and go off and make his own money?, thought Grant. Is he the real McCoy?, he thought. Grant said, "You really think there's a chance it's worth something?"

Nathan laughed again. Something below the gentleness of his laugh, something like regret or feeling something lost. Grant noted it, felt a tinge of something, felt the excitement of the good news about the print dancing with that of thinking this might end up being a *first* meeting, not simply a meeting. Nathan went on: "A very good chance, yes. It looks as though you have the real McCoy."

What do you think about that?, thought Grant to himself. He just said *the real McCoy*. What do you think about that?

Nathan continued: "So much about the image just really says it's her work in her prime. It's a beautiful image—sad, like pretty much everything she did, but it's beautiful. And you were right to notice the frame. It's a work of art in itself. It may, in fact, be worth more than the image, even though the image is by such a prominent artist. I gather you haven't taken the whole thing apart to look at it?"

Grant shook his head, knowing from Nathan's tone that he wasn't being chastised for not having a closer look. How often had he been lectured on the consequences of someone not taking care with something valuable that had fallen into their hands? He said, "No, I was going to but I got busy working with some other prints to get them ready. I thought about taking it apart and then I was afraid to. I was afraid I'd make the wrong move and ruin it some-how. Like I said, this sort of picture really isn't my specialty. The rest of my stuff is very different from this one. You won't find an-other Kollwitz among the rest of my prints."

Nathan gave a look that showed he was interested in the pros-pect of more treasures lying around, unrecognized. "What other prints? What *is* your specialty?"

Grant answered, "Much older stuff. Engravings, etchings, woodcuts, mostly 17th and 18th century, though I do have some 19th century stuff these days. You might know about these over here. French, mid-century, guy named Grandville."

Nathan nodded in recognition. He asked, "Jean-Jacques Grand-ville? Please don't tell me you found a copy of *Les Fleurs Animées* and chopped it up for the pictures?"

Grant was surprised at Nathan's knowledge. Would it be possible for him to know too much? He said, "You know Grandville? Are you a print dealer? What are you into?"

Nathan shrugged. "Well, if the subject is still collectibles, lots of things. Good taste, honesty, oddness. I buy what I like. Mostly deal in 20th century stuff: mostly Secessionist, Art Nouveau, art deco, art moderne. But I'm really interested in anything that's good design. So, bearer of untold treasures, are you a destroyer of old books?"

Grant felt the accusation hit its mark. He had, in fact, torn up more than a few old books for their lithographs until he came to realize what a crummy thing it was to treat a book like a carcass. With a bit of shame, he said, "It came to me already in pieces. And it wasn't *Les Fleurs Animées*. It was a partial copy of *Scenes From the Public and Private Lives of Animals*. I can't think of the real title in French. The binding was shot; the images were frayed. Matting them was the only way to save them, at that point."

Nathan sensed the truth, let it pass. He actually found it charming that Grant would allow himself to be found out in such an obvious fib. Boys that pretty don't lie, he thought, not until they've really pissed you off. He sighed and shrugged and looked back up at the woodcut, saying, "What a wonderful madman Grandville must have been! Forgive me if I sound strident, but I'm sure you know what happens with a lot of the print art that shows up at shows like this."

Grant paused over the word *strident*, thinking: I bet this guy spends a lot of time by himself, unless he lives somewhere outside the South, but he doesn't sound homogenized enough to be living somewhere else. A loner, then. Probably lost somebody. Recently? Or is it an old wound? *Who's been hurting you, pumpkin?* "You're right. I love old books. It's a drag so many of them get torn up to make powder room art. So, anyway. What do you think I ought to do with the lithograph?"

Nathan shrugged again, thinking for a moment. He said, "It's a woodcut, not a lithograph. First thing I'd do is take it down for now and, when you have some time, think about getting the whole thing cleaned. You're going to have to be very careful with it. But I would get it out of here as soon as possible and proceed with great care. Do you mind if I asked how much you paid for it?"

Grant couldn't believe how the day had turned. He tried to contain his excitement. "No, not at all. I paid about fifty dollars for it, as I recall."

"Fifty dollars? Hah!" said Nathan. "Almost like winning the lottery. What a nice surprise all this is. You ask me, it's what the show is really all about."

Grant seemed puzzled by Nathan's comment. "What do you mean?" he asked.

Nathan explained: "Well, I mean that what most of us, or maybe just some of us, really come for is to discover what we already have. To be able to see through our own blind spots. To find in the mountains of crap you drag home something of substance. Diving for gravitas. I don't care all that much about selling junk to all these people. Do you care?"

Grant listened thoughtfully to Nathan's little speech. He said, "It's a living. I like being around all this… ."

Nathan broke in: "Stuff? You like your stuff? That's honest. The public is just a necessary evil. You come here to be with your stuff. And to find more stuff. Maybe once in a long while you might meet someone who's interesting, somehow, but given how many people happen through a place like this, they don't tend to make much of an impression, do they? Sad to say, I suppose. All these people, and they just come and go like half-formed ideas. Once they're gone, they're really gone. It isn't about them. It's about going to garage sales and thrift stores and the occasional antique mall that actually sells antiques and on and on, and you sift through things, looking. You go out and find all this stuff, and you're not always sure what makes you buy what you end up buying, but if you're the real article and not just a hack, you buy a lot of what you buy because you like it, because *you* want to own it. And the really best of the best moments don't come from a sale, do they? They come from making a discovery, from finding something wonderful."

Grant found himself feeling oddly happy at the thoughts Nathan was throwing out so casually. He said, "I never heard anybody talk about it that way."

Nathan laughed at himself: "Who knows what any of it means? Anyway, enough time spent sitting in your booth thinking about it all, and the dust motes start spelling out messages from the beyond."

Grant found himself thinking less about the woodcut and more about Nathan: he wanted to know more about this guy. It had been awhile since he had met anyone who made him want to talk seriously about anything. Nathan had the kind of charisma you only really noticed once you started talking with him. Even more interesting, it appeared he didn't know this about himself. Grant asked: "How long have you been at this?"

Nathan smiled at the question. He answered, "Doing the show or blowing hot air? Oh, let's see, a few hundred years or so. Long enough. You?"

"I got into the show circuit about two years ago."

"Ah, you're still in the larval stage. You have a day job?"

"I have a little shop here in town. Prints and framing. By the way, what's your name? I can't believe we've been talking all this time and I haven't introduced myself."

"It's the times, I'm afraid. I'm Nathan Greenwood. Glad to meet you. And you?"

"I'm Grant Barker. Nice to meet you. Listen, it really is good of you to tell me all this stuff."

"Well, when advice is free, you can't help but get your money's worth. The pleasure's mine. Anyway, what makes you so sure I'm not feeding you some kind of line?"

"What do you mean?"

"How do you know I'm not conning you?"

"Why would you do that?"

"As a matter of fact, I wouldn't. But how do you know I wouldn't?"

"I don't know, I guess. I mean, we just met. Thought didn't occur to me. Anyway, you don't seem like the type."

"What type is that?"

"The type to try and pull a con."

"Wouldn't the type to pull a con seem like anything but?"

"Well, if you thought the woodcut was worth something and you were a con artist, you could've just kept your mouth shut. You could've made me come down on the price, and you'd be on your way with a fat little bargain, maybe."

"What if it's not the print I'm interested in? What if I were trying to con you for something else?"

"What else is there? It's either this print or another. All my stuff is pretty reasonable, I think, given what it is. Oh, I get it. So maybe you saw something else you really want, and you're distracting me by spinning a yarn about this worthless piece of crap so I won't notice when you pay me ten bucks for the Delacroix I didn't know I have and walk out of here like...."

"Like the Queen of Sheba? You never know, do you? I mean, look: I prance on up from nowhere and start spouting all this chin music and you pretty much buy it, don't you?"

"Well, yes. I mean, no! Wait a minute! What is this? First you tell me about the print and now you tell me not to believe you?"

"It's just that you were so willing to believe me, I couldn't help but encourage you to take a more critical view. You have to be careful in places like this, you know."

"Thanks! I'm not stupid. I think I can take care of myself okay. So was all that stuff about the print just some kind of joke or something?"

"No. It wasn't. Look, I'm sorry. I do think you might have something of value here. It's certainly worth investigating. Forget all that blah-blah I just spouted. If I have any credibility left here, I honestly think you should have this Kollwitz piece checked out. It might wind up yielding you a nice return on your reasonable investment. Really, I have no intention of ripping you off. Who knows? You might be in the money!"

"It's okay. Anyway, you're right. I look around me at all these old guys sometimes and think I'm probably out of my league."

"Well, on behalf of the good old guys, or at least, on behalf of the old guys who try to be good—"

"I'm sorry, I didn't mean that! I mean, you're not that old. You seem pretty nice."

"No problem. You don't really think I'm nice, do you? Nobody else does."

"That didn't come out the way I wanted it to."

"Don't worry about it."

"Anyway."

"Listen, do you want to have a look at this thing?"

"What do you mean?"

"I mean, take it out of the frame and have a good look at it?"

"Well, yeah! Sure! Okay, then, you think we should do it now?"

"No. It's too dusty here and there are all these awful people hanging around. You really need to clean it on the outside before you take it apart. Let me suggest this: I'm staying with some friends near downtown, about fifteen minutes from here. Two dykes, known 'em forever. Nice people, really. I'll give you directions, we meet there after the show, and we'll take it apart on my friends' dining room table and see what we see. You have plans for dinner?"

"No, not really."

"Where are you staying during the show?"

"Actually, I live here, in town."

"That's right, you have a shop and all that. Well, like I said, my friends are nice people, they'll cook us dinner and we can open a bottle of wine and we can get out the x-acto-knife and see what kind of story little Katy has to tell. You game?"

"Gosh, I don't know."

"Gosh? Did you say 'gosh'? How charming."

"Stop. Be nice."

"Oh, relax. Free dinner offer, free expert advice?"

"Wait a minute, you've got me going in circles. One minute you're a nice guy, the next minute you're all hand buzzers and squirting daisies. Where are you from, anyway?"

"Oh, I wish I had a hand buzzer! People play with such dreary toys nowadays, don't you think? I grew up here, but moved away the day the music died. A long time ago, that is. Now I live in a shack on John's Island, in Charleston. What makes you ask?"

"I guess I'm just checking you out a little. Do you mind?"

"No. Not at all. So you have my general coordinates. Next question?"

"Why didn't you make me an offer on the print?"

"Because I'm not a crook. Next question?"

"You really think I have something extraordinary on my hands, don't you?"

"What makes you think that?"

"Well, if you thought it was nothing much, you wouldn't have spent all this time talking about it, would you? And why would you be willing to make your friends mad by inviting a stranger home for dinner and dragging my stuff into their house?"

"Mercy, you're a fast learner. You might have a future in this business. If you do, I hope you don't pick up a sordid past along the way, like most of us. If you do happen to acquire a sordid past some day, however, I hope you'll tell me all about it. Just don't let your soul get all dried up or pickled hanging around all these crafty old gargoyles."

"So tell me, aside from the two dykes, do you have many friends?"

"Dear boy, I have a public. Any more questions?"

"Yeah. But I don't want to use 'em all up, just now. You sure your friends won't mind?"

"No, they won't. Dinner and x-act-o, then?"

"Well, yeah, I guess. I mean, thanks, I'd like to. Very much. That'd be nice."

"You're welcome. Well, then, it's time for me to go slop the hogs and feed the polo ponies. You have a pen?"

"Oh, sure. Here."

Nathan "So, it's all settled. In case we don't catch up with each other by the end of the day, here's the address and phone number. I'll go call Becky and Alice and tell them to fumigate the leznest for your arrival. I think we're having pork chops for dinner tonight. That okay with you?"

"Sure! Can I bring something?"

"Oh, no, nothing at all. Let me tell you, you're in for a treat. Those two bulldaggers can cook to make your tongue slap your brains out!"

"I'll be sure to wear protection."

"Always a good idea, isn't it?"

"Yes. Yes, it is. Well, thanks for the invitation."

"You already thanked me. And it's my pleasure. All the more so, since I'm not cooking. And don't worry about the girls, they'll be tickled to have a guest. Honestly. Salt of the earth, those two. Well, it's time for me to go now. Whatever comes up, it'll be a nice evening."

"Whatever comes up."

"Bye for now, then. Oh, let me give you my card."

"Great. Bye."

As Nathan walked away, Grant looked down at the card and gasped. The card read:

Wretched Excess
Antiques, Collectibles, Quick Snacks, Hair Styles, and More!
Booth 240
Centralia Antiques Festival
Nathan Greenwood, Proprietor

Chapter Five

Nathan made his way towards the exit. He breathed deeply to flush out the impression made by the innocent with the lithograph. *These kids today*, he said to himself. He was trying to walk off the impression of sweetness left by this Grant Barker person, this pretty kid with evidently no facial pores, green green eyes and hair a shade of really it was a deep auburn that couldn't come out of a bottle and oh, those cheekbones and, goodness, those lips and did you see the size of those hands? When is it in life, Nathan asked himself, that the switch gets thrown and people go from having no visible pores at all to having all those craters? And he was charming, that boy; what a surprise to meet such a creature and to have a talk! My god, it talks! And its feet actually appear to tread the ground, which only gives the lie to all those Greek myths. Awful people, Greeks—so sleazy. Something must've happened to the gene pool—some horrible invasion.

But, I digress, thought Nathan as he wandered on down the aisle. Oh, that boy. I wish I'd never seen him, now. So much to look at and try to not get caught looking at: the roughly cut mane framing the pair of wide green eyes set against an unspoiled pallor, hubba-hubba! Let us pray those were not contacts. No, they couldn't've been—it wasn't Prell green, it was a real live human eye green. The glint of lunacy shining in them, twin Granny Smiths full of the moon! The way those delicious episodes of embarrassment animated his skin--how easy it had been to make his cheeks catch fire! The gorgeous twang in his voice. A real Southern boy; I don't think he was raised around here, not with that accent; no, he was from the real South, maybe Cuthbert? Thomasville? I don't think he's from above the gnat line. So much to see and sort out, so much. Wonderfully lanky he was, but not sticklike, lanky and still graceful, that's how he looked; the forms of his shoulders, chest, and arms draped in an old coat, the baggy trousers belying a narrow waist, strong thighs and calves, thrift-store-shod feet as big as a field hand's. Mercy!

I'll bet the second toe of each foot is longer than the first, thought Nathan. He saw Grant at a high school swim meet curling them over the starting board, arching forward. As he walked Nathan traced the imagined curve of the long muscle flowing down Grant's pale, imagined side, flexed in the posture of the impending dive. He saw the ribs push against the broad white back, animating a mole on the middle right area of the back, where the lat muscle begins to taper inward, panned to view the one neat crease just above the bellybutton, looked up at the softly panting abdominals, then the hairless brown nipples that stood on point, then fell fainting to see the flowing rise of the quadriceps and fell further to see the soft luxurious bag held tightly between the straining legs, then floated up the back and studied each gentle knobby rise along the spine, rising to hover at the back of the boy's head, the dimpled shoulders poised to take flight as Nathan looked out above him over the hushing water. Then the arms flexed, pushed forward, and the full, tight, twin loaves rose, fell, disappeared as a thick black neck of Speedo hung for an instant, then carved into the breaking, foaming blue-green gulp.

Suddenly Nathan found he had made his way outside the building. He had no idea how he'd wound up where he now found himself. It was an odd sensation. As he came to his senses he was just about to bump into someone. The unfortunate greeter, a hefty old queen, stood before Nathan, struggling with one hand to get a small dog on a leash under control, holding in the other a large, newly-purchased dreamcatcher. "Good grief!" Nathan said out loud, taking in the scene before him with truly horrified indignation. "This is grotesque!"

The old queen looked back at Nathan in wounded disbelief. "Well, Mary, you're not exactly Gordon Scott, yourself," he said, and stormed off, spitting curses, dragging the dog.

Nathan took a moment to recover from the encounter. He chastised himself and thought for a bit about rushing after the man he'd just insulted to explain, forgive me darling, I wasn't talking about you, really. Thinking there was no way such an attempt could end well, he tried to shrug off the unfortunate accident and go on about his business. Dreamcatchers aren't antiques, anyway, he thought to himself, that person needs to go to a shopping mall, not a place like this. As he continued walking he distracted himself by thinking about things other than the boy's imagined body. He thought about the matter at hand—for the moment, it was the lithograph. He mused over how many treasures he had all but given away because of being inexperienced and getting the wrong—or no--information. Knowing what something is worth can be very tricky, especially if you choose to deal in something about which you know very little. Dealers are notoriously unscrupulous, and the law does little to protect the public against them. The avarice and ignorance of the buying public only makes it easier for some dealers to rationalize passing off junk as treasure. If people make it so easy for you to steal from them, why not steal? The best museums in the world get duped into buying fakes, so why should the general public be any safer? Despite their best efforts at damage control, museums as rich and powerful as the Ghetty in Los Angeles and the Tate in London couldn't keep the public from finding out they'd paid scores of millions of dollars to first authenticate and then to buy a *kouros* or a Rembrandt that turned out, on further investigation, to be a fake. If the Tate can be duped for millions, how much more easily can the amateur collector be taken?

Apart from the matter of fake collectibles, thought Nathan, it is astonishing how much money a person will readily give up to buy a piece of worthless garbage—think of Thomas Kinkaide and the rotten crap he keeps crapping out onto the landscape—and think of how people line up to buy shit like that. Yes, if you offer trash for sale, you will never be without a public to buy it. Astonishing as that is, it is just as astonishing how people will turn their noses up at a genuine masterpiece.

Nathan thought about the times when his friend Mark (aka the Empress) and he would go on road trips to antique malls throughout the South. The antiques malls they scoured were usually an old storefront or house converted into a number of booths operated by independent dealers. Experience had taught them that, when they went shopping, it was always important not to fix their sights too narrowly, but rather to keep an open and alert mind, looking for anything with a touch of style. As they looked over the shelves of all the shops and booths along their way, they found that labels frequently lie. They also found that the truth about the provenance of an object often reveals itself in minute details of execution. In their travels they found a truly amazing number of objects that were labeled and priced as genuine antiques, bearing nonetheless clear characteristics of reproductions. Nathan and Mark joked among themselves that they ought to take a pen and mark FAKE on the carefully hand-printed labels. There were, in fact, well-known establishments along the southeastern coast where they were banned from shopping.

Nathan thought to himself about the time he had seen an ornate bed in some greedy little dealer's booth. It was displayed with a sign that read "early 18th century French bed, $24,000 FIRM." Nathan knew little about the period—only that he loathed it. Nevertheless he felt confident, after looking the bed over with a look of undisguised revulsion on his face, that 18th century French artisans probably were not accustomed to using steel machine screws and aluminum hasps to fasten the pieces of a bed. He felt reasonably certain that the statement of origin given on the sign was, as he liked to say, "nothing more than a miniature fiction inscribed and left by accident near the object it was subsequently taken to represent." Such accidental arrangements were commonplace. Whole fortunes were made and broken by them.

Returning to his own booth, Nathan surveyed his collection of wares: a brace of 50s lamps, some pretty nice pieces of Tiffany and WMF silver, a Herman Miller office desk from the late 40s, a pair of Czech art glass candlesticks and a motley assortment of other objects (a Maori flaying knife carved out of a human thigh bone, an autographed photograph of Tony Dow with hand-painted eyelashes and a number of b-movie posters chief among them). He felt bothered and somewhat stricken with a sudden fit of anxiety as he thought how little he would probably sell this week-end. He felt just as certain that the snotty bastard with the fake chi-chi bed had probably gotten his asking price. Twenty-four thousand dollars for a piece of nelly catalog furniture! For Nathan a good show would bring in about $2000 for four days of mostly deadening, empty chit-chat with hundreds of people, maybe ten or twenty of whom might actually buy something. Out of that sum he had to pay his booth rent and numerous other expenses associated with making the three-hundred mile trip just to take the gamble he might actually make something. A good show came along a few times a year. The rest he survived somehow and tried to forget.

For a normal person it would have been a rough life. What made it bearable for Nathan was the knowledge that, having done this sort of thing for as many years as he had—twenty or so—there was simply nothing else that he was cut out for. Over the years he had held the usual assortment of nowhere jobs: waiter, restaurant manager, bellhop. The only straight job he ever held was a one-year stint as an art teacher fresh out of college. The sheer misery of trying to hold it together while presiding over a roomful of willfully ignorant, spiteful suburban Centralia teen-agers had sent him fleeing into the wide, vast world of dead-end jobs.

In his twenties Nathan had shown some promise as an artist—his formal education had trained him to be a painter of paintings. During the early morning hours he painted pictures in his apartment, looking for a breakthrough that would let him know he was on his way. In the afternoons he catnapped to prepare himself for nights of white-tablecloth pretense, slinging overcooked, confused food to squawking hordes of the upwardly mobile. His experience in food service made him wonder, at times, why the People's Workers Party wasn't the primary political force on the national scene. "In Centralia, you are what you drive." He overheard a patron saying those words one night as he was pouring a glass of La-Fitte-Rothschild that his employer sold at $95 a bottle. At the Kroger down the street you could get the same bottle on sale for under ten dollars. The best thing about the world of work as it is commonly lived, he concluded, is that none of it encourages anyone with his head screwed on straight to believe that any of it matters.

Nathan had drawn and painted since he was a child. Luckily for him, his father raised no objections when Nathan decided to study art at the University of Georgia. At Georgia Nathan met and became enthralled by two remarkable artist-teachers: Hadley Smith and Jim Herbert. Arriving at Athens for the first time in fall of 1970, Nathan had the good fortune to fall in with a group of art students and other people who exposed him to all the forbidden fruit that he could scarf up. Through Herbert he became fascinated with De Kooning, Rauschenberg and Oldenburg, and his studies led him further to discover Francis Bacon and David Hockney. The energy of their art made them his new heroes; that energy percolated in his mind and challenged him to begin to ask what he would make of himself. Through his friends he discovered the wonders of youth in the early 1970s: pot, Captain Beefheart, dada, Janis Joplin, acid, Billie Holiday, Marcel Duchamp, David Bowie, low country cooking, quaaludes, Philip Glass, living with multiple roommates, Man Ray, blowing a shotgun hit, Laurie Anderson, John Waters, Luis Buñuel, mescaline, Antonio Gaudì, Martin Scorsese, road trips, Jean Cocteau, Little Walter, the endless beauty and variety of men's dicks and the transformative experience of giving and taking one up the ass, Etta James, the 1939 World's Fair, peyote, Big Maybelle, the power of drag, Howard Finster, the romance of fashion, the persistence of plastic and the possibility of all things. Having grown up in a sad, quiet house, his university life made him feel the urgency of making an imprint on the world.

During his last year at school he had begun to paint in a way that hinted that he might be getting somewhere, might be doing something worthwhile. Enlivened by what he saw in De Kooning and Herbert, he was stretching their styles into something like his own. But before much time had passed after he left school, he just got lost in what he was doing as a painter. What had come alive for him during art school quickly became diffuse and troubled after his rotten year as an art teacher. After that, beset by confusion and un-certainty as to whether he could make his life as an artist, he stumbled through his twenties, dabbling at his art. He displayed his work in shows. He got invitations to paint sofa paintings, but he couldn't bring himself to do it. He began to falter at figuring out what to do with the education that had awakened him.

Nathan graduated from Georgia in 1974, moved back to Centralia and settled into a suitably odd attic apartment that overlooked the downtown skyline, which he referred to as the putrified forest. By the time he left teaching a year later, he was faced with the ne-cessity of figuring out what his life would be amidst the consider-able distraction of the booming gay social life in Centralia. Life in college had been idyllic. One by one, though, the members of his college clan graduated and scattered into accidental lives, so that he was left, after a time, a little more worldly and fairly alone.

As easy as it had been to find sex and romance in Athens, Na-than was astonished at the explosion of opportunities that met him back in Centralia in 1974. In the year of his return to his hometown, disco culture was going strong. The Centralia of this time was a full-throttle party town. Disco culture seemed to have sprung out of nowhere, spawned by a single Donna Summer song, complete with an endless supply of good-looking, frisky and mostly friendly men who seemed to want to go out, dance, play and bounce from one bed to another six nights out of every seven. Between the bars, the bathhouses, the dbs (Nathan's acronym for the dirty book store) and the numerous cruising areas throughout midtown Centralia, the opportunity to gather all types of sexual experience seemed to beckon from everywhere. Whenever in later years he tried to explain his life during this period to younger friends, he said it was like finding yourself at the fire sale of the century, loaded with cash and someone else's plastic.

Times being what they were, Nathan even found himself not infrequently meeting men on the bus or on a walk. Hardly a month went by without his making a detour to or from this errand or that to meet someone without intending to, find a quiet place (not always indoors) and engage in a little distraction before continuing with his daily chores. The salad days of a spontaneously born Babylon with outposts in every major city in the western world, they led him further from his art, further into a casual, careless existence he would never have thought of settling into. By the time things started to get grim in 1981 when people started talking about the gay plague, he had all but stopped painting, even though he had had a number of gallery shows, all of them well-received. He got recognition for his work, but few sales. And he couldn't bear to produce what he was being asked to produce. As he fell away from making things, he consoled himself by collecting them.

As he took a seat in his booth Nathan thought, crimony, it's Saturday and I haven't made a good sale yet! No lamb chops this month. Oh well, maybe Sunday magic will kick in, who knows? For Nathan, Sunday magic was the occasional miraculous last-minute flurry of purchases between two and four o'clock on the last day of the show. A few poker-faced patrons would have cased his wares over the previous three days of the show, not showing any interest, then show up at around four o'clock on Sunday, frantic to buy this or that. Often the bulk of Nathan's take would come in during Sunday magic, but just as often, things would be so dead he'd be packing by three, thinking about the dish queens, waiting long before the doors closed to get his van in the building to haul ass.

As he made his way to his booth, Brenda Tarpington, a silver dealer and an old show pal, came up out of nowhere and said, "Nathan, where you been? There's a lady was here just a minute ago, real interested in that Herman Miller desk and the two Atomic lamps. She had a wad o' money, babe. Where the hell you been so long?"

"Oh, I was just taking in the sights. So, where is she? Come back, Peggy Guggenheim, come back!" Nathan was irritated at himself for staying so long away from his booth, but his fatalism made it impossible for him not to make light of the situation. The sale in question could fill his freezer and give him mad money for a month.

"Naw, doll, I don't see her now. She's a big girl, well-dressed, dyed-red hair, nice shoes, lots of jewelry."

"Oh, another faux-punk socialite from Chislington out trolling for something for her rumpus room. How nice. Well, c'est la vie, n'est-ce pas? Anyway, thanks Brenda, you're a better neighbor than I deserve." Nathan shrugged, shook his head and walked into his booth to sit down. Perched on his chair, legs crossed, hands clasped over his knees, he looked up and out over the vast hall, echoing with PA system noise, chatter and the general hum of a big, enclosed space, and he felt the humming of his lungs as he sighed deeply. For a moment he wished he could make everything around him disappear, people and treasures alike, and just sit with his own thoughts. He closed his eyes for a moment, trying to blot out everything unpleasant about the show, and in his mind's eye he saw again the form of a young man's body slicing through the water—for a second he even thought he could smell the chlorine in the pool. Unfortunately, just at that moment the dreaded Wigletta appeared, his latest piece of street trash toddling close behind.

"Nate, Nate, I been tryin' to catch up with you for the past three days!" Wigletta, whose real name was Barry Williams, was a furniture dealer who had moved from Hahira, Georgia to someplace in one of the land-locked states and who wore the nastiest toupee Nathan had ever seen.

"Barry, if you don't quit calling me 'Nate' I'm gonna rip that road kill right off of your shiny pate and throw it in the garbage where it, and you, belong! Now, go away, you're scaring the customers. Matter of fact, you're scaring me, so get out of my booth!"

"Oh, Nathan, I had an experience, you might say, and you gotta hear about it!"

Nathan resented having been disturbed from his reverie, so he wasn't in the mood to show any mercy. He said, loudly: "Barry, by now I would think you'd realize that yet another recounting of how you have met yet another sad sack living in his car sporting a ten-inch beercan dick and who used it to make your eyes pop out on stems would fail to hold the interest of even your most patient and all-too-captive audience! Go away, shoo! Do you hear me? And take your factotum with you!"

"Nathan, I been given a vision of God."

"No, Barry, you've been sniffing wig adhesive. Put it on your head, not up your nose. READ THE LABEL. Now shoo!"

"You are NOT gonna cast me out, 'cause I got a message from God Almighty."

"Oh, now, Barry, this really is the limit! You can't be acting up like this with real paying customers wandering around. Someone's gonna come and take you straight to the bin, you hear me? Stop this crap."

"Now, listen! Last week I was in my house, me and Duane was in the living room watching the tv, and all of a sudden, pebbles started to come raining down from the ceiling, bouncing on the floor, and then the windows took to rattlin', then a glass pane broke out, and it started to hail outside, and them pebbles was bouncin' 'round all over my livin' room floor, comin' right out o' the ceiling, which I saw with my very own eyes, and I was so scared I like to have died, 'til Duane got up from where he was sittin' and said, God Almighty make it stop!, and soon as he said that, the whole congregation just quit it! Now just what do you think of that?"

"Well, Barry, I think you should fire the maid, because she's obviously not cleaning worth shit. Or maybe you should call the Vatican and ask someone to look up indoor pebble showers and see what they have to say. Now, is that all?"

"Is that all? Is that all? Well, listen, mister godless His-name-in-vain-takin' homo, don't you see the sign? He's tellin' me somethin', He's issuing me a wake-up call, He is blessin' me by castin' stones so I would go out and spread his gospel! I got a new life, Nate, and I'm here to hep you find your way to yours!"

"Barry, what did I just say about the N-word? And just who do you think you're calling a homo, missy?"

Nathan's neighbors were stopped in their tracks by the spectacle of Nathan's rising with a speed that no one thought him capable of to place both hands on his visitor's head, yelling *Heal, in the Name of Jesus, this roadkill-besmattered sinner! Cast out these lacre-incrusted demons, My Savior!* and then a painful snatching sound as the appliance was ripped from the visitor's head, accompanied by a high-pitched shriek from the latter, who stood there stock still all the while with his hands held up in surprise, his mouth agape. A sharp round of applause arose as Nathan held the wad of fake hair aloft, and another afternoon of tedium was briefly stripped of its pall. For awhile, Nathan allowed himself to forget about the boy and the Kollwitz piece.

Chapter Six

Later that Saturday Grant got into his truck and took off to find Becky and Alice's house. He felt a bit uneasy about what kind of evening was ahead of him. On the one hand, he felt anxious as he thought about the prospect of spending the evening with two women he didn't know. On the other hand, he was also looking forward to spending an evening with Nathan. He was attracted to Nathan on several levels, and he felt hungry for contact with someone who wasn't a barfly. He also thought to himself that Nathan was attracted to him, but fighting it.

Grant arrived at Becky and Alice's house without problems; Nathan's directions were clear and the route was familiar. As he got out of his truck, Grant looked up at the huge, old house and smiled at the sight of it. The house was a craftsman bungalow with cedar shingles, a broad verandah wrapping around the front and right side. The porch was heavily laden with potted plants; it was littered with old-fashioned porch furniture; a gaggle of wind chimes hung from the eaves around the porch; and there were even a few painted concrete gnomes in view. The front yard was enclosed by an unpainted picket fence. The yard was full of large old azaleas and boxwoods, all of them unpruned, overgrown. There was a small pond with a moss-covered statue of St. Francis standing slightly atilt, overlooking the water. From the street it was an inviting, comfortable-looking house. It gave the impression that the owners had lived there a good many years.

Grant drew the lithograph out of the passenger side of his truck and went through the gate. He walked up the short flight of stairs that gave entry onto the porch, and then went to the front door. The door was open, allowing him to see through the screen door into the front room of the house. What he saw made him think of Nathan's calling the place a *leznest*: a well-worn living room full of treasured clutter arranged on the walls, the floor, and hanging in the windows. Inside he could see a number of unframed canvasses on the walls, striking in their subject matter: a dwarf shaking hands with a giant, a gooey-looking landscape that appeared to be studded with giant teeth, and a portrait of a woman with a large, very strange-looking face that looked as though it was about to explode. As he stood at the door, he could hear music—Marianne Faithfull singing about strange weather—and voices coming from the back of the house. He felt a tingle in his belly as he knocked first lightly, and then loudly. Before long a large woman appeared at the front door, barefoot and wearing a bright, printed cotton dress. She looked as if she'd just been interrupted in the middle of cooking.

"Hi, you must be Grant. I'm Becky Turner, come on in," she said with a deep warm drawl. Her voice was full of sincerity. That was a good sign, but Grant knew that among Southerners, sounding sincere is often an expression of the deepest loathing. Wait and see, thought Grant. He pulled open the screen door and maneuvered the lithograph into the house.

"How are you?" continued Becky, shaking his free hand.

Junior League meets "The Killing of Sister George," Grant thought to himself. "Okay, I guess," he said. "You sure I'm not imposing?"

"Oh, no," said Becky, breathlessly. She certainly seemed to be genuinely happy to see him, as if they'd already met before. She continued: "It's no trouble at all. We're glad to have a real guest. Nathan's like family, of course, so he doesn't count. Except on special days. We don't get out much, so a real newcomer is a treat. Come on in and let's get you something to drink," she said, smiling in a way that made Grant feel at ease. He liked the sound of her voice, deep and soft. He liked the way she pronounced the word *on* as if it were *own*. Becky was forty-three, looked younger. She had long curly blonde hair and a freckled face. She gave the impression of someone who'd grown older but not up.

"It's really nice of you to let me come," said Grant. "And your house is cool."

"Aren't you sweet?" said Becky. "We've lived here a long, long time, so we've had the time to do it up like we want. Here, let's take the artwork into the front bedroom for now and I'll close the door while we're having dinner. The place is overrun with animals, and I'm afraid they'll all try to mess with it if we leave it out. Nathan says it's a lovely piece, and I'm so excited for you," said Becky, leading Grant through the living room into a large, cozy bedroom. As he listened to Becky, Grant thought to himself that she sounded like an old-money socialite, her accent evoking the South that middle-class people banished from their voices.

As they made their way into the bedroom, it was obvious that this was the room where Nathan slept while he was visiting. Realizing this, Grant felt a little odd for a moment. He found himself quickly looking around the room for clues that would tell him more about Nathan. Noticing a stack of books on a night table, Grant quickly surveyed the titles, but only caught the words "true crime" on the topmost volume. So, Nathan liked to read about real criminals? He couldn't help but be a bit amused and, naturally, taken aback by such a prospect—a far-ranging connoisseur who made bedtime stories out of books about serial killers? Not your average trade, he thought.

After they put away the lithograph and closed the bedroom door, Becky led Grant back through the house into the kitchen, quickly managing to ask him where he was from and who his people were. He was being quizzed. So, Nathan must've said something.

"Look who's here," said Becky, entering the kitchen where Alice and Nathan were working at putting together what looked like dinner for ten.

"Hey, Grant," said Nathan, turning from the counter to flash a smile. "You made it."

"The directions were great, and it was no trouble to find," said Grant. He walked over to Nathan. "Hey," he said, looking Nathan right in the eye and smiling broadly.

"Hey, yourself," answered Nathan.

Grant leaned over and kissed Nathan. Nathan was handling some pork chops, so all he could do was either allow himself to be kissed or turn away. He allowed himself to be kissed.

"Well," said Nathan. "For that you get two helpings of pie at dessert. If you want, you can have them both now."

"Hi, Grant, I'm Alice Turner," said the other woman, a small, slight person who, like Becky, looked to be a well-kept forty-something.

"Hey, Alice, thanks for letting me come," said Grant, shaking her hand. Well, I guess she's the *daddy*, thought Grant. He stood by

Nathan as the latter continued working on a marinade for the pork chops—mangoes and something else, he smelled. Becky made everyone a drink, lit a joint and served as interlocutor, asking Grant more about himself. Becky and Alice took turns telling Grant embarrassing stories about Nathan. They had a pleasant time laughing and talking about the characters who hung out at the antique show, and by the time they sat down to eat, Grant felt completely at ease. He was impressed by how long the three had been friends—Becky and Nathan had known each other over twenty years, and Alice had known Nathan since grade school—and he envied them the history and the continuity.

When dinner was ready it took all four people to get the food on the table. For meat there were pork chops marinated and batter-baked, fried chicken and boiled shrimp; for vegetables there were collard greens, mashed potatoes and carrots with butter and gravy, green beans, and yellow squash casserole and there were fresh sliced cucumbers and tomatoes in balsamic vinegar as well; there were home-made biscuits, bran muffins and pan-fried cornbread; there was blueberry cobbler and apple pie, and there was iced tea to drink. It was a meal like none Grant could remember, especially for an informal Saturday evening.

"Man!" said Grant, looking in astonishment at the food on the table. "Y'all always eat like this?"

"Oh, sometimes," said Becky. "We needed to clean out the fridge. It's nothin' special. Alice, honey, would you say grace?"

Alice, sitting at the head of the table, her head not all that far above the height of the food, bowed and lead the dinner party in a prayer. Afterwards she raised her head and, in a commanding tone of voice, said, "Dig in before it all gets cold or the cats come and take it off."

"Yep, you're on your own from this point on, Grant," said Nathan. "Grab it or lose it."

Thereupon everybody at the table started reaching for food and passing dishes, doing a decent job of not getting in each others' way. To keep the conversation going, the two women resumed their accounts of Nathan's exploits. Alice took great delight in telling Grant how, in the sixth grade, Nathan had been called upon to give a report on the Statue of Liberty: "Being an idle child with an over-heated imagination," she said, "he was bored with what he found in the encyclopedia, so he decided to skip the research and make the whole thing up. When it came time for him to give his talk," she said, 'he started by saying, 'The Statue of Liberty is the world's largest emerald,' and spun a yarn—completely off the top of his head—that left the teacher—it was Mrs. Jordan, remember, Nathan? The one who carried her tampons around in a grocery bag?—anyway, left her speechless. Of course, the other kids didn't know any different, so they just sat there and took it all in. And, and this is the part I've never figured out, his teacher never said a word to him about it afterwards. How'd you get around gettin' your ass whooped, Nathan?"

Nathan squirmed visibly as his prank was held up before him, but he managed to endure the whole retelling as he saw that it enter-tained Grant. Before he had a chance to answer Alice, Becky broke in: "I figure she knew what she was dealing with: not a lie but an invention, a bit of juvenilia in the life of an artist. Obviously, she was a discerning woman. Probably an old carpet muncher who real-ized she had a budding faggot in her care."

Blushing, Nathan looked at Grant and asked, "aren't they colorful, these two? Such a charming variation on the theme of the Southern rustic." He then tried to take control of the conversation a moment, saying, "Well, girls, thanks for telling Grant what an accomplished liar I am. I'm sure it'll help Grant put things in perspective when we sit down and try to authenticate the lithograph. For your information, Grant, they left out the worst ones they know to tell, I'm assuming because you're a first-time guest. And girls, you will never, not ever, as long as either of you lives, no never know the really worst stories there are to tell."

"Damn!"said Alice. "I hate it when he says that!"

"There's plenty of time for more stories," said Becky.

"Yep," said Alice drowsily, "you got that right. Why didn't you tell him about the time we were all doing psyllicibin and wound up in the field full of angry bulls?"

"What?" asked Grant.

"Oh, it'll keep," said Becky. "Just means Grant has to come back sometime to dinner. So Grant, you live in town?"

"Yeah," said Grant. "Midtown. Corner of 4th and Durant."

"Oh," said Becky. "Is it that cute little brick apartment building, across from the Cuban grocery store?"

"Yes," said Grant, surprised she knew the place. "I guess y'all know your way around town pretty well."

"I just love the sandwiches Mr. Diaz makes. We go there to buy mole and coffee, when we're in the neighborhood. Your folks live in town?"

"Well, not any more. My folks died when I was a kid. I was raised by my aunt."

Becky felt awkward at having brought up an unpleasant subject, so she sought to divert the conversation. "I'm so sorry. Your aunt and you must be very close."

"Actually, she passed away three years ago," said Grant, feeling peculiar at being the center of attention.

"Oh, dear," said Becky, vexed with herself at managing to stumble into the double tragedy of Grant's life.

"Leave the guy alone," said Alice. "Your interview isn't going too well. In case you hadn't noticed, Grant, she's trying to check you out. Don't pay any attention. Did you know Nathan's an orphan, too? What she really wants to know is if there's any insanity in your family."

"Alice, honey, don't say 'orphan,'" said Becky. "It isn't nice."

Grant laughed at Alice's deadpan comments. "No, I didn't know," said Grant. "As for the insanity question: not as far as I know," he said. "My folks died in a car accident when I was eleven, so I went to live with my father's sister, my aunt Mary Lou. She took me in and raised me. I guess I was a real handful for awhile. Got into some trouble shoplifting, breaking into houses, that kind of thing. Lucky for me, my aunt never gave up on me. She saw I liked to draw, and she encouraged me to keep at it. Got me involved with the swim team, too."

At the mention of the last item Nathan choked on his food. Becky took advantage of the short pause to add, "Nathan lost his mamma when he was a little boy. I guess you two have something in common."

"No two losses are the same," answered Nathan in between large gulps of water. "And I still have Daddy."

"That's right," said Becky, glad to hear the conversation turn away from death. "How is he?"

"Last time I talked to him, he was having a ball," said Nathan.

"Nathan's daddy is a gem, Grant. You'd love him."

Grant felt glad that the attention was turning away from him, and he took the opportunity to lighten the conversation by pursuing Becky's lead. "Oh yeah?" he asked.

"Tell Grant about your daddy, honey," said Becky.

Nathan felt pleased that the conversation had been salvaged, but he didn't feel like talking family history any more. He said, "We don't want to bore Grant with the details of anybody's family life. Anybody seen a good movie, lately?"

"Well, then, I'll tell," said Becky. "Nathan's daddy is the most darling man. After Nathan's mamma died Mr. Greenwood moved the family here from Alabama, thank God, and worked at the bank for years. He never remarried, just kind of worked and was a daddy and didn't do much of anything else. I think he grieved a long time for Mrs. Greenwood. She was very beautiful. People say Nathan takes after her a lot. All along Mr. Greenwood kept at his hobby, which was playing the base fiddle. Jazz. I mean, here was this quiet, nice man who worked a regular job, but he always kept at playing his bass. And to look at him you'd never think in a million years he'd be the kind of guy who'd play the base fiddle. I mean, you look at him and maybe hear him speak a few words, you think, Auburn University Sigma Nu bank executive. Case closed. Except, I guess, bass players are usually big men, I think, I mean, they have to be, don't they? I never saw a really small man play the bass, and whatever about all that, anyway, Mr. Greenwood is tall. Taller than Nathan by a few inches. So, when he retired, when was it, Nathan?

Five years ago? He started playing with a group in a neighborhood bar on week-ends, and now he's *touring* with them."

"Wow," said Grant. "That's great. You ever see him much, Nathan?" asked Grant.

"When I can catch up with him," said Nathan. The mention of his father seemed to spark something strange, but Grant couldn't make out exactly what it was.

"Well," said Becky, "he may be retired and all, but he's one of the youngest people I know."

"That's great," said Grant. "I mean, that he was able to pick up his dream again, even if it was late in life."

"There's a lesson to be learned there," said Becky.

At length Alice began to yawn and Becky announced that the two of them were going, as she said, to go set their teeth to soaking and go to bed. As they cleared the table Alice and Becky both invited Grant to stay the night, and Grant stammered that he didn't live that far away, but thanks anyway. After the two women went to bed, Nathan and Grant went into the living room and sat on the couch for awhile, basking in the glow of food, pot and conversation, talking about the house and about what good people Alice and Becky were.

Chapter Seven

"I hope you weren't embarrassed by Becky's interrogation," said Nathan.

"What do you mean?" asked Grant.

"Oh, you know," said Nathan. "All those nosy questions about your background. She can't help it. She's just trying to figure out if you're a nice guy."

"Oh," said Grant, understanding the why behind Becky's wanting to figure him out. "Well, for what it's worth, I gave up breaking into houses a long time ago, and I haven't stolen anything since college."

Nathan laughed at Grant's response. It felt good to laugh like that.

"So," said Grant at last. "Anything else about me you want to know?"

"Whatever you care to share," said Nathan.

Grant smiled at the answer. They sat for a moment just looking at each other, and it was becoming clear to both of them that they liked what they saw.

"Well, let's see," said Grant. "I've lived here all my life, except for college, done a little traveling: Europe and Central America. I've known I was gay since I was about fourteen, been pretty lucky with friends. I guess, in a way, I was lucky that my Aunt Mary Lou was the one who raised me."

Grant's casually announcing his being gay startled Nathan for some reason. He found the younger set difficult to read; for all he knew, Grant could be straight or, worse, a virgin. "How do you mean?" asked Nathan, feeling his face flush a bit, hoping it wasn't noticeable, sure that it must be.

"From what I remember about my folks, they were really type-A people. I think if they'd raised me, I'd probably be married now and working as a lawyer or a stockbroker, screwing around with guys on the side and anaesthetizing myself by drinking and buying more and more stuff."

"Mercy," said Nathan," "ça fait trés Eugene O'Neill. A life of duplicity and conspicuous consumption," said Nathan.

"Yeah," said Grant. "SUV's, substance abuse, vacation homes and fake friends. Yuck! No thanks! So, you speak French? Of course, the Grandville prints. Anyway, my aunt was a free spirit, so I was lucky to have her raise me. She knew how to bring out the best in me."

"Did she know you were gay?" asked Nathan.

"Sure," said Grant. "I told her when I was sixteen. She said she knew it, but she was glad I told her. She joined PFLAG and started marching in Gay Pride."

"What a difference twenty years can make," said Nathan.

"Twenty years?" asked Grant.

"The difference between your age and mine, I would reckon," said Nathan.

"You don't look forty-five," said Grant.

"Come to think of it, you don't look twenty-five," said Nathan.

"How old do I look?" asked Grant.

"That was supposed to be a joke," said Nathan. "Actually" he continued, "you have one of those faces that's hard to place in terms of age. But I would place you at somewhere between twenty-three and thirty, if I didn't already know how old you are."

"Why twenty-three?" asked Grant. "What's the difference between twenty-three and twenty-five?"

"Oh, there's a big difference," said Nathan. "Not a teen-ager anymore, not yet hurtling towards trolldom, either."

"Are you hurtling towards trolldom?" asked Grant.

"Yes, I think in general I've crash-landed in the middle of trolldom," said Nathan.

"That's not right. I don't think you're a troll," said Grant.

"Thanks," said Nathan. "But I think I am officially the room troll tonight, given that it's you and me alone." He felt his face flush again: stop it! he thought to himself. "Much as we ate tonight, my vanity was still feeling a bit peckish. So, tell me more about yourself."

"Not much to tell, really. I had a lot of fun as a kid, got interested in art, graphic design, went to art school, did the straight job thing for awhile, then when my aunt died, she left me some money, so I bailed from my day job and opened a shop, got interested in old print art and that's how I make my living, now."

"That can't be all there is to tell," said Nathan. "No boyfriends? No romance?"

"Oh, sure," said Grant. "I was in love with this guy in high school, he was a jock and really cute, really a sweet guy."

"So, what happened?" asked Nathan.

"Things kind of fell apart when I went away to college. He stayed here. It was just too easy to drift apart. I don't think either of us could have known how much we'd change during the first couple of years of college. We both just started running with different crowds, didn't connect anymore. It was okay when we broke up. I mean, we're still friends and all."

"And yet," said Nathan, "all this couldn't have been all that long ago. Maybe you'll come back into each others' lives."

"I don't think so, not to any really great degree," said Grant. "He's a circuit boy, works as a personal trainer now. Don't get me wrong: we had a great time when we were together. We're just not in the same world, now."

"So," said Nathan, "if it isn't too rude to ask, surely that's not the only romance in your life?"

"No," said Grant. "I've dated some people. Few months here and there. Guys are funny these days, though. The psychotics and spouse abusers want to get married after the first date, and most of the rest just want to fuck and run out the door."

"I don't suppose dating has ever been anything but very ugly business," said Nathan. "You've got your youth, though, and you're a good-looking guy."

"Thanks," said Grant. "Do you think that's all there is to it, being young and good-looking?"

"No," said Nathan. "From the perspective of someone who grew up through gay lib, it certainly seems sad that now it's harder rather than easier for men to figure out how to couple. I don't understand how any of it works anymore. The whole mating game makes no sense to me. I don't understand very much about how being good-looking, being attractive, attracted, how all that stuff works. Gay men are peculiar creatures in the way they select their mates. It's a very tricky process, no pun intended. I look at who's coupled with whom and say, Why? See who's single, ask the same thing. So, is there anyone in your life right now?"

"I've been seeing this guy for a few weeks," said Grant.

"Oh? How's it going?" asked Nathan, immediately mad at himself for feeling disappointed at this bit of news.

"Okay, I guess" said Grant. "We met at a party, been out to dinner and stuff a few times."

"What's his name?" asked Nathan.

"Darren," said Grant.

"Hmm," said Nathan. "D's, so many gay men with d's in their names. Darrens, Devins, Darryls, Dons, Davids, lots of Davids. You ever go out with a David?"

"Yeah, as a matter of fact."

"So, why aren't you with David tonight?" asked Nathan.

"You mean Darren. Well, you invited me here, for one thing," said Grant. "Anyway, he's out of town. He goes on the road a lot. He sells software."

"Oh," said Nathan. "That could be a good mix, actually, might be some room for a little chemistry. I read somewhere that computer people tend to be into heavy kink."

"What do you mean by kink?" asked Grant.

"What was it?" asked Nathan to himself. "I think the thing I read said that somebody did a poll and found out that more computer programmers are into cross-dressing than any other job group, or something like that."

"Where'd you read that?" asked Grant.

"I don't remember," said Nathan. He was enjoying the thought of Grant's new boyfriend sitting in a room in a cheap hotel with a trick he'd dragged home, watching soft porn in a bra and panties and getting the crap beaten out of him as entertainment.

The conversation lulled for a moment. After a bit of time had passed Grant said, "So, now it's your turn. Tell me some more about yourself. You have a boyfriend?"

Nathan smiled at the question, felt his heart skip a beat. Recovering himself, he said, "no, not for a while."

Upon hearing this, Grant shifted in his seat. He asked, "So, you were in a relationship before?"

"Yes," said Nathan.

"Go on," said Grant. He shifted his position on the sofa again, ending up perhaps just the slightest bit closer to Nathan, Nathan tried not to notice. His mouth went dry. Grant said: "Tell me about it."

"Ok," said Nathan, hearing his voice crack. "Let's see, where to begin. When was it, 1979? Was it that long ago? That would've been what—about the time you were issued your first big wheel? I was waiting tables at night, painting during the daytime."

"Painting? Painting what?" asked Grant.

"Pictures," said Nathan. "Pictures of people, mostly, but sometimes other things, as well. I went to the University of Georgia School of Art—did I tell you that? Go, you hairy dogs! Ha! I majored in sodomy, drugs, and rock'n'roll, and ended up by some inexplicable accident with a degree in art education, ready to take Rauschenberg and Rothko down a rung. Those are my works on the walls. This house is full of my stuff, paid-for by my two principal patrons."

"I like them," said Grant, looking at the paintings about the room. "I'm surprised that I do, but I do. You still paint?"

"Surprised? You're surprised you like them? Hmm. No, I haven't painted in awhile. Not for a long time," said Nathan. "Anyway, I had a few shows back then, sold some stuff, but not enough to make a living. I suppose I was lucky to be selling anything, but I was impatient, kept thinking more should be happening with all that. So, there was one show, Halloween 1979, if I remember right. It was a group show, half a dozen artists, and everyone was dressed up, you know, on account of it was Halloween. Everyone was having a blast. I was shitfaced, having a good time, talking trash with all kinds of people, really full of myself. Actually had some people buy my work right off the walls, so I would've been flying even without the booze and drugs.

'And there was this guy. Showed up out of the crowd. Dressed as a faun. Actually, dressed as Nijinski dressed as *the* faun. Doing a very good job of being Nijinski as the faun."

"Wait a minute," said Grant. "Nij-nij-ewski? Who is that?"

"Nijinski? You don't know Nijinski? You know who Barishnikov is?"

"Barish—who? Who is in this story? I've forgotten who we're talking about."

"Well," said Nathan," I don't think I got to that part yet. A famous and very pretty male dancer. He was dressed like a famous, very famous, male ballet dancer. This guy. But that's not really the story. So there was a guy dressed like a faun, you know, half-man, half animal. It was a wonderful costume, home-made, very simple and clever. He was gorgeous, this guy, and I have no idea why but I went up to him and said, Hello, my name's Nathan Greenwood. And he said, my name's David Lattimore. And I fell in love with him, right there on the spot. We went to the men's room and we did

MDA and we made the beast with two backs, which everybody there knew and thought it was a real hoot, except for a few people who really had to pee at a certain point."

"MDA?" asked Grant. "What's that? Is it like acid?"

"Umm, well, come to think of it, it's been a while since I've done anything like that, I guess I don't even know if MDA is around anymore. As I recall, it was supposed to be a mixture of cocaine and speed and probably animal tranquilizer. It made you very silly, and if you were the shy type, as was I, it was just the thing to make you overcome the more or less perfectly natural tendency to behave yourself and instead of behaving do what you really wanted but never, ever actually should do. Which is what we did, that's for sure. So, afterwards we went home together and I called in sick the next day. We stayed in bed for a couple of days, and finally I had to go to work and we parted company. My boss was mad as hell because I'd skipped work and I told him to piss off, so he fired me.

'I didn't hear from David for a week or so and thought, oh well, another one bites the dust. We had fun, so what? I felt shitty and stupid for awhile, tried to keep at painting, got another lousy job working as a bellman in a snooty hotel uptown—all this was happening here, in town, by the way, forgot to mention that—and the job involved working so many hours that I was painting less and less. At least, that's the excuse I gave myself. Anyway, a couple of weeks went by, and I really felt hurt that I didn't hear from David, called him a number of times and then said the hell with it, though I still felt mad.

'Then one day, I can't remember exactly how long it was after we'd first met, I got this frantic phone call and who should it be?

David. Hey, it's David Lattimore, remember me? He said he was in trouble and he needed a place to stay. His roommates had kicked him out, and could he please come stay with me? And, horny, desperate fool that I was, I said, sure, thinking, *the poor lamb* and also thinking, yippee!, more great sex! Anyway, David showed up sometime that evening with a suitcase and a story about how he'd written a check at the grocery store and it bounced and before you know it, the sheriff showed up at his doorstep with a warrant for his arrest. Luckily for him he wasn't there at the time the cops showed up with the warrant, so his roommates had to deal with the police drama, which didn't sit too well with them. And David said it was all a big mistake, the check was bad because someone had written *him* a check which he'd deposited but then it bounced and somehow the bank hadn't let him know that, but he couldn't get the check covered because the person who'd written him the bad check had skipped town. So here he was in this terrible fix with the sheriff and the Kroger store gunning for him and didn't know what to do.

'So, guardian angel and horndog that I was, I offered to cover the bad checks, and I got David out of trouble. Even got my father involved."

"What? Your father? How was that?" asked Grant.

"My father worked for the Citizen's State Bank. He was a manager downtown. He pulled in a few favors, and David was off the hook."

"Did your father know about you and David?" asked Grant.

"We never talked about it out loud, but yes, he knew. My dad and I have never talked about my being queer. He's too old school to be able to say the words involved," said Nathan.

"But he obviously supported you," said Grant. "I mean, he must've realized he was taking a chance on this dude."

"Yeah," said Nathan, "*dude*. That's exactly what David was. It was an odd arrangement, what my dad and I had. I don't think he really cared that I was gay, and I don't think it bothered him all that much that I had a boyfriend. As long as he didn't have to get too close to the details. In retrospect, I can't believe I had the moxie to ask him for help. But, like I said, I was in love, and deep in lust, and David was gorgeous, in a William Higgins kind of way."

"What's moxie? Who's William Higgins?" asked Grant.

"Moxie is balls. William Higgins—porn movie director, mostly pre-AIDS," said Nathan. "Think bareback sex, handlebar mustaches and great big wang-dang-doodles."

"Oh," said Grant. "So then what happened? Did you and David stay together?"

"Yes," said Nathan. "David couldn't ever seem to find a job, so I supported the both of us, working for tips, dressed in a grey polyester monkey suit. I was in love, and we had lots of sex, even when we were fighting we had great sex. We probably fought at least once a day. And we'd screw sometimes two or three times a day. So I convinced myself that everything was fine. How could anything not be fine? We were screwing as much as any four people that either of us knew, and that's counting the four of them AND their tricks, so things must be all right. Remember, this was 1979, before Satan and the evangelicals had co-opted sex."

"Was David in love with you?" asked Grant.

"Whenever the question came up, he changed the subject," said Nathan. "He was always uncomfortable talking about it. But he loved to pretend to be the lock while I played the key, that's for sure. And he stuck around. Of course, where was he gonna go? As I was saying, I held our little domestic comedy together on the strength of my own talent for self-delusion for awhile, until one night I came home and David wasn't there, which was pretty un- usual, as he generally made sure he was home when I got home. David couldn't drive, did I mention that?"

"No, I don't think so," said Grant. "You mean he didn't have his own car?"

"I mean he couldn't drive. Far as I know, he still can't, if he's alive. Never learned to drive a car. He always got people to take him places or took the bus, so he never had to learn. As I said, one night I came home from my wonderful job as a bellhop, and David wasn't there, which was odd. So I waited up and it got late, and I got worried. I got so worried I called the emergency room to see if he'd been admitted, but they didn't have his name."

"So, what happened?" asked Grant.

"About four or five in the morning, David finally showed up. I'd dozed off, and woke up to hear banging at the front door. It was David. He didn't have his keys. He'd been beaten up. He looked like hell. He gave me some story about getting on the wrong bus and winding up in a bad part of town, and when he got off to get on a bus back into town, he got mugged. It was a really touching story, as I remember. I was all full of indignation and motherly love, and I took care of him and vowed to bring the ruffians to justice. He was hysterical, because his face was busted up pretty badly. Anyway, even though at the time I thought there was something not right about what David was telling me, the episode gave me another op- portunity to play the nursemaid, which I did very well. David had no insurance, so we had to go to the county hospital to get him stitched up. He was very afraid he'd come out of it looking like a gargoyle, but that's not what happened. By the time he healed up, he had a small scar over his right temple, and that was pretty much all he had to show for it. The scar just made him more irresistible. The trauma gave him the excuse to stay at home, though, because he was too distraught to go out and look for a job. I ate it up. I worked double shifts to make ends meet.

'We continued life in this way for a year or so, and there were no more calamities for awhile. David was a stay-at-home husband, and I was a working stiff. I didn't mind, really, because I was in love."

"Excuse me, but it doesn't sound like there was very much to him," said Grant. "What was it that made you love him so much?"

"I know, it doesn't make much sense," said Nathan. "I bet by now you can guess the rest of the story—at least, the long and short of it. I don't think it gives anything away if I admit we're not heading towards a happy ending. What did I love about David? He was so incredibly beautiful, we were both young and full of energy, and he never got tired of having me pound his ass. He had jet black hair, the bluest eyes I've ever seen, and he had the body of a movie star, even though he never worked out. He ate like a horse, too. Nothing but junk food. Cokes and hamburgers and that was pretty much it. Fries, cereal. Very little else. He wasn't very bright, that I knew, but he was just sweet and kind of helpless and loved to have a good time. Great dancer, of course. And in bed he was incredible. We'd go at it for hours, and he'd beg me to drill him again, sometimes two or three times in a night. I fucked him until *I* was bleeding. We were in our twenties, remember. Certainly kept me in shape. Picture me with a twenty-eight inch waist and a decided bounce in my step.

What can I tell you? I was spellbound by this vacuous beauty who never read a book or did much of anything except watch television and listen to Donna Slumber records and wait for it to be time for the next party."

"Donna who? Never mind. So, then what?" asked Grant.

"Somewhere along the line, I forget exactly when, a woman I know who lives in Charleston invited us to come and stay for the 4th of July. I had been to Charleston and liked it, and David had never been, so we went. It was a four-day party at some big old place out in the country, I can remember there was a swamp and there was talk about, don't go off by yourself 'cause there's gators and wild pigs eat you up in a skinny minute, and there were hundreds of people, lots of booze and drugs, and it was just the kind of time that we both needed at the moment. At the end of the week-end we both decided we were taken with Charleston, so we made plans to come back to town here, tie things up, move to Charleston and re-invent ourselves. We didn't have a real plan except to move to the place and soak it all in, on the basis of one wild week-end, but that was enough, then.

'So I broke my lease, which cost me a lot, but I still had enough in savings to keep us fed for a few months, and I managed to summon the chutzpah to get my woman friend to let us stay with her in Charleston until we found our own place. Within a few months after moving to town I had found us a place on Ashley Avenue, a dump but a pleasant dump, and I was slinging hash at a trendy restaurant, while David was still officially looking for a job. I worked, we fucked, got high and went to parties, went to the beach, and made lots of friends. We had a good time.

'Another year or so went by and I got a wild hair to go into business for myself. I had been collecting all sorts of garbage for years, and people I knew told me all the things I'd collected would sell for big bucks to the right people, which meant tourists from up north, as real home-grown Charlestonians wouldn't have touched much of anything I liked. At that time rent was cheap in downtown Charleston—we're talking circa 1982 now—so I was able to find a place that was reasonable on King Street that had a lot of traffic and was lots of fun to fill up with junk. I started going religiously—and I use the term advisedly—to yard sales and that sort of thing, and before long I had enough tchotchkes and what-nots to fill my store. Next thing you know I had a real clientele—dealers and serious buyers—who'd come in looking for something or other in the vein of early-to-mid-twentieth century oddity that had become my specialty and, lo and behold, I was making money.

'For awhile I was actually holding two jobs, working the shop in the daytime and slinging hash at night, and finally I figured out I could quit the waiter job, so I did. Nervously. Very scary move, that."

"What happened with your painting?" asked Grant.

"Oh, by that time I'd given it up. It just disappeared into the whirlwind. I didn't care too much, because it was so much fun to go around buying stuff, learning how to work auctions, making contacts, learning about stuff, finding all kinds of collections of extraordinary things being hauled out of old ladies' houses from all over. I was having a ball, and I was amazed that we weren't starving to death, and there were always lots of incredible people around, and it was wonderful. I was feeling passionate about what I was doing, and it all seemed to be coming so easily."

"So what did David do during all this time?" asked Grant.

"Well, my success finally gave him a vocation: he became a sort of social secretary. Being the sort of business that it was, buying and selling collectibles, I made lots of contacts through social events, some of them at the shop, some of them at our place. So it sort of became David's job to organize parties and be the pretty boy who made everything look nice and made sure that there was enough food, drink and marijuana and blow to keep everybody happy. It suited me fine, and it made us both finally feel as though we were developing into a partnership, though we never really talked about it."

"Wow, Nathan," said Grant. "You were like, living the life"

"I was a gay brigand, darling, back then there were lots of us. Anyway, this went on for years, this partnership of ours, let's see: when did the big boom come down? It was 1986, my annus horribilis. I think 1986 was a tough year for a lot of people. It helps to remember that. Everything was going along just fine: the business was cranking along, I was working like a field hand, David was closer than ever to having a real occupation, and I thought we were doing as well as a modern couple could hope. Nothing seemed to be in our way. Then one day I was in the shop and some queen I knew who was a pretty regular customer came in and struck up a conversation—he had a gaggle of his nasty, hissing little friends with him, of course—and started making all these remarks about how David was banging so-and-so on a regular basis and hanging out at the Battery, shame of shames, and picking up trade and blah-blah-blah and wasn't it just awful!

'Of course I just dismissed it as hateful chatter-queen mischief and acted like I didn't believe a word of it. This is, what, seven years? after we had first gotten together, David and I. So I didn't pay it any attention.

'Had you been faithful to him all that time?" asked Grant.

"Figure it out for yourself," said Nathan. "I was working twelve to sixteen hours a day, six days a week, and for the last few years we were together, rarely went out except with a crowd of people, including David. Hell, back then, even going to the grocery store was a mob scene. I thought we were happy and I thought I was being a good boy, a hard-working homo entre-freaking-preneur. I didn't have time to got out looking for snatch, matter less the desire. So, as I said, I didn't pay the rumors any attention. Finally, some time after the chatter-queen bit, I ran into my friend Clare, who was the manager at the last restaurant I worked at before I became a shopkeeper, and she asked me to go out for lunch. It'd been a long, long time since we'd spent time together, so I decided I needed to do it.

'We had a pleasant lunch. Caught up, promised we'd make an effort to see each other more often. Then Clare told me she needed to tell me about something. She said it was common knowledge all around town—including up and down King Street, which was a very chatty crowd at the time—that David was boffing everything he could find that had a pulse *and* a dick. Like I said, David believed it was more blessed to receive than to give. He was *devoted* to this belief—truly committed. Of course, I didn't believe her, so she gave me the names of half a dozen people who were willing to recount intimate details of the moves David favored while getting his clock punched, and after enough testimony, though I was stunned, I had to accept it."

"So what did you do?" asked Grant.

"Oh, I did the whole nouvelle-vague, forlorn-waif-wandering-the-streets bit for a few hours or so, finally made it back to the shop, which I'd left closed all afternoon, and found a few notes on the door from customers, went inside and locked myself in, had a good cry.

'I made it home after dark that evening and David was there. I confronted him, and he didn't deny any of it. He said I'd abandoned him and made it clear that the business was more important than he was, and he'd tried and tried to do what he could to make me stay interested in him, but when he saw it wasn't working, well, he just went out and found himself someone to fill the gap. We argued for hours, and it got nowhere, and finally I got a blanket and made a bed on the couch.

"Why did *you* end up sleeping on the couch?" asked Grant.

"I said something like, there was no way I'd sleep in the bed where he'd done it with his white trash tricks during the day while I was out earning a *real* living, blah-blah-blah, and he said, fine, being in bed with me was worse than being alone, and we cornered off for the night. The following day I got up, didn't sleep a lot that night, of course, and got ready and went to the store. I stumbled through the day and went back home reluctantly, not knowing what to expect. It was an hour or so before I noticed that David wasn't there. Once I realized I was alone, I spread out in the apartment a bit and sat down and went through it all in my head. I thought about how I was the one at fault, how he was right that I'd neglected him, how we'd been together for so much time, and I thought well, this doesn't have to be the end of the world, I mean, we've never had a really big fight before, maybe this is just normal, for where we are now. So I waited up for David to appear, only he didn't appear.

Another night of waiting for David. Naturally, remembering the mishap on the bus, I began to get crazy again, wondering where he was, and I called tons of people, and told a few of my so-called friends what had happened, dodged a few rounds of ain't-it-awful with them, and passed the evening waiting for my beloved to show up. He didn't.

'The following day I made it in to the store and went about my business, feeling like shit, rehearsing how I'd go over it all when I saw him that evening. At one point I sat down to balance my checkbook, because I'd bought some stuff and hadn't entered it into the check register, yet. There was something I couldn't get to tally up, so I called the bank to get my balance. My balance: what balance? I called the bank again, asked to speak to the manager. She got on the phone. I told her what an odd thing it was that my account was showing a zero balance. It should have had about seven thousand dollars. The balance was zero, she said. How's that, I asked? A check was drawn against the account the previous day, emptying the account, she said. How could that be, I asked? But even as I asked, I knew: David had signature authority on all our accounts. He'd emptied the business account. So I checked my personal account: same story. Zero. I knew then and there he'd taken the money and was off on a tear, wreaking revenge on me for being an absent husband.

'I tried to find David, but no one knew where he was, no one had seen him. I drove down to the Battery that night, talked to a couple of rental boys, none of them knew a thing about David. I could tell they were lying, but what could I do? So I went back home that night, sat down and tried to think about what to do next."

"Did you call the police?" asked Grant.

"Are you kidding?" asked Nathan. "That bunch of good-for-nothings? A few years before all this happened, all this awful business, something similar happened to a friend of mine. It was on a somewhat smaller scale, mind you. When he called the police, they treated him like dirt. Blew him off."

"Blew him off?" asked Grant. "How?"

"They basically refused to fill in a report, told him it was a domestic dispute, and anyway, it was his fault for giving his boyfriend the power to write checks. They were pretty nasty to him. No, I didn't bother trying to fill out a police report."

"But what he did was embezzlement," said Grant. "Or theft by taking, or something."

"It didn't matter," said Nathan. "It would have been a mess, trying to go after him, so I just got myself together and went about salvaging what I could."

"What did you do?" asked Grant.

"Well, I had to give up the shop, sold a lot of my stuff at auction to raise enough money to get by, and I got a booth in an antiques mall in town. I squeaked by, crawled into myself and just worked, went to auctions and kept at it."

"Did David ever show up?" asked Grant.

"I wrote a letter to his folks, who lived in Murphy, North Carolina. I didn't let on about the money, just told them David had taken off and I was worried about him. I asked them to get in touch with me and let me know how to contact him."

"So, did they write back?" asked Grant.

"No. I did get a call from his mom, and she said she had heard from David. He was living in New York, working in a hair salon. He told her he owned the place. He told her I beat him and ran around on him until he couldn't take it anymore, so he took what was his and left."

"Do you think she believed him?" asked Grant.

"No," said Nathan. "David's mom and I were always on pretty good terms. She knew he was rotten. She even, poor woman, spilled her guts and told me he'd gotten into trouble a number of times with the law before I'd met him: bad checks on more than one occasion, and public indecency."

"Public indecency?" asked Grant.

"David was a hustler," said Nathan. "That's the real punchline to this joke. I was too stupid to see it. He'd been a hustler when I'd met him. The beating episode? Probably a fight with a trick. Definitely not a commuting mishap. The first bad check story? It was part of a pattern. David's m.o. He had a habit of writing bad checks, it seems. I wouldn't be surprised if there were still warrants out for him in all kinds of places. If he's still around, he's probably living on bad checks and the kindness of meatheads like me."

"And you haven't been involved with anyone since then?" asked Grant.

"Not seriously," said Nathan. "Ever since then it's been tricks and videos and a long relationship with Ultra Glide."

"But all this happened over ten years ago," said Grant.

"And your point is? I guess I'm not as tough as I look," said Nathan.

"Hmmm," said Grant, nodding. "Maybe it's time you got tougher."

A pause ensued. "Maybe it's time we had a look at the woodcut," said Nathan. "It must be after midnight." At that Nathan got up and shuffled into the kitchen. Grant thought about Nathan's story as he sat alone. What would it be like to grieve for ten or fifteen years? The thought made him angry.

Nathan came back into the living room with two glasses of water. "You think you can do this tonight?" he asked.

"I'm fine," said Grant, looking up at him and trying not to let his exasperation show through. "But, I tell you what."

"What's that?" asked Nathan.

"Why don't we bag it and just spend a little while longer, together?" asked Grant.

Nathan looked perplexed at the suggestion, handed Grant one of the glasses of water. "Aren't you worried about feeling like crap tomorrow?" Nathan asked. "It's almost one a.m." Then Nathan sat down on the couch beside Grant.

"No, not really," said Grant. "What about you?"

"I'm okay," said Nathan. "I won't go in until around ten tomorrow. I have a feeling it'll be a slow Sunday, anyway."

"Probably right," said Grant. He looked at Nathan and felt a strange mixture of emotions. Pissed off at knowing Nathan had given so much of his life to grieving for a jerk, anxious to get inside. Finally: "Nathan?"

"Yeah?"

"Are you gonna make me ask if we can cuddle?"

Silence. Nathan looked quickly at Grant and then away again. Then: "I'm HIV-positive."

An invisible hammer hit Grant on the chest. "Oh," he said.

A long silence. Then Grant asked, "How long have you known?"

"Found out in 1986," said Nathan.

"David?" asked Grant.

"Who knows?" asked Nathan. "Maybe, maybe not. I went on a sex binge after he disappeared. I don't blame him, if that's what you're getting at. Not for the HIV, at any rate. Is this really your idea of a fun evening?" asked Nathan.

"Nathan?" asked Grant. Nathan was looking very nervous.

"Don't you think it's getting kinda late?" asked Nathan, fidgeting.

"Nathan, I know you're attracted to me," said Grant.

Nathan was very much afraid he was about to break down, right in front of this beautiful, clueless young idiot he'd just met. "Did you hear what I just said? I'm HIV-positive. And I'm forty-five years old. And you've got a boyfriend. I really think we ought to call it a night, don't you?"

Nathan got up and started to tidy up the coffee table. "I can get someone here in town to look at the woodcut for you. That'd be a better idea, anyway. She's an appraiser. She knows her stuff."

"Nathan."

"Yeah?"

"So, are you taking anything for it?"

Nathan found himself laughing at the question. "What's so funny?" asked Grant.

"I'm sorry," said Nathan. "It just sounds like the punchline of a couple of hundred jokes I've heard in movies. Yes, I'm taking the cocktail—you know, couple of thousand dollars worth of toxic waste every month. Doctor says I'm fine, despite the odds."

"So, the outlook is…"

"Good, indefinitely. The outlook is indefinitely good. As long as nothing happens. All things considered, I'm fine. Considering."

"Nathan."

"I don't know about you, but I think I've finally worked off dinner."

"Nathan."

Nathan, standing in the middle of the living room folding a newspaper, looked at Grant, who sat on the couch, looking at him. Looking at Grant now, Nathan found he couldn't let himself turn away. Grant sat on the couch, looking very large somehow, stretched out, looking straight at him. Looking straight at Nathan, a look of openness on his face, pale in the lamplight, breathing lightly, slowly.

"How could I possibly get from where I am to where you are?" asked Nathan, surprising himself with the question.

"Put down the paper, walk around the table and sit down," said Grant. "Here." Patting the place on the couch next to him. "Come here."

Nathan hesitated, put down the paper where he'd found it, walked around the coffee table and sat down next to Grant. Nathan was shaking. Grant sat looking at him, not moving. A few long moments went by, and Nathan finally looked at Grant.

"Hello," said Nathan.

"Hello," said Grant.

No, they didn't fuck, you filthy bastards. There was arousal, to be sure, and there was cuddling, and there was talking, and there was, sigh, much kissing and holding onto. But no fucking. It was the kind of sweetness Nathan wouldn't have allowed himself to hope for, and the kind of tenderness Grant would, perhaps, not have admitted to giving so unself-consciously. They got to know each what the other smelled like, and they got to know a few things each about how sexy the other was. It was a fine beginning.

Chapter Eight

The following morning Alice got up to let the dogs out and make coffee. She was always the first to get up, as Becky slept soundly. Hearing Becky snore as she tried to get out of bed quietly was one of Alice's favorite pleasures. There were nine animals in the house to contend with as part of the daily rising ritual: six dogs and three cats. The cats moved about during the night, waking to eat, use the catbox and take a drink of water—like middle-aged men, thought Alice, waking up to take a leak and wander around the house a bit. By morning the cats had always settled, it seemed, in some corner of the bed where they passed out and stayed immobile until they heard the sound of the can opener running in the kitchen. The dogs—all six of them—cooperated pretty well in keeping the noise down, so that despite the wagging of tails thonging against the cast-iron frame of the bed, Alice was able to crawl out of bed, open the closet door, find and put on her robe, her slippers, shuffle out the bedroom and nudge her way long the wagging-dog-crowded hall towards the kitchen without waking Becky up.

It was chilly in the large kitchen, but Alice still felt good being there. It was her very favorite room of the house, with a large double window centered over the sink that looked out the back yard across the bricked terrace and into the small yard, surrounded by a weathered, moss-covered old unpainted wooden privacy fence. Alice loved everything about the view out the kitchen window: the rusty lawn furniture, the bricks on the patio, the potted plants and plots here and there of flowering things mixed with weeds, a couple of Japanese maples close to the house, a small expanse of grass growing in the part of the yard that was always sunny, up towards the left corner, opposite the shady side on the right, shady because it was shielded by the branches of a very old oak tree. There was nothing really beautiful about the view, not in any formal sense of beauty, but it always held Alice when she looked out through the window, whether rain or clear, and took her in as nothing else she'd ever seen.

Maybe it was seeing out the back window in the kitchen that made her such a good cook, made her coffee taste so good, made everyone end up in the kitchen. This was where Alice entertained, this was where she spent as much time as she could, in the big old kitchen in the back of her old house.

As she was first up, Alice took the opportunity to make coffee and begin making breakfast. After getting the coffee started, she asked herself, Wonder if that Grant guy ended up staying the night? She smiled and bit her lower lip slightly the way she had when she thought about wicked things like Nathan *getting it on* with another guy.

Nathan woke up with a slight headache; from the wine? He asked himself. He slept on his left side, facing the window that looked out the back side of the house. He saw tree branches from a large old dogwood and a small patch of blue sky. He didn't want to get out of bed yet. He wasn't sure how the morning would play out. He figured from the amount of light coming in through the window—he hadn't yet turned towards the dresser to look at the clock—that it was late enough so that there was a pretty good like-lihood that at least one of his hosts had already arisen. Nothing to be done but face another day, he thought as he rose.

Nathan made his way into the kitchen, where Alice sat reading the paper. Nathan knew she was dying to get a report. "Good morning," he said.

"Morning," Alice replied. "Sleep ok?"

"Yep," answered Nathan, "except I have a bit of a headache. Red wine. Otherwise, not too bad for an old fairy. You sleep ok?" He bent over her and kissed her on the head as he shuffled towards the coffee pot.

"Same as ever," she answered. "You know me. I'll sleep through the Apocalypse, probably."

"That's not entirely true, dear," said Nathan through a yawn. "Dubya is still in the White House, and he's declared the First Re-public of Gilead. And you're awake. Had you forgotten?"

"No, I hadn't," answered Alice, "and if I had, you'd be there to remind me. You hungry?"

"Toast and jam, maybe, but the first thing is coffee," said Na-than. "We must first worship the coffee pot, and after we've said our prayers, then we can break the fast. He isn't here, by the way. Didn't stay the night, we didn't fuck. So that's that."

Alice looked up, blushing slightly, smiling through her reluc-tance to be caught smiling. "Well, thanks for the update," she said. "You didn't even get to first base?"

"Gay men don't have first base, darling," said Nathan, "with us it's either home run or strike out. There was no sex. You know me, if the earth had trembled, you'd have heard me."

"Well," said Alice, "things change. I thought maybe I'd just slept soundly or you guys were being extra polite, which would've been wasted. So, why not?"

"It didn't come up," said Nathan. "After you all went to bed, we talked for awhile, and then decided it was time to pack it in. Meaning, call it a day. He took the woodcut and left. We never actually got around to looking the thing over."

"Oh," said Alice. "So, you think there's no prospect there?"

"Of what?" asked Nathan.

"Romance, silly," said Alice, folding the section of the paper she'd just read and then dropping it onto the floor beside her. "You remember romance?"

"Only too well," said Nathan, drawing up a chair across from her, snatching a pile of New York Times sections before he sat down. "As I recall it's the last sign on the road to hell."

"Not all men are like David," said Alice. "You've got to get over that one of these days."

"No, they're not," said Nathan. "They don't have to be all like David. I don't know how to explain it to you, darlin. Anyway. I'm fifty and he's twenty-five. That makes me old enough to be his father. Literally. And I don't get that kind of vibe off of him, anyway."

"Well, there it is," said Alice.

"There what is?" asked Nathan, leafing through the arts section.

"You just admitted you're attracted to him," she said.

"I did not," said Nathan emphatically. "Don't be absurd."

"Oh, yes you did, monkey doodle," said Alice, getting up to refill her coffee cup. "I think I'll have to start another pot for Becky, in case she ever gets up. Are you going to drink more?"

"I did NOT say or imply I was attracted to him, and I think I might have another cup, yes."

"But you did, Nathan. You said you didn't get 'that kind of vibe off him.' How would you know that unless you were checking for it? And why ever in this wide, wide world would you be checking for the vibe from a handsome, sweet, interesting young thing like that?" Alice knew she had him. Winning an argument with Nathan was like a month in the country. Nathan sat there and said nothing, glowered and turned a dark color, shuffled the paper and continued reading silently. Alice knew she'd hit her mark a bit too squarely and immediately felt sorry for what she'd said. She got her coffee quietly, then came back and sat down, picking up another section of the paper. "There's nothing wrong with admitting you think he's cute," said Alice, "especially since he is."

Becky finally shuffled into the kitchen. "Hey, pookie, hey, Nathan," she said. "You get it on with that dude you brought home last night, Nathan?"

"SHUT UP!" said Nathan and Alice in unison.

Nathan got cleaned up and drove to the show. It was Sunday, so people would already be pulling out, even though the rules said people weren't supposed to start packing up until after three in the afternoon. Sundays at the Centralia show always felt odd. People were tired, disappointed at the way the show had gone for them. Often it seemed the people who had done the best at the show were the dealers who had no business being there in the first place. Some time back Harold Farmer, the show manager, had begun to allow vendors into the show who weren't selling actual antiques. At first this included vendors who were selling reproductions of antique furniture produced in Asia. Nathan cringed when he saw the vendors wheeling in obviously new rosewood furniture, cheaply made and badly finished, probably using slave labor forced to work under inhuman conditions. Long-time vendors complained about the reproductions, first because they weren't antiques, and second because the public started to flock to buy the stuff. Why buy an old dining room chair when you can have a new one that looks old? Everyone knew there was a lot of hypocrisy surfacing when this conflict arose. The matter wasn't so much a defense of good craftsmanship. After all, many vendors of real antiques had plundered markets in Europe to find their furniture—they had bought from people who were under financial stress and were literally selling their own beds, tables and chairs to be able to afford to eat. Antiques from Europe were generally sold either as estate lots or as distress sales, so they were generally pretty good bargains for the buyers intending to send them to America. Vendors of real antiques, in other words, were generally people who profited well off of other people's misery—they fed off of death and decay. So who could take them seriously when they stood forth to object to selling reproduction furniture bought virtually directly from the factory? In any event, Farmer's argument was that he needed to fill booths to pay his rent on the fairgrounds—an obvious lie, as he rented the fairgrounds for a nominal fee, and everybody knew it.

The vendors realized that they had no power to affect Farmer's decisions, so some of them shrugged and went on with life. A few vendors left the show, opting to set up shop at a rival weekend show. Farmer showed no signs of concern about the vendors leaving, letting it be known he had a long list of people waiting to get a space in the show. This did little to help moral among the dealers.

Things got worse when Farmer allowed new crafts into the show. One such vendor had old turpentine buckets—all right, they were old objects, but would anyone call them antique? The bucket vendor made decorative cuts in the old buckets to make lanterns out of them, painted some with flowers and animals, and still others he just filled with artificial flowers, which he also sold at his booth. They sold like crazy, and the vendor reported that during one show he pocketed upwards of forty thousand dollars. His investment in old buckets, paints and silk flowers had been minimal. To dealers like Nathan, who found their wares by scouring thrift stores, estate sales and auction houses, the advent of the painted bucket dealers was very bad news.

So, everybody's chickens came home to roost on Sundays at the show.

So far Nathan hadn't had a very good show, either. When he got to his booth, he immediately felt a sense of pain and dread. He hated the thought of boxing everything up again, getting covered in newsprint, getting a hundred paper cuts, wondering why this or that hadn't sold again, wondering why he had sold what he had.

He thought about going to look up Grant and talk about getting the woodcut examined, perhaps by someone at an auction house. Nathan wasn't even sure what kind of response a Kollwitz would elicit these days. He had been living so long among collectors of crafts that he felt completely out of touch with the world of art galleries. For all he knew, Kollwitz was out of fashion, thought it didn't seem likely that that could happen. All he knew was that he didn't hang around painters or print makers or collectors of paintings or print art, and hadn't done so for quite some time, so he thought that, if he ended up helping Grant somehow figure out the true worth of the woodcut, he'd be almost as much a beginner at the process as Grant himself was.

Nathan thought again about the conversation he'd had that morning with Alice. Of course, he had to admit to himself, he found Grant attractive. Of course. But so what if he did? What was the point of pursuing anything with a guy like that? He really didn't have any sense that Grant was interested in him. Well, that wasn't true, was it? Grant had spent the previous evening with him, and things did get pretty heated up towards the end of the evening, didn't they? So what if they did? Grant was a young man and it was Saturday night. Maybe all he wanted was to get off, what was it Nathan heard some young guy saying the other day? Bust his nut, that was it, bust his nut. What a horrible expression, bust your nut, are these guys kidding? Sounds like someone kitting himself in the balls with a sledgehammer. What kind of image is that supposed to be? I mean, I don't get any part of it. Orgasm equals busting your nut? That just doesn't make sense, it's too violent and stupid, too childish a concept. Wait a minute, Grant never said anything like that, and here I am, getting all worked up over it and deciding there's no way anything would ever work out, what the heck do I mean by work out, anyway, on the basis of something Grant never said? So, there it is, the real reason why it would never work out is that I'm crazy and he's better off without me. Without me as if there were some remote possibility that there would be something more than a brief session of 'nut-busting,' I mean, really, nut-busting? something that might last for awhile, a couple of months, who knows? Hell, why not go for broke since we're talking nonsense anyway, a couple of years maybe ten or so? So no, it could never last that long and why? If not because I could never make a guy like that happy, could never manage to keep it together, could never make it work, if not for that obvious reason then because he'd never think about it in the first place, would he? The whole thing is just too fucking absurd, it's really pathetic, I mean, listen to me.

"Nathan." Nathan heard his name being called. He was standing in his booth and holding something, and he didn't know why he was holding it or how long he'd been holding it and standing there. He felt deeply embarrassed and wondered if he'd been muttering out loud the thoughts he'd just been lost in, please God, may the God I don't believe in please protect me from it's being true that I've been standing here muttering all this crap while someone's been standing here. What the fuck is wrong with me?

"Nathan?" It was Grant. He was standing right in front of Nathan.

Nathan wanted to disappear. He was certain he'd just been muttering out loud all the idiotic things he'd been thinking. At this moment he couldn't imagine being more humiliated or more naked. He found it difficult to speak or to move or to do anything at all.

Grant looked at him with an expression of puzzlement. He looked searchingly at Nathan for a moment, clearly waiting for Nathan to speak. But Nathan couldn't speak. He was seized by the realization that he had just spent a block of time, maybe minutes, ranting to himself, possibly out loud, and now the subject of his rant was right here in front of him. He simply couldn't speak. Finally Grant said something: "Hi."

Nathan didn't reply right away. He was feeling overwhelmed, as if he'd just been hit by a wall of water, as if he'd just come up for air after being hit by a huge wave. He thought he might get sick in a moment. He wanted badly, badly to just disappear.

"Nathan, are you all right?" asked Grant. He looked more concerned than puzzled now. Nathan was not sure how he might extricate himself from this conversation, but he wanted to do so as quickly as he could. Maybe he hadn't been talking out loud. Maybe Grant hadn't heard any of what he'd been muttering. That didn't really matter at the moment. It was enough that Nathan knew now what he felt. He realized that he wanted to try and make Grant want him. He wanted to make contact with Grant and find that Grant wanted it, too. He wanted Grant to become connected to him, and stay that way. And wanting all of this, Nathan knew, was utter folly and hopeless, helpless self-deception. There is no balm in Gilead, he thought to himself, and this *is* the Republic of Gilead, isn't it? He collected himself. Grant wasn't leaving. He collected himself and made up a story.

"I was just lost in thought," he said, "Trying to remember what I did with my sales record. All my business information is in that book, and I must have lost it a dozen times this weekend. It's driving me crazy." He sounded convincing to himself, though he wasn't sure what must be going on in Grant's mind at the moment. Oh, well, he thought, the damage has been done. In a few hours I'll be packed up and waiting for old man Farmer to send around his minions to start helping people get out of this dump. I can do that, he thought, I'll be home by one a.m.

"Well, what does it look like?" asked Grant. "Maybe I can help you find it."

Nathan hadn't anticipated this response. Of course he hadn't lost his sales record book. It was an obsession with him to build a number of rituals around keeping the little beaten-up red spiral notebook in a special place so he could never lose it. There was nothing much wrong with Nathan's memory when it came to things like sales record books. And now this tedious young man was actually offering to help him find it. What a bother! "Oh, don't bother!" said Nathan. "If it turns up in all this mess, it'll turn up when I start packing."

"But what happens if you make a sale this afternoon?" asked Grant. "Won't you need your record book to, well, to record the sale?"

Nathan looked exasperated. Grant was getting on his nerves. In fact, Grant was already very badly on his nerves, and Nathan was not sure how long he could hold out without telling Grant to shove off. It hurt to look at Grant. He had no idea why Grant was there and he didn't want to know. He only knew that it hurt to have him standing there. All he wanted was for Grant to go. How could he make him go?

"I'll worry about that if it happens," Nathan finally said. "Which I doubt it will. I think I will start getting organized to pack up, if you don't mind."

Grant was no longer puzzled at Nathan, he was insulted. Nathan hadn't said a proper hello, hadn't asked Grant why he was there, hadn't mentioned the evening before and their visit. Nothing made sense about the way Nathan was behaving, but Grant wasn't ready to leave. He had news, and he intended to share it.

"Well, okay, I guess I need to get out of your way, then," said Grant. "Unless you could use some help getting ready to go."

Nathan was now fidgeting with boxes under the tables he used to display his wares. It was just after noon on Sunday, a bit early to start even pretending to pack. It didn't matter at the moment. This is it, Nathan thought, if I get busy with packing up he'll eventually just get bored and go away. That will be the end of it.

"I came by for two reasons," said Grant, feeling wounded by Nathan's strange behavior.

"Two?" said Nathan, nodding. So Grant had come to thank him for dinner. Good boy. "And what might they be, then, your two reasons?"

"Well, I wanted to thank you for dinner last night and I thought I would get Becky and Alice's contact information and send them a thank-you note."

Jesus, thought Nathan, I can't do this much longer. I'm going to go off the deep end and it will indeed be my fault, because he is just being a nice guy. But I may have to just kick him to the kerb. "I'm sure they don't expect a card," said Nathan, "though it's very nice of you to offer. I'll tell them you said thanks, and so you don't need to worry about the card. That all right?" he asked, smiling a pretty good Miss Manners smile--mouth only, no eye involvement.

Grant understood now that he was being urged to leave. He was baffled; not quite ready to believe that he was being shoved away. He had no idea what he could have done to merit such treatment. "I'd prefer to thank them myself," he said.

Nathan stopped what he was doing and got a piece of paper, wrote down Becky and Alice's address, their full names, and their phone number. "Here," he said, handing the paper to Grant. "That about do it, then?" Nathan asked.

Now it was Grant's turn to be headed towards speechlessness. He watched while Nathan puttered and fussed in his booth, opening and closing empty boxes, rummaging through piles of newspaper, and generally moving about without really doing anything. "Well, actually, I was going to ask you about the woodcut," said Grant. He wasn't sure what to do. He didn't like being pushed away like this, and after the conversations he'd had with Nathan the previous day, it didn't make sense that Nathan was behaving the way he was. Something had happened, but Grant couldn't figure out what it might be. He tried to think whether or not he'd misbehaved in any way the previous evening, and he couldn't think of a single point where he'd gotten the impression he'd said or done the wrong thing. So why was Nathan acting like this? Like what? Like they'd had a fight. A fight? They hadn't fought, they'd had a great visit. It seemed they were off to a good start. Quick snacks and hair styles—they had that in common. How could it be that Nathan was pushing him out the door now?

Nathan didn't respond to Grant's statement about the woodcut. Instead he fidgeted. He seemed to be getting more agitated as he did so. Grant wondered if it was becoming noticeable to the people in the adjoining booths. He looked around to see if anyone was taking notice of their conversation. No. Grant began again: "I was going to ask you about the woodcut, and tell you the oddest thing happened when I came in this morning."

Nathan was sitting on the floor in one corner of his booth, taking wadded up newspapers and stuffing them into an empty box. He was beginning to get dirty from handling all the news print. He hated handling news print. He thought to himself from time to time he'd probably end up dying of cancer from spending years handling news print and getting covered with newspaper ink. No such luck, he thought, I'll probably live to be a hundred and two, spend the last twenty or so of that crazy as a shithouse rat and hooked up to fifty different contraptions. No suck fucking luck, he thought.

He looked up at Grant and saw that Grant was hurt. He felt a pang of pain in his belly when he looked at Grant. He felt his eyes sting and his throat go dry. He felt suddenly very, very tired. He felt like going to sleep. Of course, he couldn't sleep. Of course. Of course. He looked at Grant again. Grant seemed to be waiting for something. It was almost unbearable, seeing Grant standing there. What is the point of all this? Nathan thought to himself. So I can reach out and try to grab something so it he can just run off laughing? That's the whole thing, right? I reach and he runs and laughs. Okay, then, I'll reach, so he can laugh and run.

"I'm sorry," said Nathan "I'm not being a very good host, am I? I guess I must be preoccupied with getting this show on the road. It's a long drive back to Charleston, and sometimes it gets to me to have to face it. So you were saying something about the woodcut?"

Grant wasn't buying it. He kept the ball in play, though: "Well, yes," he said. "Soon as I got to my booth today I found a note from some lady who said she wanted to make me a deal on it."

"Is that right?" asked Nathan. "Way to go, Grant! Did she mention a sum?"

"She's offering me two thousand dollars for it," he said. "She came by a little while ago, asked me if I'd sold it because it wasn't in my booth any more. I said no, I hadn't sold it."

"Well, then," said Nathan. "Congratulations. She seem to be on the up-and-up?"

"I guess so," said Grant, shrugging. "It's just, I've never had a sale this big, so I'm just wondering."

"Wondering?" asked Nathan. "Wondering what? Maybe we stumbled on a marketing technique. Put your stuff up in your booth, and then take some of it down to make people think you've sold it. Might help more people come down off the fence. Can't believe I never thought of that. Maybe you just made a sale *and* invented a new sales technique. Wouldn't that be something?"

"Well, do you think I should take her offer?" asked Grant.

"That's up to you, Grant," said Nathan. "It's your woodcut. Is there any reason why you wouldn't want to sell it? Didn't you say it's not the kind of thing you usually buy?"

"Well, no, it isn't the kind of thing I usually buy," said Grant. "But didn't you say we ought to take it apart and look it over?"

"Well you might learn something by doing that," said Nathan. "But if it really isn't your thing, why not accept an offer from someone who obviously wants it? Did this woman tell you what her interest is?"

"Yes," said Grant. He was sounding very unsure of himself.

"And?" asked Nathan.

"She's a lawyer from out of town. She collects art by women artists. She knew Kollwitz, and said she was familiar enough with her work to presume it was the real thing, the woodcut," Grant said.

"Perfect," said Nathan. "So you have someone who evidently knows Kollwitz who is confirming what we thought—that it's a genuine early impression of one of her works. Pretty easy money, if you ask me."

"But Nathan," said Grant, "are you sure I wouldn't be better off holding onto it and looking it over really closely?"

"What for?" asked Nathan.

"I don't know," said Grant. "It just seems to me that if this woman appears out of the blue and offers me two thousand bucks for it, it might be because it's worth a lot more than that. What if there's something about the woodcut that is unique? You said her work can bring up to ten thousand dollars or so."

"All of that is true," said Nathan.

"Well, then, I'm asking you now, because you know the artist and the period better than I do. Do you think selling to this woman is the right thing to do?"

"Grant, I can't tell you what to do," said Nathan. "It's your piece. What if I tell you not to sell and you find out that two thousand is a good price for it? What if your lady goes away and you don't find another buyer for it? How will you feel then?"

"I'm not trying to get you to tell me what to do," said Grant. "It's just that I don't know what to do, and I was hoping you could help me get a little more certain about it."

"I do believe you should trust your instincts," said Nathan. "If you don't think you should sell, don't sell. If you think it's a good sale, take it."

Grant was sure there was something wrong, but he had no notion of what it could be. Something had happened, but what? Was it that they hadn't fucked the night before? Was Nathan pissed off about that? But it had been Nathan who had pushed Grant away. Grant hadn't been really focused on the idea of their having sex, but once they got talking, once he sat with Nathan and listened to his story, he found himself really looking at Nathan, watching his eyes, his facial expressions, the little movements he made as he talked, the way he breathed. He found himself drawn in by everything he could see, could sense about Nathan, and he knew he wanted to know more. And there was that business card. They never got around to discussing how it was that Nathan had found his way to the same place by the side of the road that Grant had; how it had made an impression on Nathan the way it had on Grant. A small thing, a stupid thing, but no, it was the kind of thing that defined a certain kind of person, and that had to mean something. Something. Grant knew something about Nathan that Nathan didn't know about him. Grant knew they shared something silly and whimsical and very, very small, but if it was small, it was a small opening into something big, perhaps.

So Grant wasn't ready to let Nathan push him away. It didn't matter if it was about not fucking the night before. It didn't matter what it was. Nathan was clearly about to come out of his skin about something, and Grant knew that it involved him.

"Well, then, I guess I'll just have to make my own mind up, then," Grant said. "So, are you leaving town tonight, or staying over until tomorrow morning?"

Nathan couldn't believe that Grant was still hanging on. Was he really going to have to just tell Grant to leave? Did it have to come to that? Grant wasn't an idiot, he must realize Nathan was showing him the door. What was it going to take? "I haven't figured that out yet," said Nathan. "Probably hit the road after the show ends."

Grant stood there, hands in his pockets, watching Nathan fiddling. It was beginning to look comical, because Nathan had spent the better part of the last fifteen minutes doing nothing more than wallowing in news print. Grant smiled and said, "Well, it would be nice to keep in touch, you know?"

Nathan looked up at Grant. He couldn't take this any longer. He looked up at Grant, and he saw a stray dog sniffing at the doorstep. Entreating, starving, needful eyes. "Grant, I'm the worst kind of mess you could ever hope to get messed up with. I don't do lots of drugs, and I don't drink, but I don't have to, because I have enough shit weighing me down to make up for all the other vices people usually use to ease themselves into their graves. If you want a friend, or a big brother, or whatever it is you want, go find somebody your own age, somebody who doesn't have all this baggage. It's not worth it."

"I don't understand," said Grant. "Yesterday you came to me, you showed me what I had, and you could have gotten it for cheap, but you didn't. You did a kind thing, and you offered to help me more. And then you invited me to your friends' house, and they were kind, too. I thought it all went pretty well. I thought we were starting a friendship. That's not something that happens every day, Nathan. You know that. Lots of people are full of bullshit, and pull all kinds of stunts and treat each other like dirt, but I didn't think we were off in that direction. I thought, well, Quick snacks, hairstyles, Nathan!"

Nathan was startled. "What? What did you say?"

"I saw that same sign a few years back, on a road trip. On US 1 near St. Augustine. Right? Isn't that where you saw it? Right, Nathan?" asked Grant.

Nathan was completely taken by surprise. What sort of person was he dealing with? "That's right," he said.

"There's so much of life now that is crap, pure crap, and so many people who are just, well, fucking empty, nothing, all surface and just nothing else. Everything seems disposable. Almost everything. And you came along and saw that sign and it made you smile, and it stayed with you and you think about what's behind it. And I had the same thing happen, Nathan, I saw that sign, too, and I began to think about how things are fake and how so little innocence is left in the world, and what's left is lots of crap and a fake sense of play, a childishness in everyone and everything, at least that's how it seems at times, and that sign made me think, where is there something that's really sweet in the world, something where there really is a genuinely sweet kind of whimsy and play, and if you can find something like that, doesn't there have to be something good behind it? You don't play sweet if you're mean and full of shit, do you? You play sweet if you really like play, if you love something. That sign stayed with you, Nathan, and it stayed with me, too. So, yes, I was hoping we could be friends, because I need to be friends with someone who saw that sign and held onto it, someone else who did that."

Nathan had to see that Grant didn't care that he was crazy, that he was eaten up with all the damage that had been done to him. Grant was an entirely new species for Nathan. He was a young man who appeared, really appeared, to be honest, to be comfortable with honesty and to expect it. Other young men Nathan knew were shockingly duplicitous, always faking everything about themselves, it seemed. Nathan could barely stand to talk with someone below the age of forty for this very reason. But here was Grant, and there was no explaining his existence or his presence. How on earth could such a creature have arisen, thought Nathan. "So what is it you want from me, Grant?" asked Nathan.

"I need, I would like your friendship, I think," said Grant. "And if you're crazy, well that's fine, unless you need to be in a hospital, because if you're that crazy, I just don't think I can take it. But if you can manage it, I would like to see if we can try to be friends."

"Friends?" asked Nathan.

"Well, you want me to say here and now that I want to go to bed with you? I'm not going to do that," said Grant. "But I'm not ruling it out, either."

Nathan was chastened by Grant's forthrightness. The day before Grant hadn't seemed like the kind of person who could be so demonstrative and so clear about his feelings and his intentions. They'd only spent parts of one day together.

"I'm sorry to be such a cunt," said Nathan.

"Don't say that word," said Grant. "It's a mean word. Don't call yourself that."

"Sorry," said Nathan. "So, you want to keep in touch."

"I want you to be my friend," said Grant.

Nathan saw the earnestness in Grant's eyes. More than that, he saw something in the way that Grant was standing in front of him. There was something utterly unprotected in the way Grant stood there, asking for his friendship. Nathan felt humbled by it. The more he saw of this young man, the less he understood. He could feel himself growing numb from the encounter. It was too much for him. He could feel his own craziness lowering over him like a bell jar. He didn't know how to stop it. He didn't want to leave the moment he was having, but he didn't feel particularly all there, either. He didn't know if he had the courage to do this with Grant, even though he really had no clear idea what "this" might mean. It didn't appear that Grant was asking him for a sexual relationship, and after an evening like the one they'd had the day before, Nathan couldn't imagine their having a sexual relationship. It was far more difficult than that. Grant appeared to be openly, desperately asking for friendship. The real thing. Why with Nathan? On the basis of that silly card, that stupid business name? Nathan felt sick to his stomach. He felt his head pounding and his jaw tighten. He feared the worst. He feared he was falling in love, and he was sure that if he were, there was no place it would end up but in a burning pile of debris.

"Grant, I don't know what kind of friend I can be," he said at last. It seemed as if hours had passed since Grant had last spoken. Nathan wondered what it looked like to passers-by, two men in a booth, one standing and one crouched on the floor, just staring for long stretches of time at each other, saying something once in a while. Nathan wondered if it looked any odder from the outside than it felt from the inside.

"Well, Nathan," said Grant, "There's only one way to find out, isn't there?"

"Why are you being so persistent?" asked Nathan. "What is it you want or hope to get?"

"I think there are a lot of shitheads in the world, Nathan, and I don't think you're one of them. I think I can connect with you, and I really want to give it a try." Nathan heard Grant's words as if they were spoken from a distance, or as if he was remembering hearing them spoken from some time years ago. "And I think you might connect with me," Grant continued. Nathan had the odd feeling of being slapped on the forehead or the face, as if he were just noticing something or someone had just hit him in the head. Finally, Grant said, "I guess maybe for the moment I'll just have to settle with the fact that you haven't said no," he finally said. "Are you going to give me your phone number? Maybe your address, too?"

Nathan got up from his pile of papers, covered in filth from handling the newspapers and the dusty boxes. He looked like a collier, he was so dirty. As he stood up, his lower back hurt as if he had a rusty ice pick stuck in between the vertebrae. "Oh, my GI back," he said, wincing at the pain. The pain of his back brought him out of his numbness, made his awareness shift. He went over to a tackle box he used as a briefcase, opened it, and pulled out his sales record book. It was a red binder notebook with the word "Sales" emblazoned on it in large, black capital letters. He opened the book, pulled an ink pen out of his back pocket, wrote some scribbles on a piece of the paper from the notebook, tore it off and handed it to Grant.

"Looks like you found your sales record book," said Grant as he took the paper. He was smiling, looking at Nathan, thinking how beautiful Nathan was, his large, sad brown eyes looking right into Grant's. Grant looked at the paper to make sure he could read it. He folded it up and put it into his wallet. "I guess I need to get back to my stuff now," he said. "I'll give you a call." And with that he turned and walked away.

Nathan watched Grant leave. Grant walked like an athlete. He had an easy, fluid gate, the kind of walk that men have when their strength is something they're comfortable with and modest about. There was nothing battered or torn in his walk. It was the walk of someone who was healthy, young and strong; of someone who hadn't learned to be afraid of things or people. Nathan watched him leave and asked himself what on earth had just happened to the both of them.

Chapter Nine

Grant woke up Monday morning feeling a little queasy, as if he'd spent the night out drinking wine and smoking. He hadn't done either. On Sunday evening he packed up from the show, came by the shop, unloaded, and then went home. When he got home he listened to music, channel-surfed, flipped through the new *Smithsonian* magazine, read an article on hippie settlements in Patagonia, then had a bath and went to bed before midnight. A very tame evening. He had no reason to feel queasy or hung over this morning, no reason to feel bad on any account.

The show ended pretty well for Grant. He had decided to take the woman's offer on the Kollwitz; she had given him a check for $2000.00, so that was that. The sale made it one of the best shows he'd ever had. And in August, too. Not the usual turn of events. As the dealers were leaving the show, many people were saying they hadn't made a dime through the whole weekend. There was the usual talk of defecting to one of the other weekend shows, as the Centralia festival, by all accounts, was going downhill. Certainly Grant had no reason to complain. He had no reason to feel cruddy, and he had every reason to be as perky as if he'd gotten laid that weekend. It didn't make sense to him that he felt as lousy as he did.

For one thing, Grant didn't feel at all like going into the shop. Maybe it was the heat at the show that had gotten to him. He'd worked at the shop all week, then gotten his part-time help to watch the shop Thursday and Friday while he packed up, drove to the fair-grounds, set up, and then worked the whole weekend. Wasn't that enough to make him feel like not going anywhere or doing any-thing? He wasn't sure. He just wasn't up for it. Why couldn't he just not open for one day—just go by the shop and hang a sign say-ing he was out on business or something? Mondays were slow; he might sit in that damn place all day and not see a soul, except maybe around lunchtime. Just him, the radio, his cds, and all those frames to cut. And if anyone were to come in on a Monday, who would it be? People walking off their lunch at Mama Jack's, the diner down the street. Aside from the foot traffic at lunch, he might not see anyone. Then he thought: shit, I have that lady coming in to pick up those Cunard line posters I framed last week! If I go in, she won't show; if I stay home, she'll bend my ear tomorrow. Not much choice, he thought. Oh, well, he thought, at least I didn't fuck up and forget about her, the old bag.

The old bag was one of his best customers, a woman Grant ac-tually liked quite a bit. She lived in Chislington; her name was Janet Mackey. She started coming into his shop one day after lunch at Mama Jack's. She was a lawyer, or as she said, an *attorney*; she evidently had lots of wall space, and she paid good money. She was affable enough, and always made a point of chatting with Grant when she came in. Even though he had good reason to try and like her, Grant just couldn't bring himself to do it. He had the impres-sion he was one of her pet fags, and that bothered him almost as much as her voice, a very loud, high, whiny nasal voice, so typical of the kind of voice young women affect these days. What demon is responsible for the fashion so regrettably current among American women of talking in loud, piercing, whiny voices through their noses? It certainly wasn't always that way. Name me one woman in a prominent place in popular culture—at least in the United States—who doesn't sound like a cat being strangled when she talks, and I'll give you a dollar.

Anyway, none of that mattered. He just had to go in. What was wrong with him to think he could just not show up and open shop, just because it was Monday and he –poor thing who'd just raked in nearly four thousand dollars in a weekend, poor thing just didn't want to? What did he have to do that was so pressing that he couldn't go in? Beat off and go back to bed, and that was pretty much it. The fact was, he had had an unusually good show for the end of summer, which was usually a dry season for selling junk at weekend shows; he should be full of energy at the thought of going in to his own business and running his very own shop. The god of capitalism was being kind to him. What was he whining about? He went on like that while he got himself ready to go in. He was in a foul mood, and either going in or not going in wasn't going to change that fact.

He tried to think positive thoughts about the money he'd made from the woodcut. Should he give part of it to Nathan ? Like a commission? They didn't have any agreement like that, did they? And why wouldn't Nathan say what he thought when Grant asked him for advice about whether or not to sell? Why did he pull back like that, just when Grant really needed advice on what to do next? Grant knew he was out of his depth and he said so. And Nathan had started it all. If he hadn't opened his big fat know-it-all mouth, Grant wouldn't have known what to expect for the woodcut. Stupid, Grant thought, how dumb did I look to Nathan? He blushed to think about actually showing up in at a major antique show with a piece by a well-known artist and pricing it like yard sale art. How could he have been so stupid? But then again, he had bought it in a yard sale, and he'd made good money off the investment.

It really bothered Grant that he'd shown himself up like that to Nathan. Still Nathan hadn't been at all nasty about it; he was the one who said—in so many words—that Grant needed schooling in that kind of thing. Which was true, Grant admitted it freely. He couldn't know everything about every piece of print art. Nobody does. I'll bet Nathan has made all kinds of stupid mistakes, thought Grant. And it was Nathan's idea to invite Grant to dinner; he didn't have to do that. That was not just a polite gesture, it was a friendly one. So why be friendly first and then just go cold without any warning? Like turning a switch—soon as a possibility for a real deal shows up, Nathan acts like it's all none of his business. Grant couldn't figure out what had happened to make Nathan shift the way he had.

Nathan had helped him see what he had, and thanks to Nathan, Grant had positioned himself to get two thousand dollars for a fifty dollar investment at an estate sale. So why didn't Nathan tell him to sell the piece outright when a buyer showed up? Why did he go out of his way to be a good guy and save Grant from selling the piece for nothing, then draw back and act funny when Grant asked what he should do about the sale? Wasn't it possible, didn't Nathan say it was possible the piece was worth much more than two thousand? Did Grant do the right thing by selling it? Should he have held onto it? Why was it so difficult for Nathan to say outright, don't sell it to this chick, hold onto it and have a look around? Wasn't that what Nathan was sort of implying, though? So, why did Grant turn around and go ahead and sell it? Was that the right thing to do? It's worse having something valuable than having nothing, Grant thought to himself. I hate this shit, he thought to himself. So much for thinking positive thoughts.

Anyway, it was done. The woodcut had been sold, and the woman had taken it with her. Her check was drawn on a local account, her ID matched the information on the check, on and on, so what was the problem? He would deposit her check today, and that would be that. Thinking about it wasn't helping. It was a deal and it was done.

Grant got to his shop, parked his truck in back of the building, went in through the back, turned off the alarm and began to go about getting ready for the day. It was almost nine-thirty when he got in, so he would have to hurry to be ready to open by ten. He went through his usual morning ritual quickly : make coffee; set up cash register; check phone messages; look at calendar. For a young man of thirty-four, he was pretty responsible. For a young gay man of thirty-four, he was the picture of rectitude. He struggled to make his little business work, he kept his shoulder to the grindstone, he didn't snort or drink his profits, and he led a quiet life. He read all the time about print art of the seventeenth, eighteenth and early nineteenth centuries, almost obsessively studying the periods he admired. He spent little time reading about other periods, only the occasional magazine article. He believed it was important for him to stay focused on learning his way through the periods he had chosen, so he could really become an expert in the art of that time.

He thought about branching out from his current work and getting into doing art appraisals. Maybe he could sell his shop and go to work for Sotheby's or Christie's. that would be a very different life from the one he had been leading all this time. It would mean leaving Centralia, almost certainly. Not at all a bad prospect. He really couldn't expect to learn a whole lot living in a city like Centralia; if he were serious about becoming a major expert in old print art, he would need to spend time in New York, London, Paris, Berlin—staying his whole professional life in Centralia wasn't the route to becoming a world-class expert in anything.

But thinking about it all rationally, was he already too old for all that? Weren't the people he read about in the business coming right out of Ivy League graduate schools and going to work in major museums, learning the crafts of preservation and identification of old art, learning to appraise art by actually working with the best academic resources available in universities and other public institutions? How could he find anything like that in Centralia? It was a second-rate big city with few cultural resources; even among cities of its size and wealth, it didn't rate highly in its public art institutions. Denver, Dallas, Houston, Cleveland, Minneapolis, Seattle—all of those were mid-sized cities with much better resources for learning the trades related to appraisal than Centralia. Centralia was notoriously stingy when it came to supporting the arts. Boosters loved to talk about how forward-looking the city was, but compared to cities like Houston, Dallas or Seattle, cities of similar size, Centralia was a cultural backwater. He was in the wrong city in the wrong line of work on the wrong track to building a career worthy of great ambition in anything related to art. So where was he going? What was he doing? What kind of life was he building? Selling frames and old prints for the rest of his life? Was that what he wanted? Well, Grant thought to himself, it's a good thing you finally shook off that negativity thing you were on this morning.

He paused in his reverie long enough to consider, yet again, that he was in such a crabby mood at the end of a very successful show. He had made a good deal of money, and he had learned something, truth be told, from Nathan. He had every reason to be feeling good about his business and his prospects for development as a business man. Instead he was feeling like arguing with anyone who dared to open his mouth, and since he was all by himself, he argued with himself.

Ten o'clock came, Grant opened the shop, and braced himself for the coming day. It was very quiet in the shop when he opened. There was virtually no traffic sound outside, and he was aware of how still everything seemed. He even felt a slight sense of panic, very briefly, as he noticed the stillness about him. Noticing that he was noticing this, Grant asked himself what could be the problem? He had no idea at all why, but he felt like crawling into bed and sleeping for the rest of the day. Skip beating off, just sleep.

At length Grant decided the only way he was going to get through the day was to get busy. He looked at his calendar, saw what was due when, and started planning his day. He cut frames and mats, he put pictures into the mats and frames he'd made, and he wrapped them up and put them with the paperwork he'd drawn up for each order. Despite his feeling lousy, he actually began to get things done.

And so the day went by fairly uneventfully. The attorney showed up to pick up her vintage posters. She talked on her cell-phone all the way through the transaction. Though Grant found the behavior distasteful, he was glad he wasn't obliged to make small-talk with her. She waved and made faces on her way into the store. She chatted while she pawed in her purse and found her credit card.

She plopped it down and he ran it through the machine. Grant used hand signals to tell her where to sign the sales receipt. She tucked the phone in the crook of her shoulder and took up the two posters, blew Grant a kiss and tottered off in her very high heels. All the time she stayed focused on her conversation, which apparently involved something about "discovery" and the "other side." Blah blah blah, thought Grant, thanks for the business, now get out. Once she actually came and went, Grant felt a sigh of relief. Not so bad, after all. What was I griping about this morning?

Other than a few tourists, there were, indeed, very few visitors to the store that day. It was very hot outside, after all, so Grant wasn't surprised that relatively few people were stirring. It gave him time to think about how odd it was that people had rushed to move to the South, when they absolutely could not stand the weather. The bugs, the mind-killing heat, the humidity were all far more than most of the transplants could bear. During the warm weather, most people—not just transplanted Yankee trash, either—dashed from their cars to the nearest shelter to avoid having any contact with the heat and the humidity. It seemed to Grant that there was really no difference between living in a city in the South and living in someplace awful and frozen like Chicago or Minneapolis, places where people drilled holes in the ice to go fishing. It didn't matter whether people lived north or south, most of them couldn't handle the reality of where they ended up—but it did seem to Grant that the way people ran from the weather in the South was unusually silly, since they'd been warned by the news and by much of American literature what they were getting into long before they arrived. People are so stupid, thought Grant. Every fucking one of us is as dumb as a mud fence, as dumb as a sack of hammers, as dumb as a village full of idiots. Grant loved the heat. He rarely ran the air conditioning at home, and kept it running at work only because he knew people really couldn't stand not to have it. Being pretty lean and having grown up in the region, he didn't sweat a great deal or generally feel at all bothered by the heat. In fact, he found August one of his favorite times of year, mostly because it was so quiet, so relatively untroubled by an excess of visitors and other people milling about. The general weakness among people that he laughed at inwardly also, in other words, made his own life a good deal easier.

Once he started thinking about thin-blooded Yankees and their horror of Southern weather, Grant could barely be stopped from thinking worse things about what the invasion of newcomers was doing to his hometown and the region. All in all, he didn't care much for what was happening to the South. True, it was good that the city was becoming more diverse, that it was getting easier and easier to actually taste and otherwise learn about the world at large through what immigrants were bringing with them into the region. On the whole, it wasn't the immigrants that bothered Grant. The Asians, latinos and Africans were far more interesting to Grant than the people from Pennsylvania, Ohio (is there anyone *left* in Ohio, Grant thought from time to time), Michigan and New England who were pouring into the South. It seemed to Grant that, among the domestic newcomers to the South, most of the people who were moving south were people with dark pasts and serious personality problems. They brought with them their resentments and their brutality, their pushiness and their cockiness, an overriding arrogance based on what? Having found themselves unemployed or no longer able to endure life where they'd been plopped onto the earth? So what did they do when they came South? They mostly appeared to have brought the rust and decay and anger they'd ostensibly tried to leave behind. The South isn't growing, thought Grant; it's just disappearing, being buried under the weight of all the crap these losers are bringing with them from the awful places they've already turned into ruins.

Nathan came into his mind, at length. A Southerner, an interesting person, the kind of person he would like to have as a friend. Was that all there was to it? Grant going to bed with Nathan—what would that be like? Grant wasn't into kink. He was pretty straightforward in his sexual tastes: hugging and smooching, sucking and fucking, lots of cuddling. Wonder what Nathan was into? He certainly had a much more developed sexual history than Grant would have. After all, Nathan had come of age before AIDS, and he was, in fact, HIV-positive. The being poz part didn't bother Grant, at least as a point to make him decide for or against having sex with Nathan. Grant knew how to take care of himself, and he got the sense that Nathan did, too. Did that matter, Grant wondered. That Nathan appeared to be a certain way? Grant was old enough and experienced enough with men to understand that their sexual natures have very little to do with the rest of their character—you can't spend any amount of time with a guy in a non-sexual encounter and figure out what his sexual predilections are. Grant had learned that if there was a rule of thumb about men and their sexual practices, it's that the kinkiest ones are usually the ones who seem the least inclined to be kinky.

But then, how was the subject of sex coming up at all? He had had to practically pin Nathan down on the floor to get his contact information. It was clear, at their last meeting, that Nathan was reluctant to have further contact. Why? He really seemed disturbed, agitated, and for no reason that Grant could discern, except that somehow, in some way, Grant thought that Nathan's agitation was somehow connected to him, to Grant. Grant only knew that he hoped they could be friends, and as far as he was concerned, the prospect of their having sex wasn't out of the question.

Late that afternoon the phone rang at Grant's shop. Grant stopped working on a frame, picked up the phone. "Hello," he said.

"Grant," the voice said

"Nathan?" Grant was utterly surprised. "Did I give you my shop number?" asked Grant. He couldn't remember having done so. He felt himself blushing for some reason.

"How many frame shops are called 'Quick Snacks, Hairstyles and Frames?'" asked Nathan.

"Well, just one in this town," said Grant. "Are you in Charleston?"

"No," said Nathan. "I stayed over. I was too tired to face that drive. And I realized I don't have to rush to get back home, so I thought I'd putter around town for a few days, maybe do some shopping. You have time to get away from the shop and go with me?"

Grant thought, well, here we go again, he was all cold and weird yesterday and now he seems to be warming up. again Maybe this time we'll figure out what we really want. "I could probably get someone to watch the shop tomorrow afternoon," he said.

"You want to run around with me, then?" asked Nathan.

"Sure," said Grant, "that sounds nice."

Chapter Ten

Smith's Bridge Road was an ugly stretch of low-lying storefronts and warehouses that had been part of gay life in Centralia since the 1970s. Winding in an arc through the northeast part of town, it connected midtown Centralia with the smart neighborhoods of Chase Run, Tuscany Hills and Chislington. Smith's Bridge Road got its name from the first bridge built by early settlers to cross the now all-but-lifeless Kennechopke Creek, a meandering tributary of the Kennechopke River. Situated by well-paid Department of Transportation engineers so as to make use of the creek as an open industrial sewer, the Smith's Bridge Road industrial area saw a decline in the sixties following the general trend that drove businesses to eat up more unspoiled land and water in the suburbs, farther and farther away from the city too busy to hate.

Benefiting from this decline in property values, gay businesspeople moved in during the seventies, opening up vast, cavernous discos and adult bookstores in several of the warehouses left vacant by the white-flight exodus. Following the lure of the bars, the glory holes and the peepshows, gay men moved in great numbers into the apartment complexes and tract houses that bounded the area so that, by the beginning of the eighties, the area began to feel the resurgence in property value that seems so often to accompany patterns of gay migration. As property values continued to rise, straight people started moving back into the area, drawn in by the charming and often naughty little shops, hair salons and restaurants that sprouted in the area as accompaniments to all the gay traffic.

Capitalizing on the passing away of the men who had bought neighboring houses fairly cheaply, fixed them up and then died, the new mix of residents in the late eighties exerted a pressure on the area that resulted in the demise of most of the gay bars, all of the adult bookstores and most of the better restaurants. At the conclusion of its gentrification, all that remained of a gay business district in the area at the turn of the century were a few clusters of antique malls, an adult toy store and a couple of gay bars, one of them among the most notorious sex dens in the Southeast.

As Nathan and Grant drove down Smith's Bridge Road, Nathan thought about poor little Suzie, the chimpanzee who had escaped one night in the early eighties from an exotic pet store that adjoined one of the primo gay bars. Little Suzie, who was fully grown at the time of her escape, had gone into heat and, it was surmised, was driven to her breakout by the noise and the soupçon of testosterone leaking through the walls. She made her way up the street unnoticed, as it was very late when she broke out. Finally making her way to the intersection of Smith's Bridge and Piedmont, she hid in the bushes in front of an old church near the intersection. Unfortunately, things turned sour for Suzie when, driven by lust, she started dashing out from the bushes to attack several men staggering home in the wee hours from a night of frolic. The police were summoned before long, and Suzie was shot dead. Shortly thereafter, the pet store was closed. As a memorial to the tragedy, the carwash next to the church set up a large mechanical gorilla that beckoned patrons ever since the night of Suzie's murder.

"Are you shittin' me?" asked Grant as Nathan told him about Suzie.

"Of course not," said Nathan. "Why would I make up something like that? Do you think I spend my time dreaming up stories about cruelty to animals? Has it ever occurred to you why there's a gorilla in front of the carwash?" Nathan asked.

"No," said Grant. "I just assumed it was a stupid gimmick."

"It *is* a stupid gimmick," said Nathan. "Only it's a stupid gimmick with a history."

"What made you think of it now?" asked Grant.

"I don't know," said Nathan. "I find I've been thinking about the past a lot since I've gotten into town. I guess, for one thing, it's been a long time since I've spent any time in this part of town. Usually, when I come to do the show, I hang out with Becky and Alice and that's about it. This time, I guess you could say I'm revisiting some of my own past, and things just seem to be springing up: memories, thoughts about things that happened when this was my playground. It's pretty breathtaking, how much has passed away."

Grant could hear the sadness in Nathan's voice. It made him think how much less of a past he had than Nathan did. He cast a glance at Nathan and said, "you don't like being here very much, do you?"

Nathan turned to Grant and gave a quizzical look. He said, "What do you mean?"

"This town," said Grant. "It's not your favorite place, is it?"

Nathan sighed and thought for a moment, looking very far away. "It's hard to describe. I have a lot of history with this place. Most of it's sad, I have to admit. It's hard not to notice, all the reminders. It must seem strange to you."

"Well, I did grow up here, you know. I have a lot of history here, too. This town *is* my history. And you've been away from here a long time. What is it—fifteen years since you left town?" asked Grant.

"Longer than that," said Nathan. "I suppose it's that, well, to put it bluntly, this is where I spent my youth, most of it was a disaster, I'm not a young man any more, and now here I am again, and it does feel strange being here. I know I'd never want to move back here, that I can say for sure."

They made their way to a row of antique shops, parked and got out. As they got out of the car, Nathan said, "Okay, so this is our first outing together in the land of junk. I should have warned you, I tend to linger."

Grant smiled and said, "No problem, I can deal with it. You realize there are two more places down the road we could hit?" Grant was saying, diplomatically, that it would be a mistake to spend the whole afternoon pawing through the booths where they were.

"Oh," said Nathan, realizing he hadn't given much thought to where else they might be heading. "Well, are you looking for anything in particular? I don't want you to have to slug through while I troll for kitsch, especially if there isn't likely to be anything here you're interested in."

"There are a couple of places in here that have good print art from time to time," said Grant. "If I'm lucky, I'll find enough to keep me occupied while you look for your stuff. What are you looking for?"

"Oh, I never know," said Nathan. "I just cast out my net and see what turns up. Ooh! Look at those chairs," said Nathan as they approached one of the storefronts, where a pair of orange and black op art plastic swivel chairs sat in a window. "Those are nice! Probably cost a fortune," he said, standing in front of the window. Grant looked at the chairs in horror. He was honestly stunned by how ugly they were. As he recovered from the shock, an image flashed in his mind: the two of them, both older and a good deal pudgier, engaging in a heated domestic dispute over how to make yet another pair of ugly plastic chairs fit in with an antique sofa. The thought made Grant shudder, and he tried to make it disappear by thinking of the two of them on vacation on a desert island: no furniture.

As they went into the store, Grant told Nathan he was going to head over to one of the booths that sold print art, leaving Nathan to wander slowly. Nathan went through the booth nearest the entrance quickly, making a few faces at the collection of reproduction Louis Quinze furniture. "LEVITZ fire sale!" he said a bit too loudly as he passed the fake stuff. He went on, picking up a few books to look at them, finding nothing of interest and then continuing down the aisle. He came to another booth where he found a display case that was largely full of crap: lousy art glass rip-offs, old lady porcelain, souvenir spoons and Depression glass. Then he looked down at the shelves close to the floor and his eyes got large as he noticed a few pieces of what looked like a Mayan Revival desk set. He quickly knelt down to have a look, and was delighted to see an entire set of copper and bronze desk accessories. The design was very good quality, and the set was in very good condition: an inkwell, a letter opener, a perpetual calendar, and a fountain pen. He looked for a price tag and was annoyed to see none visible, so he went to the front of the building to the check-out counter to ask someone to open the case. A pleasant old queen opened the case and waited while Nathan examined the pieces, finding a price tag under the calendar: ninety-five dollars for the set. Nathan asked the queen what the dealer price would be: eighty-two fifty. As Nathan peeled off the bills from the wad he'd brought with him, he felt the day was off to a good start. With luck he could double his money on the set. If not that, he could keep it, which was what he thought right away was what he might end up doing.

As he completed his purchase, Nathan thought to himself, Okay, *that* was for me, maybe. From here on out, it's strictly business. He made his way through several other booths, admiring a few lamps, a small naugahyde sofa and a set of highball glasses, and finally came to a booth where he saw an amazing monstrosity: it was a set of wrought-iron furniture, complete with bedstead, night-stands and dressing table, all fashioned in a bizarre sixties moderne pattern that evoked some kind of Salvador Dali floral fantasy. Nathan had never seen anything like it. The bedstead was appointed with an iron headboard shaped in fanciful swoops and meandering curlicues that formed an asymmetrical pattern he could only describe to himself as sixties arabesque. He thought to himself that it must be a relic of some Floridian vacation home, and wondered what kind of person could have ever had it in his or her home. For that matter, what must the rest of the place have looked like? He imagined a modern ranch with a slanted roof and a fake suit of armor in the hallway and an antiqued bronze wall relief of Greek horses mirrored on a glass oval coffee table that stood before an angular, gold-brocade sofa, a sunburst wall clock somewhere close by and a large floor model hi-fi playing Ferrante and Teicher, Percy Faith or Martin Denny. In such a place, there must also be a large white poodle having a hysterical pregnancy and someone named

Babs or Linda primping her bouffant and talking on a pink telephone at all hours of the day, a thick crust of make-up on mouthpiece of the receiver.

Before he could make his way into the kitchen of the imagined house, Nathan was interrupted by Grant, who came up next to him and said, "Any luck?" Grant had a parcel under his arm and looked at the furniture with an expression of horror that was inescapable. To Nathan it seemed as if Grant were being obliged to look at the scene of a bloody disaster. Nathan smiled and looked back at Grant, saying, "just a few odds and ends. What about you?"

"I found a couple of nice prints," said Grant. "Some engravings. So what's this?" Grant looked at the grotesque headboard and did his best to show some interest.

"Have you ever seen anything this nuts?" asked Nathan. "I'm trying to figure out what made someone make this stuff. So far I've been channeling some mafia dons from Miami, but I'm not sure. Just not sure."

"Well," said Grant, "I don't know where to being trying to guess what kind of person this was meant to appeal to. I mean, it looks like it was meant to cater to a very specific taste, wouldn't you say?"

Nathan thought about Grant's observation. Actually, it made a certain sense. Perhaps some record mogul or cruise director had had the suite made for his girlfriend or mistress. Better yet, maybe it had come from a whorehouse. It certainly would have fit in a brothel. "Do you suppose this stuff came from a house of pleasure?" asked Nathan.

"Well," said Grant, "I don't think it came from a monastery. Are you thinking about buying this?" Grant looked at the furniture as he posed his question, and it was obvious he found it astonishing that anyone would pay money for such a collection of things.

"I don't know," said Nathan. "I'm still adjusting to the fact of its existence. You have to admit, it certainly is unique. I haven't even looked for the price tags." Grant stood by as Nathan slowly moved to the headboard and examined the piece more closely. Grant found himself embarrassed to be standing next to such wildly tasteless objects, and asked himself what it meant that Nathan was drawn in by objects that were so intensely ugly. As he watched Nathan inspect the furniture, it occurred to Grant that Nathan seemed a little stunned, or could it be that he was awe-struck?

Nathan bent over the back of the headboard and found a tag, read it and reported back: "The tag says it's French, made in the sixties. It's part of an estate. Good God, what else must there have been in this lot?" Nathan stood up and backed away from the furniture, looking at it studiously. Grant began to feel himself panic a little, thinking of what their house might wind up looking like. He wondered whether you'd wake up covered with bruises after a night of sleeping on such a bed.

After a time Nathan sighed and said, "Well, it's no use. Sure as anything if I bought this stuff, I'd wind up having to keep it. I bet you could unload it in New York real fast, though." Grant sighed with relief.

"So, what next?" asked Grant.

"Oh, I don't know," said Nathan. "I found a couple of nice things. How would you feel about bailing?" Grant was surprised that Nathan was suggesting they leave. They had been at it for no more than an hour, and yet from the sound of Nathan's voice, Nathan was suggesting that they quit the hunt for the day altogether. It didn't sound like a bad idea at all to Grant.

Chapter Eleven

It was about 4:30 when they left the antique mall, not very certain about where they'd go next. Grant suggested they stop in at Trembling Earth for a drink. Nathan didn't know the place, as it had arisen since he had stopped going out to gay bars. Nathan shrugged and said that was fine with him, maybe a cocktail would be just the thing.

The bar was in a strip mall next to a health food store, which made Nathan comment, Something for the vegans, something for the serious meateaters. Grant chuckled and leaned over to peck Nathan on the cheek, which made Nathan blush. "What'll people think?" said Nathan.

"Probably that we're not vegans," said Grant.

"You want me to blow you right here in the parking lot?" answered Nathan.

"I'd like to see you try," said Grant.

After the commotion in the car they got out and Grant tucked his t-shirt back into his trousers. "That reminds me of a friend of mine," said Nathan.

"What does?" asked Grant.

"You tucking your shirt back in," said Nathan.

"So tell me," said Grant.

"Friend of mine in high school used to talk about how, when his father would take the family out to dinner every Friday night, he'd unbuckle his trousers before he got into the car so his belly wouldn't bind," said Nathan. "Then when they'd get to the restaurant, he'd get out of the car and tuck himself back in, right there in front of God and everybody."

"You know what, Nathan?" asked Grant.

"What?"

"You've got too much time on your hands," said Grant, shaking his head as they went into the bar.

Inside the bar was dark and smelled of beer. The latest Cher remix was playing on the sound system, and the place was pretty busy. They made their way up to the bar and Grant asked what Nathan wanted: a dry martini up with an olive. Grant got a light beer and the martini, and they found a place towards the back of the bar to sit at a small high table with two chairs. They sat down and looked around. "So, you come here often?" asked Nathan.

"No, not really," said Grant. "If I'm in the neighborhood. It's pretty benign, as gay bars go. Just a place to come and do some people-watching. Plus, I have a thing for place names, you know." Nathan looked at Grant as he looked around at the men in the bar. Nathan tried to study Grant's expression: bemusement, mostly.

"My favorite name for a gay bar is 'My Little Dude,'" said Nathan.

"Seriously? Where is it?" asked Grant, enjoying the idea of the place.

"Jacksonville, Florida," said Nathan. "I read about it in the *Damron Guide*, tried to find it on a buying trip. I never did make it there, but it shows up in the guides."

"There used to be a place here in town called 'Kansas Drilling Company,'" said Grant.

"Oh, yes," said Nathan. "I'm surprised you know about it. Appropriately enough, it's a steak house now. How do you know about that place?"

"A friend of mine told me about it," said Grant. "It must have been a wild place."

"You could say that," said Nathan. "There was a bathtub out behind the bar, and people used to go and sit in the bathtub and, you know, do things," said Nathan.

"What kind of things?" asked Grant.

"Tee-tee parties," said Nathan. "Water sports."

Grant didn't seem to understand the idea, so Nathan explained it to him.

"You mean some guy would sit in the bathtub and let people piss all over him and then actually go back into the bar?" asked Grant, horrified.

"It was a different time, darlin', people were sowing their wild oats," said Nathan.

"But aside from the filth aspect, I just don't get how somebody could be comfortable walking around in a bar soaking wet all night," said Grant.

"I don't really understand that scene, either," said Nathan. "Don't think I ever will. One of the principal pissees was a restaurant manager, as I recall. Maybe it had something to do with his job."

"Were you ever into that kind of thing?" asked Grant.

"Pissing on people?" asked Nathan. "No. Never. It sounds too much like the rest of life. My tastes have always been fairly vanilla, though I must admit, I did visit a few backrooms and more than a few bathhouses in my salad days," said Nathan. "Does that shock you?"

"I don't know if *shock* is the right word," said Grant. "More like, hard to picture. I mean, since AIDS all that stuff has changed."

"Has it really?" asked Nathan. "These days you have party circuits, invitation-only orgies, Jack and Jill parties, though I think that phase has died out. No one's ever come up to you and handed you a card inviting you to a 'special event' in some warehouse here in town?" asked Nathan.

"Well," said Grant, blushing. "Actually, I did go to a few of those things. It kind of freaked me out," said Grant.

"But you went to more than one?" asked Nathan.

"Three times," said Grant. "No, five. It wasn't anything I'd want to do again."

"It must be very different now," said Nathan. "My generation was lucky. All we had to worry about was syphillis or the clap. Now there's a whole catalog of life-threatening dangers, including AIDS. It's hard to convey to someone of your generation how innocent and downright brotherly all the sex dens of the seventies were. There was less focus on a certain type of body, a certain look. Guys were kinder to each other then than now, it seems to me," said Nathan.

"There's so much dishonesty now and craziness about the whole AIDS thing," said Grant.

"What do you mean?" asked Nathan.

"I mean it's clear that a good many men don't want to think about the dangers or the responsibility of sex, and when they try to put it out of their mind, they let their fear creep back into the whole business by doing crazy things, like not using a rubber."

"Well, I think it's been very crazy-making all along since AIDS has appeared, what information has come up about how people can protect themselves," said Nathan. "So much conflicting information about what constitutes safe sex. What needed to be said from the get-go was that if you have sex that involves some kind of bodily contact, you're engaging in some degree of risk, no matter what you know or don't know about who you're doing it with. Too many political agendas have gotten in the way of telling people the straight truth, and that's made it harder for people to make a sane decision about how to take care of themselves."

"Yeah," said Grant. "And young people don't think that anything can kill them, or that a miracle cure will come along and save the day."

"So where do you ordinarily go to meet men," asked Nathan.

Grant looked at Nathan with surprise. "I don't know," he said. "In the past I guess when I've gone out hunting, it's been mostly to the Heretic. What makes you ask that?"

"I guess I'm trying to fill in some of the gaps, what I don't know about you," said Nathan. "So how long since you've been, involved?"

"I dated a guy a few months back," said Grant. "Didn't work out."

"Why not?" asked Nathan.

Again, surprise. "It just didn't. The sex was good at first, but we didn't have that much to talk about," said Grant. "Sound familiar?"

"I've been out of the food chain for awhile," said Nathan. "But yes. It sounds familiar."

"Why are you interested in my sexual history?" asked Grant.

"I just want to know what I can about you," said Nathan. "Help me figure out how a man like you would end up sitting across from a man like me."

"You said yourself I have a knack for finding things," said Grant.

Just as Nathan began inching his foot up Grant's leg under the table a loud shrill cackle sounded from the other end of the bar. Nathan gave a look of horror as he turned around to look in the direction of the noise. "Oh, my God," said Nathan.

"What?" said Grant. "What happened?"

"I can't believe it," said Nathan. "It's Lady Circumference."

"Who?" asked Grant.

"An old acquaintance," said Nathan. "Well, if Lady Circumference is here, the Viatical Lover can't be too far away," said Nathan.

"The what?" asked Grant. He was struck by the look of horror on Nathan's face as the latter turned back away from the front of the bar. "Are you all right?" asked Grant. "Is this somebody you know? An old flame?"

"Worse," said Nathan. "Childhood friends." Nathan held his head low and sipped his drink, looking to his side to see if the source of the cackle was approaching. Grant watched Nathan and then looked up the bar as he saw a very large person in what looked for all the world like a caftan shuffling down the bar, hugging and slapping and slinging his drink. As the light from the door was behind the large figure, Grant couldn't make out much in the way of details. He just sat and watched the procession, a blowsy queen making the rounds with the other regulars. Grant didn't see anything unusual in the little spectacle, pretty much quotidian fare in any bar he'd ever been in. He looked back at Nathan and could see discomfort: another ghost rising up from Nathan's past, not a welcome one, either. Grant asked, "Do you want to leave?"

Nathan shook his head: "No use. Unless this place has a back exit. Anyway, if we leave now and he sees me, he'll call Becky and Alice and, God forbid, might even wind up on your doorstep. You don't want that, believe me."

Grant was took in the entire scene with incomprehension, sitting and waiting for what would happen next. Eventually the large creature made its way to the people at the bar across from where Nathan and Grant sat, Nathan with his back away from the bar. The immense fairy, whom Grant could now see more clearly, was greeting a gamy-looking guy who sat at the bar. It had lots of large rings on its plump fingers, and before long the most incredibly cloying woman's perfume wafted in Grant's direction. It stung his eyes a bit, he gasped and said, "What's that smell?"

The creature turned from the bar with a look of disbelief, obviously having heard Grant's question. Shuffling over to the table, the large man looked at him and said, "Well, honey, I reckon it's the natural scent of my twat getting worked into a froth over the sight of all these hot men. Well, I swan, if it isn't Nathan Greenwood!" And at that the big fairy flung its arms around Nathan and managed to find and tweak one of his nipples through his shirt. Nathan wrestled free and wiped the kisses off his face, then looked up at the big thing next to him and said, "Hey, Sam."

"Oh, don't call me Sam in here, Nathan! Hey, darlin, I'm Blaze Reddy. Don't I know you from somewhere?" The big fairy asked as he extended a large, puffy hand for Grant to shake. As Grant took the hand in his own, he noticed the long, fake nails on the fingers and the cheap jewelry.

"I don't think we've met," said Grant. "I'm Grant Barker."

The big queen screamed for the bartender to haul up a barrel for him to sit on, and before long a spindly little kid brought up a barstool. "Shit, honey," said Sam/Blaze to the boy who brought up the stool. "I sit on this thing long enough I'm gonna wind up wearing it up my ass. You be a good boy and get me something more substantial, now," fondling the nervously smiling kid as he spoke. The boy disappeared and Blaze settled onto the stool, remarking that he felt like he'd just landed on Plymouth Rock. "Law," said Blaze. "I'll tell y'all I'm just worn out. I's about to go to the shop this morning–in case you didn't know, Grant, I own a couple of hair salons, I bet you half the hair you see in this place is real I've burned at least once, why don't you come in some time and let me do something with what you've got?–and went out to get into the car? And somebody had keyed the whole side down the driver side? And I was just ill! Like to have took back to my bed, it just broke me up so bad, on account of the car is brand new? And it's the prettiest Cadillac I ever owned. What you think makes people do you that way? So how you doin, Nathan? I haven't seen you in a coon's age! Oops! Y'all look around and tell me any the children in here are colored."

"Sam," said Nathan, "no one says 'colored' anymore."

"Well, is that all you have to say for yourself? I swan, this boy's something, isn't he, Grant? So how long y'all been going together? Did you tell him about David, Nathan? Awful what that boy done to Nathan, Grant. Did he tell you what he did? Where the fuck is Robert? How long can it take that queen to park a car and get in here! ROBERT?" And Blaze looked around as he bellowed out the name of the unannounced person.

"Who's Robert?" asked Grant.

"Remember the other person I mentioned?" said Nathan.

"Oh, don't worry about him, he'll show up directly," said Blaze. "So tell me, Nathan, what's been happening? Looks like things are picking up, if you know what I mean?" nudging Nathan as he downed his drink and snorted, pausing with a mouthful of ice and booze to lift his glass and bellow out a refill order.

In the silence that ensued for a moment, Grant tried to find his bearings in the conversation. Luckily, Nathan stepped in: "Grant and I met at the show this month. We just came out for a drink, did some shopping first."

"Well, that's nice," said Blaze. "Did Nathan ever tell you about him and me, Grant? We known each other since we were that high. Did you tell him about David, Nathan? It's just awful what he done to you. I don't wonder you been laying low the past couple of years, he done you so wrong. Does me good to see you getting back in the saddle, you know? You hear me, Nathan?"

Suddenly a small, skinny, wizened man appeared and stood beside Blaze. Blaze looked at him and said, "well, there you are. What the hell happened? The parking lot ain't that full, what took you so long?" The skinny little man glared at Blaze with arms folded across his chest, and said, "I will not tolerate being treated like this."

"Well, what is it, Mary, did someone drop a house on your sister? What the hell's the matter with you?"

"You left me with that goddamned rental car and piled out and slung up in this bar and I couldn't get the thing into park. I am not your chauffeur."

"Robert, let's cut to the chase," said Blaze. "You didn't want to come here, I know that. You wanted to go visit your poor AIDS buddy in the hospice, and I just wasn't in the mood, I'm sorry. Robert spends more time tending to strangers on their deathbeds than he does to me. Them boys are dyin, darlin, they don't even know when you're diddlin them. Robert's got issues, Grant."

Robert stormed off and sat at the opposite end of the bar. "Good riddance to bad baggage," said Blaze.

"And yet you're still together after all these years," said Nathan.

"So, Grant, you and Nathan met at the show. You a dealer or a collector?"

"I guess a bit of both," said Grant.

"What you sell, honey?" asked Blaze.

"Antique prints, woodcuts, engravings, an occasional watercolor," said Grant.

"That don't seem to fit you, honey, not from looking at you. I'd've thought you was a carpenter or somethin, look at them hands! Hmm!" said Blaze, giving a look of astonishment and pleasure as he poked Nathan. "He's a big-un, ain't he, Nathan? Ain't he?" Blaze seemed really to need for Nathan to confirm that Grant was, indeed, a big-un.

"You could say that, Blaze," said Nathan.

"Ain't you listening, sistuh? I just did!" said Blaze, laughing far too loudly at his own wit. "Well, anyway, it don't matter, what can't fit in your mouth is wasted anyway, ain't that right?"

"Speaking of dinner," said Nathan, "you know, Grant, I think we'd better be getting along soon so we can meet Becky and Alice."

The announcement was a complete surprise to Grant, who paused for a moment to try and remember when he'd agreed with Nathan to meet the girls for dinner. Then it became clear to him what Nathan was doing. "Oh, y'all don't let me scare you off, the real crowd hasn't even arrived yet, y'all stick around maybe you can find some hot young thang to go home and do a three-way with."

Grant smiled at the suggestion, just as he saw Nathan wincing at Blaze's words. "Oh, I don't know, Blaze, I think Nathan and I can stay busy enough by ourselves. A third person would just wind up feeling left out." This comment afforded Blaze a good deal of amusement, and allowed Grant to experience up close the snorting cackle that had announced Blaze to Nathan.

Grant got up and downed the rest of his beer, said to Nathan, "You ready, Nathan?"

They said their goodbyes and left Blaze to hoist himself off the stool, thence to continue wandering from one person to the next at the bar, telling everyone hey and having a good laugh. As they reached the front of the bar, Nathan said goodbye to Robert, who sat sulking at the bar, not saying anything to anyone.

Once outside and out of earshot, Grant said, "so they're a couple?"

"Yes," said Nathan. "They been together since right out of college. Thirty years they've been tearing each other apart, driving each other crazy. Inseparable, those two."

"What upset you so much about seeing them?" asked Grant.

"Sam's been on a long, downward spiral ever since his twenties. Would you believe that morbidly obese, vulgar hayseed has an M.S. in Industrial Engineering from Georgia Tech?"

"It wouldn't have occurred to me to think that, no. Why is he a hair burner?"

"I suppose it's just his way of dropping out. His daddy died and left him some money some years back, so he went on a spree for awhile, living the party life. He quit the design business and went to cosmetology school, opened a salon and dove deep as he could into the gay life. Would you believe he was Mr. Drummer, 1979?"

"Him?"

"Him. That poor fool has probably snorted twice his present weight in cocaine over the past twenty-five years."

"I don't get it," said Grant. "So he used to be a circuit boy, gave up his profession and became a hairstylist, and then…"

"And then he fell apart. It's this town, Grant. Blaze wanted to fit into the gay life, he wanted to be the belle of the ball, so he took what he had and built himself a real gay life, Centralia-style. Boozing and parties and, somehow, a lover who stayed with him mad as hell that they weren't having the time of their lives, not willing to leave, not able to figure out what to do to keep sane. Last I heard Robert, out of spite, took to hooking up with men in the final stages of AIDS, acting as their buddy, flaunting his affairs with the poor guys just to try to get Blaze to snap out of it."

"Snap out of what?" asked Grant.

"Being an aging adolescent. Centralia does that to people, turns them into idiots or into sullen, stuck people like Robert. This isn't a town to find your dreams in, it's a town to watch them wither and turn on you."

Chapter Twelve

Grant drove back in the direction of his apartment, without thinking consciously that that was where he was headed. For a few minutes he just drove and thought about the conversations he'd had that day with Nathan. He thought about what Nathan's life must have been like as a young man in Centralia, and he tried to imagine Blaze as something other than an enormous, bloated drunk. It was all very hard and disquieting.

At length Grant became aware again that Nathan and he hadn't said a word to each other for what seemed like a mile or so worth of driving. Grant stole a look at Nathan, who seemed to be enjoying the scenery, looking out the window calmly, taking in all there was to see.

"Does the neighborhood look the same to you?" asked Grant.

Nathan smiled and looked at Grant. He said: "More or less. It's obvious the place is getting seriously gentrified. Most of the apartments are now condos, and Smith's Bridge Road is slowly moving in the direction of being redeveloped. I wouldn't be surprised if someone comes along soon and builds some mega-development soon, you know, one of those live-work-play things."

Grant smiled at the prospect. Smith's Bridge Road was pretty ugly, pretty much a wasteland of run-down buildings and liquor stores, strip joints and the occasional restaurant. He wondered if it wouldn't be better, in fact, if the whole area were bought up and redeveloped. He said, "Would that be such a bad thing?"

Nathan took a deep breath, gave a thoughtful look, and said, "well, I don't know that it matters whether it's a good idea or not. It may be enough that redevelopment has become a big enough force so that it just moves through with the inevitability of a weather front. I mean, granted, this part of town is pretty ugly, as is most of Centralia, let's face it. People don't think of this town as being a paradise of good architecture, any more than they think of it as a cultural Mecca. This town is about getting rich and moving on. It kind of bothers me, though, that the trends in development, given how much money they have behind them, seem to be moving in certain ways."

"Like how?" asked Grant.

"Like everything that's being built is fake something: fake art deco, really cheap-looking and clumsy, or fake Victorian, some of it not so cheap, but it's just so fucking safe, and it really tends to be a dumbed-down Victorian, or dumbed-down Craftsman style, or dumbed-down Mediterranean, which is really very robotic looking, I mean all of what gets built, certainly in the way of residential ar-chitecture, is just meant to not offend anyone. New office buildings are all this safe kind of postmodernist non-descript crap or dumbed-down deco. It's as if the whole landscape is slowly being turned into the set of a Japanese horror movie."

"A what?" asked Grant.

"A Japanese horror movie," said Nathan. "You know, some-thing really choice, like "The Manster," where Raymond Burr is the only actor you recognize, and he's speaking in English while every-body else is talking in Japanese, and when there's the big scene of the monster making his getaway through the streets of the city, which is already half in ruins, the cheesy background the actor in the monster suit is walking through is the model for what is getting built now."

Grant looked at Nathan as if he were out of his mind. Nathan realized the problem: "I'm sorry," he said at last, "I chose a comparison too far outside your personal frame of reference. That and I'm showing my age. Pretend I never said anything about Japanese movies, and just think, cheap, cheesy, inhuman architecture. I mean, it's really as if the whole city is being turned into the kind of clumsy, dopey amusement park crap you find in the exhibition buildings at the Centralia Antiques show, you know, the exhibition buildings. Clumsy, dumb, spiritless copies of something from somewhere and some time else."

"I never thought about any of this," said Grant. "I guess you have a view of things that's different from mine, because you've been around longer and have seen more. What I see is that the whole city is changing, pretty fast, it seems. But it's more than that—there seems to be this kind of rush to build up the city really really fast so that it really is the New York of the South, which is kind of crazy."

"I couldn't agree more. And I think that's what all this new, fake art deco is about. First of all, art deco is safe. No one is going to object to it. That, plus I think it's easy to design a building inspired by art deco elements because you can make something pretty simple that looks decorative by adding art deco touches here and there. That, and of course, when did much of New York and Chicago get built? Between the twenties and the forties. So here we are in Centralia, with lots of relatively cheap land, and this boom in people rushing southward from the rust belt, and so what are the obvious choices? Build something that looks like the places the refugees from the rust belt left; build something that allows the knucklehead boosters to say, 'See? We really are just like New York City!' But it doesn't work, it's all fake, and it looks fake. The real art deco came along as part of a social and historical phenomenon. It reflected a real set of feelings and beliefs in twentieth century modernism—awestruck faith in industry, fascination with the then-new idea of big machines, cars and locomotives and airplanes. But you start tacking that look onto the public landscape in a world that has evolved far beyond a fascination with the newness of machines, and it just all looks empty. That, and I think much of the new building, residential and commercial, is being designed on computer, and so it all has this extremely harsh edge to it, like the face of someone who's been redesigned by cosmetic surgery. It all looks too perfect, too studied, and it's all very, very creepy."

"So, I'm guessing you won't be moving back to Centralia anytime soon?" said Grant.

"I can't imagine subjecting myself to that," said Nathan. "The city is filling up with pod people moving into pod people buildings. It's the land of the body snatchers, and I won't have any part of it. Such a shame, too, because the region is still one of the prettiest I know of, the rolling hills, the beautiful forests, the old intown neighborhoods full of greenery and flowers. But the new is just repulsive and overwhelming, and I just can't stand it."

By this time they had reached Grant's apartment building. It was a two-story brick building with eight units. The building was situated on a small street in Center Town, an old neighborhood built on the site of a Civil War battlefield. Having gotten lost in the force of his own rhetoric, Nathan finally noticed they were parked. He looked around and thought he remembered a night, long ago, when he made love on a second floor balcony in the building next to which Grant had just parked. Blushing at the memory, Nathan turned to Grant and asked, "Why are we parked here?"

Grant looked at Nathan and said, "This is my place. I just kind of ended up here. Didn't think about it. I guess I was thinking about what you were saying while we were driving."

"Oh," said Nathan, blushing further. Where could this be headed? Was this Grant guy about to make a move on him? Would he be able to get an erection if anything happened, or would he be so panicked he'd just be unable to perform? "Well," he said, "It looks like a nice building. I think I might have been here before, matter of fact," he continued.

"You want to come in for awhile and visit?" asked Grant. "I could take you back to Becky and Alice, if you'd rather," he continued. Nathan thought he saw Grant swallow a lump. A lump?

Nathan thought about what he should do. If Grant wasn't moving him towards a seduction, he was laying a pretty good groundwork for a very well-performed practical joke. But there honestly didn't seem to be anything in Grant that would suggest that kind of meanness, that kind of intent. How could it be that this handsome young man was working so intently to get Nathan in bed? He was having a hard time comprehending Grant's motives, and he had no idea how he could or would react. It had been so long since he'd made love indoors, in private, with just one man present. Since David it had been dirty bookstores, bathhouses, sex clubs, and all of them only occasionally, only when the desire for contact with another man overcame his firm belief that he would never find anything of substance in an intimate relationship.

"Why me, Grant?" at length Nathan heard himself giving into the realization that he had nothing to lose by asking a truthful question.

Grant smiled. It was already beginning to be pretty dark, so Nathan could see less and less clearly the features of Grant's face. He could see the small lights in Grant's eyes, reflections of the surrounding sources of light, and he could see and, he thought, hear Grant's smile. Grant said: "I don't think I've met anyone like you before. I don't want to let you slip away. I don't just want to fuck, but I do want that. Don't you want to, Nathan?"

Early the following morning, Grant pulled up in front of Becky and Alice's house. He was bleary-eyed, as was Nathan. Nathan was slightly hoarse as he leaned over and kissed Grant. Grant said, "So, you'll give me a call when you get back to Charleston?"

"Yeah," said Nathan, still wondering whether the last twelve hours had actually happened.

"Okay, then," said Grant. He put the truck into park, leaned over and hugged Nathan, smelled his hair, which was messy and slightly scented with Nathan's smell, a smell he had already begun to commit to memory. Grant kissed Nathan on the side of the face and held him tightly. They sat there for a long time. Eventually it was Nathan who pulled back. He looked at Grant and seemed to study him.

"Thanks," said Nathan. "Thanks seems a pretty stupid thing to say right now, but, well, thanks." He kissed Grant. Their lips were chapped, they burned each other's cheeks with their early morning stubble, and they kissed a long goodbye kiss. Nathan got out of the truck and went up to the front door of the house. Grant watched him and made sure he was able to get in the house, then drove off.

Nathan walked quietly into the kitchen, greeted along the way by a host of fat, waddling, panting dogs, a clutch of cats weaving around his feet. When he went into the kitchen, Alice was there. "Where'd you sleep last night, in the gutter?" she asked, looking up from her newspaper.

"Well, yes," Nathan said, "But I was looking at the stars."

Chapter Thirteen

The rest of the day Nathan thought about the previous night he'd spent with Grant. It was hopeless, he thought to himself. Grant will get it out of his system, and in a week or two, he'll be ready for the next new thing. Nathan had seen too many men come along to think that Grant really wanted anything like a boyfriend. People don't do that anymore, thought Nathan. Dating is passé. We just had a hook-up. That's what people do nowadays, they hook up. No one has a relationship. In this way Nathan talked himself out of the prospect of believing that Grant might actually want something other than another night or two of multiple orgasms, endless cuddling and smooching, and the occasional nap. It was just the newness of doing it that had carried them, thought Nathan. It wouldn't be the same the next time they met, he thought. It was just a one-night stand, he thought, no fault of Grant's, that's just the way the world works now.

So Nathan went about his business that day, got ready to go back to Charleston, and silently talked himself out of believing that he would ever see or hear from Grant again. The whole thing had just been an adventure. So what?

That afternoon Nathan, having packed up, wrote a note to Becky and Alice thanking them yet again for their hospitality. Becky and Alice were at work, so he was by himself. As a gesture of his thanks he left them a nice bottle of white wine he'd picked up at the liquor store. He made sure all the indoor animals were indoors, all the doors were closed and locked, and then he went out the front door, locked it, and took a deep breath, thinking about the drive back. He was surprised he didn't feel more tired than he did. He wondered if the fatigue would hit him someplace inconvenient, like the long stretch of road between Aiken and Charlotte, or between Charlotte and Charleston. He got in his van, cranked it up, and drove off.

Nathan found his way to the Club Pinque, the oldest surviving gay bathhouse in Centralia. It was a relic that had survived the seventies, the beginning of the AIDS epidemic, and all the vicissitudes of economic and political circumstance that had come about over the past twenty-five years. Few people—most especially few Centralians—admitted they patronized such a place, though the parking lot was almost always full, day and night. The Club Pinque was located right next to the expressway that ran through midtown Centralia, making it very easy to find. It was owned by a mother and son team well connected with organized crime in the region. Centrally located in the middle of midtown Centralia, it was close by two major universities, and thus attracted a large number of students (and faculty), many of whom found their first experiences with gay sex inside the dour-looking building. The fact that there was an endless supply of college boys at the center of the establishment's client base accounted for its survival over the years.

In cities other than Centralia sex clubs like the Pinque tended to be more elaborate, more well-kept, more cheerful, and more—sexy. People visiting from Los Angeles or Miami, with their palatial, well-managed sex resorts, were often shocked to find what a depressing, primitive place the Pinque was. From the check-in counter to the innermost recesses of the building, the Pinque was dark and dank. The smell of mildew, industrial-strength disinfectant and patchouli incense hung over everything. The décor was mid-century retro, done very cheaply. The check-in window was staffed by a group of expressionless, wormy-looking young men who made few efforts at concealing their contempt for the habitués and occasional visitors alike. More than a few people had noted over the years, in fact, that the one good thing about the staff was that it really didn't matter who you were—they all hated you equally. Once you paid the entry fee, you were given a towel and buzzed inside, where you found a common area outfitted with lockers, vending machines, dinette tables, a large projection tv that was always tuned in to a cable sports channel, and a couple of dingy restrooms. If you paid the basic fee of twenty-five dollars, you got six hours worth of access to a locker, where you stored your clothes and put on a towel. If for some reason your towel became soiled, you had to pay extra for another one. Pending availability and your willingness to pay a higher rate, you could get a room or even a suite. Having stowed away your belongings in whatever accommodation you had chosen, you kept your key on a rope that fit snugly around your arm or leg, and you then wandered through the building, visiting its various amenities. Woe betide the guest who lost his key: fifty dollars and a conversation with the manager, a very nasty man who seemed to be there twenty-four hours a day and who was also breathtakingly repulsive. Most visitors spent their time wandering the halls past individual rooms or suites, where men lay in various states of play. If the signs were favorable you might enter a room and play along.

The rooms and suites were on the upper level. There was also a lower level where there was a large swimming pool, a sunning area, a set of restrooms, a steam room, a sauna and a set of showers. Men had sex in the pool, the sauna and the steam room, and sometimes in the showers. Occasionally the manager came through and discouraged people from having sex in the open, and if a patron was found doing something unkind or unclean in the sauna or steam room, the manager broke it up and threatened to throw the offending party out. There was, then, a kind of nagging dishonesty about the place: everyone who came there came to have sex—not a soul ever came to enjoy the steam room or the pool. Even so, the management, which had no illusions about why the place was in business, gave lip service to the notion that sexual activity was not allowed on the premises.

Nathan hated the Pinque, but he found that as he left town, he was in such an agitated state that nothing seemed more natural than to do something that would agitate him even further. If pressed at the time to account for his actions, he would have probably said it was just a last-minute impulse.

Nathan paid his twenty-five dollars, got his key and his towel, and went inside. He changed clothes, noting as he did so that he was being spied on by a small group of youngish men lurking in the shadows where the common area gave access onto a corridor leading to rooms and suites. Nathan went about his business, neatly undressing and folding his clothes, stacking them in the small locker: shoes on locker floor, socks tucked into shoes, jeans hanging on the one hook in the locker, shirt hanging on the same hook as the jeans, and finally, briefs on top of the shirt, so the briefs would be the first things he'd put back on when it was time to leave. As he stood there in front of his locker, naked, he folded his towel so he would be able to wrap it around himself in the most comfortable way possible, given the towel's length, width and texture. This was a skill he'd learned many years before, in his twenties, when he started going to sex clubs: how to fold and wrap so the towel looks right and stays on without your having to fidget with it all the time. This skill has no name, Nathan thought for the first time in his life, there is no way to name the skill of folding and wrapping your towel in a gay men's club. Isn't that odd? He thought to himself. We have names for everything imaginable related to sex except this. How did it get overlooked? He heard the hissing of whispering voices as his dick and ass were being assessed by the boys in the shadows. He finished folding his towel, then he wrapped it and tucked it in so that it wouldn't fall off as he strolled around the building.

Nathan made a point of walking past the group of whispering boys as he made his way out of the common area and into the corridor. "Excuse me," he said as he passed. The group of young men stopped talking abruptly as he passed, being careful to look anywhere but in his direction. What do young men think they're doing when they pretend you're not there by refusing to look at you? He thought to himself. He was feeling anxious and a little dissociated as he made his way into the corridor. He knew it was a bad idea to be in this place. It was as if his body were moving without his intending or directing it. How odd, he thought to himself, moving into the dimly lit hallway. It feels as if I'm not here, but watching this on remote camera, like that guy who explored the Titanic with video robot.

Watching it all on remote, from a safe distance, he thought. But am I safe? Of course not. Could there be a less safe place for anyone? Maybe a North Korean nuclear reactor or an exotic contagion research lab at the CDC? Why did I come here, he thought, and in thinking that thought he had accomplished his reason for coming, for he could not honestly remember why he was there. Having realized he could not remember why he was there, however, and knowing he was in a bad place, he did not leave. He thought to himself how dimly lit the place was. Dim, he said half aloud: like this city, and dim like the people in it. For that matter, like the whole country. For that matter, like me. Dim. And dreary. As he walked he saw various vignettes through the open doorways: an enormous black man lying in a small bed, stroking himself and looking languidly at nothing at all; a sepulchrally wasted white man, standing in the small space beside his room's small cot, lighting a cigarette; a beautiful young man getting a blowjob from two muscle boys who were vying for the space between his legs like baby piglets at their mother's teat; an alarmingly muscular, very hairy man, with telltale bulging, sinewy belly, standing in the doorway of his room, his gigantic dick hanging low between his legs, a thick Prince Albert dangling from the head; three young, skinny queens perched on a cot, laughing and talking in high, whispering hisses; a closed door behind which could be heard the thumping of limbs and the loud, urgent moans of a man getting fucked; and through the doorway of a suite, the sight of a lone, thirty-something man lying on a bed, hands propped behind his head, watching a re-run of "The Andy Griffeth Show" on TV. With every step he took, Nathan regretted more deeply having come to this place. He thought to himself: *"Th'expense of spirit in a waste of shame,"* indeed. But he did not leave. He wandered the halls awhile, looking into doorways, stopping to watch the pornography on the banks of TVs built into the walls at intervals, and found himself thinking about less and less, except noticing once in a while how utterly suffused with boredom the whole place was—as if boredom were a scent, a mind-numbing perfume, that had been pumped in through the ventilation system. *Luxe, calme et volupté*, he thought to himself. *Well, actually, one out of three*, he corrected himself silently. The music being played over the PA system helped with the sense of mindlessness: the usual trance mix, the staple of all sex clubs, dirty bookstores and gyms, full of urgency and repetition, a sonic depiction of hotness considered singly or in congress with other hotness. As the background sound of a scene that offered mostly vacuity, the music, in its driving urgency, only served to accentuate the fact that nothing much was happening there. Men walking past each other, for the most part pretending not to notice each other. *There really is an epidemic of that*, Nathan noted to himself, *and certainly not just in bathhouse, Note to self: What is it with this whole "You can't see me because I'm not looking at you" thing?*

Nathan came to a room where a young man was lying on a bed, alone. He was well-built and had his towel draped over one leg so that it obscured his dick. He was lying flat on the bed, smoking (a habit Nathan despised), half-watching porn, half-eyeing the doorway. Nathan stopped to watch him, finding him attractive. The man was fairly young, blonde, with a hairless body, very athletic. The young man seemed not to mind Nathan watching him, so Nathan stayed, trying not to appear too interested, lest he wear out his welcome. After a few minutes of this staring contest, the young man moved his towel to reveal his dick: pretty, about average in overall dimensions, uncut, surrounded by a very blonde bush. Nathan found himself becoming more interested, a fact the front of his towel began to display for him. The young man smiled as he saw the evidence of Nathan's growing arousal. He made a gesture inviting Nathan to come in. Nathan entered the small room and closed the door behind him. "Want some company?" he asked, removing his towel to reveal a very full erection.

"Sure," said the young man.

After the briefest of hellos, they laid down onto the tiny bed and made out for awhile. Nathan enjoyed the making out stage and the oral sex stage. He knew the stage after the oral sex stage would be where trouble might crop up. Sure enough, when it got to that point, the young man wanted Nathan to fuck him bareback, but Nathan insisted that a rubber was indispensable, as he himself was positive. The young man said that didn't matter, because he was, too. Nathan said it did matter, and after a few awkward minutes, during which the young man lost his erection, Nathan suggested that they "take a break."

"That's cool," said the young man, clicking the channel changer as Nathan clambered out of the bed. He arranged his towel, said his Thank Yous and left the room, leaving the door open, as the young man instructed him to do.

Nathan thought that it was a bit of a relief to have gotten the matter of sex out on the table, especially since his first encounter hadn't ended with a proper orgasm. This meant he needed to decide whether he was going to devote the rest of his evening to finding a suitable partner—or a succession of them—and orchestrate a tremor or two. He had been bone tired when he came into the place, but now that he was awakened to the hunt, he felt very awake. Still, it was a Sunday night, and he knew, from years of hanging out in places like this, that it could just as easily be busy and fun as still and boring. Or worse yet: if a covey of circuit boys all cranked up on tina were to blow in, then the party would be over. They might scurry about and chatter like witches, so they would provide some diversion, but it wouldn't be about sex, in any literal sense of the word.

The place didn't seem to be terribly busy, but then it was not much later than about ten o'clock. Things wouldn't get cracking until after midnight, the faggot's dawn, so there was really no telling what was likely to happen. Often, when Nathan sought out comfort and forgetfulness in a place link the Pinque, he found that he had the most fun, the most tender, satisfying encounters, when there were relatively few people out and about. The worst time to come to a place like that, in Nathan's view, was Saturday night, when virtually everyone in the city was so heavily drugged that there was no telling how they would behave. Sundays were always something of a surprise. Another Sunday surprise, Nathan thought to himself, as he wandered.

He decided to go downstairs to the wet area. There was a large pool, heavily chlorinated to neutralize the great quantity of body fluids that had been released into in every day. There was also a steam room, a sauna, and a place to lie out under the sun (or the stars) and relax. If the place hadn't been so ugly and so badly maintained, these areas would have been pleasant places to pass the time. As it was, the steam room smelled alarmingly nasty and the pool was so full of chlorine that swimming in it felt like swimming in pure bleach. Nathan opted to go into the sauna, reasoning that it, next to the outdoor seating area, was the cleanest corner of the place. He thought it might do him good to sweat a bit.

When he went into the sauna he was the only person there. That was fine. It let him be alone with his thoughts which, for the moment, was not an unpleasant prospect, since his mind was almost completely blank. He thought that it would be good to get home to his shack, and it appeared he would be doing that sometime Monday, assuming he spent the night at the baths, which was very likely. He felt a tinge of guilt at not driving home straight from the show, as his cat, Widdybug, would be—certainly not waiting, but he felt guilty at leaving the cat alone. Of course, the cat wasn't alone, because Edna Sykes, his next door neighbor, was looking after the whole place, as she always did when Nathan went away for the weekend. Missykes, as he called his neighbor, doted on Widdybug, as she doted on all cats, her favorite being her twenty-eight pound prince, Buster. Nathan allowed himself to think for a moment what Missykes was doing that very minute with Buster. Well, owing to the hour, probably nothing, but if it were still light outside, she'd be sitting out on her screened porch, reading the newspaper or the Bible to her cat, who would be lying there lazily watching birds and bugs, flicking its tail every once in a while. Buster was so fat he looked like a pinhead, Nathan said to everyone but Missykes. The cat w as so fat its belly dragged against the ground whenever it got up to move around. Nathan knew that when he got back he'd have to deal with the fact that, in a show of affection, his neighbor would have fed Widdybug all manner of unhealthy food—bacon and heavy cream and fat trimmed from pork chops—so that he would have to endure a few days of bowel and nausea issues with his cat. At least she was kind enough to take care of the cat, and that even though she had been inside Nathan's house and had seen how he lived, a feat not accomplished by most of his friends and all of his family.

It wasn't just that Nathan wasn't a particularly scrupulous housekeeper. He kept people out of his house because he was half afraid if people saw the inside, they'd have him locked up. This was owing to the fact that, as an independent dealer of collectibles and oddities of all kinds, Nathan had filled his house with the oddest of the oddities he'd found. After nearly twelve years of living in the little house, Nathan had turned the house into a personal paradise. Though he thought it was a haven, he feared most people would think of it as a grotesque pile of evidence pointing to a depraved imagination. He had a collection of 1939 New York World's Fair artifacts, a number of paint-by-numbers paintings and paintings by convicts he'd bought at yard sales and thrift stores, furniture, sculpture and incidental decorations from the ranging from the Vienna Secession to the Eames studio—all in all, a brilliant and daring combination of objects crammed into a small house. He also had collections of far more preculiar things: large bowls of teeth and desiccated animal carcasses, sex toys and other accouterments he'd bought in various dirty book stores, newspaper clippings, and even odder things. In his bathroom there was a whole wall of letters and photos of serial killers, some of them autographed and addressed to Nathan: John Wayne Gacy, Ed Giehn, Albert Fish, all of them were plastered on his bathroom wall, interspersed with religious icons, prosthetic devices and marital aids. It was an unusual approach to interior design, he knew, but it was somehow necessary. Still, he knew he had to be very careful about who he let in the place, as it was just not the sort of collection of collections that one could expose to the general public. Missykes had come to be a confidante only because when she had a stroke a few years back, Nathan looked in on her, and she had showered him with gratitude ever since her recovery. Whether the stroke had impaired her faculties or for some other reason, Missykes, once allowed into Nathan's house, had never made a single comment about any of the remarkable objects inside.

Sitting in the heat felt good. Nathan began to warm up, and before too long he noticed he was dripping with perspiration. He found he was getting a bit too hot, so he left the sauna and showered off in cool water for a few minutes, then went back into the sauna for another sweat. Shortly after he went in the second time, a nice-looking, if somewhat portly, young man came in after him and sat down on the ledge next to him. He let his towel fall open, revealing one of the largest human penises Nathan had ever seen. It was a horse dick, plain and simple. Nathan, great admirer of dicks that he was, made no effort to conceal his fascination. The young man seemed unaffected by the attention. Of course, thought Nathan, he must be used to it, given how truly big his dick is. Nathan thought for a minute about that old story that circulated among intellectuals that the one sentence from "A Rose for Emily" the publisher had refused to print was something like "He had the biggest dick in the county." Wonder if that's true, asked Nathan to himself, or is it like all those stories queens used to tell about Tallulah Bankhead?

Nathan felt himself getting hotter and hotter, but of course he had no intention of leaving the sauna until he got either a chance to play with the wonderful giant dick or the opportunity to watch it in action with someone else. The dick's owner looked to be in his mid-thirties, so Nathan's best guess was that he, Monsieur Priape, would probably not be interested in any attention paid him by a fellow like Nathan, a greybeard faggot of over fifty. After some time of sitting in silence, Nathan finally spoke up:

"You doing all right this evening?" Sufficiently manly vocal tone, establishing himself as a Southerner and a real man. Well done, Nathan thought to himself.

"Not bad," said the stranger, looking at Nathan briefly and then looking back straight ahead. "You?"

"Ok, I guess," said Nathan. Thinking there was no prospect of having sex with Monsieur Priape, he decided to take the innocuous role of the honest, plain-spoken old fairy. He said: "It was a mistake for me to come here, of course. But then it's a mistake for anyone to come here."

"Why stay, then?" asked the young man with the big dick. Nathan was surprised the fellow was answering him. Surprised he hadn't already gotten up and left. "Why not go home and go to bed?"

"That would be a roughly five-hour trip, to Charleston," said Nathan. "Just didn't feel like making the drive tonight. Or at least, I'm not resigned to it, yet. You from here?"

"Yes," said the young man. "Charleston, South Carolina? Great city," he continued.

"It was really pretty nice before the Yankees all moved in, started snapping up the old places, driving up the cost of living and trying to refashion the place as a New York suburb." Nathan couldn't help but respond with his usual bitterness at what was happening to Charleston: the city was being invaded by rich people fleeing the rust belt, and gradually it was losing its charm, its sense of uniqueness, like much of the rest of the South. It was becoming just another American city, Nathan thought to himself, a homogenized, blank mess. He hated what was happening. On that count, he hated Centralia perhaps most of all: aspiring to be the New York of the South, it had ended up looking more like Disneyworld.

The young man looked at Nathan and smiled. "You're right," he said, "it's awful what's happening. But look how much worse it is here. They keep talking about Centralia as the next great international city, and it's laughable."

Now it was Nathan's turn to look at the young man and smile. "Oh, my," he said. "A Centralian, but not a booster? Are you on the run from the law? I thought your kind had been stamped out. Don't tell me you're a *native*."

"I am, indeed. Born and raised. I love the region," said the young man, "like the climate, most of the time. But I hate what's happening to the city."

Nathan was feeling very uncomfortable from the heat, but he was enjoying the conversation. He did his best to hold on, thinking the next few minutes were probably the best contact he could expect to have all evening. In response to the young man's last comments, Nathan asked, "What don't you like about what's happening here? Aren't you happy Centralia has gotten to be a real big city?" As he asked his question, he couldn't help but notice that the young man was slowly playing with his dick, which was responding. Odd, thought Nathan, as he began to loosen his towel: a young man who gets aroused talking about urban affairs? Is this something new he's brought back from the west coast? The next step beyond fisting?

"The problem is, it's *not* becoming a *real* big city," said the young man, slouching and spreading his legs as he began more openly to stroke the enormous dick. "The problem is, it's not real at all. It's fake." He looked at Nathan and smiled lazily.

They played for awhile, until Nathan declared he couldn't stand the heat any more. They left the sauna together, showered, and went outside to the seating area. There were a few men lying in lawn chairs, smoking. Nathan and his new acquaintance took up lounge chairs side by side. Seeing there was company, Nathan didn't think that the play would continue. He was wrong. The young man threw back his towel, and quickly became aroused again. The other people present noticed and took up positions close by. The young man allowed himself to be serviced as he continued his conversation with Nathan, who was too uncomfortable to join in. The conversation was so good, though, and he found himself so hungry for a good talk, that he couldn't tear himself away.

"Where were we?" asked the young man, spreading his legs wide and allowing himself to be serviced by a pair of men.

Nathan thought back for a minute. He said: "I believe you were indulging in a great heresy. You were saying that Centralia is fake. How can you question the excellence of this mighty city?"

One of the men worshipping Monsieur Priape's dick popped up and looked at Nathan. The worshipper said: "You're not kidding. This town has more phonies and assholes per square mile than any place I've ever been."

"Where are you from?" asked Nathan.

"Chicago," said the worshipper.

The other worshipper, who had been nursing Monsieur Priape's balls, popped up and said: "I love Chicago!" He then resumed his ministrations.

Nathan then asked the first worshipper, "If you like Chicago so much, why are you here?"

Out the side of his mouth, the first worshipper lisped one word: "yob." *Job.* Nathan didn't pursue the matter further, as it was clear the worshipper was trying to concentrate. He turned to Monsieur Priape and said, "that pretty much sums things up, don't you think?"

Monsieur Priape nodded. He said, "That's what happens to make most people come here. Some may like all the greenery at first, but they soon discover there's not much going on here in the way of city life. It's five million people trying to ignore each other."

Nathan responded, "Well, with the exception of a small number of American cities like New York, don't you think it's pretty true of most American cities that the city itself, the inner core, is usually run-down, more or less irrelevant to the life of the region? American cities are suburbs arranged around despised, empty cores. Do you think it's fair to pick on Centralia?"

"You're right," said Monsieur Priape, "Centralia is a sewer of crime, bad government and dirty dealing, with a bunch of sprawling suburbs attached to it like a bunch of ticks. Five million opportunists cluster in this place, curl their lips and say, I hate you, I owe you nothing at all. And that's the story of American cities, Centralia is just one of a species."

"Do you think it might change?" asked Nathan.

Monsieur Priape shrugged and said, "it could, of course. But will it? Do *you* think it will? Do you see life getting any better here? Do you see it turning into a real city?"

"What is a real city?" asked Nathan.

"A place with a soul that isn't mean and crazy," said Monsieur Priape. "A place where people can feel encouraged, loved and recognized."

Nathan nodded. He watched a bit longer, as the two men continued to blow Monsieur Priape. Then he said his goodbyes, went upstairs, got dressed, and left.

It was nearly one a.m. when he left the bathhouse. He hadn't had a single orgasm. He felt the need to get back home and just be there, cocooned in his own little place. He needed to get out of town fast. So many memories, he thought. So many, many memories.

The drive back to Charleston wasn't as difficult as he had expected. Light traffic and a clear, moonlit sky helped. It also helped that he was alert and awake, for some reason, despite the late hour. He stopped for coffee in Augusta, then stopped for breakfast in Charlotte, then headed down I-26 all the way into Charleston, making it into his driveway around six-thirty in the morning, just as the sky was beginning to brighten. He left the van full, locked it up, went inside, breathed a sigh of relief, and fell into his bed. He didn't wake up until almost four in the afternoon.

Chapter Fourteen

Nathan drove into his driveway early the next morning. He got out of his van, locked it, went inside the house, undressed and went to bed. When he woke up late that afternoon, the sun was white-bright. It was hot as an oven inside the house when he woke up, because he'd forgotten to turn on the air conditioner when he fell in his bed early that morning. He got up, made a pot of coffee, put on some shorts, put some music on and shuffled out to the mailbox. There was the usual assortment of bills, circulars and credit card offers, and a a post card from a friend from college he hadn't seen in awhile: it was from Ken in New York, a homemade card showing the infamous Dawn Langley Hall in bed with her two shar-peis, on the reverse side an obituary notice for Dawn and a brief, surprisingly sentimental note from Ken, reminding Nathan of the time the two of them had visited Dawn, down on her luck but still gracious and entertaining. Nathan felt a quick rush of sadness as he read the card: it had been so long since he'd seen Ken that he couldn't remember how just how long it had been. A voice from the past, recalling to mind the more distant past. Why, he thought to himself, does it sting to remember?

Still, it felt good to be back home in his little tumbledown house, so eaten up with Formosan termites that there were rooms even he no longer went into. Situated on a dead-end road near the marsh, it was remote enough to be comfortable, and close enough to the Folly Beach Road to give him easy access to the rest of the world. In bad storms, the area sometimes went under water. Nathan knew that it was just a matter of time before he'd have to find another place to live, because the house was so precariously situated and in such bad shape. He dreaded the thought of ever having to move, shuddering at the thought of what it would take him to pack. How long had he been there, renting the little house? He had trouble remembering, finally gave up trying. Where had the time gone?

Then it came back to him: he moved into the house in May 1989, not long after David disappeared. On the heels of that disaster, there was another: in September of that same year, Hurricane Hugo hit Charleston. The storm was so destructive that it nearly wiped out the beach communities along the South Carolina coast. The storm did so much damage to downtown Charleston itself, the old section on the peninsula, that it was feared at the time the city would never be able to rebuild fully. Nathan rode out the storm in his little house. After David left him, especially the way he left, Nathan was pretty torn up, so when the hurricane came, he simply wasn't able to get himself together to leave. The house was little more than a shack made of wood planks nailed to a simple frame, so that during the worst of it all, Nathan could feel the spray of water coming through the walls. The house, had survived, he believed, only because it was nestled in a copse of old live oaks and cedars. Either that or God, knowing Nathan was inside, wanted to make sure the house rode out the storm so that Nathan would feel every bit of its force as directly as possible without dying. The house was situated in a group of old live oaks and cedar trees, and that had probably protected it from the storm's full force. Had it been out in the open, it probably would have blown away, as so many others had. Nathan still thought about the storm from time to time, picturing himself found dead in the remains of a shack that had been blown all the way to the beach. Hugo was a beautiful spectacle, but it was also the most terrifying experience Nathan had ever had. Yes, he thought to himself, Hugo was the worst I've ever lived through; even David doesn't come close.

See what happens when you start thinking about the past, Nathan asked himself. It all begins to open up, like a box you take down from the top shelf of a closet, which then perversely tips over and spills out its contents—and as they spill out, they seem to grow in number, and before you know it, you've blown a whole afternoon or evening picking up crap you can't remember having a reason for saving. Better never to have touched the box in the first place. Better still to have thrown all that junk away. Nathan put the card from Ken back with the stack of mail, and then noticed the neighborhood cats were swarming around him, waiting to be fed. Inside the house, Little Jimmy Scott was singing "Holdin' Back the Years." Nathan started as he heard the lyrics, feeling his face heat up briefly. Never mind, he said to himself, never mind. He got the food for the outside cats, working to keep Widdybug from fleeing to the outdoors so he could beat the shit out of all the strays. Then Nathan sat on the front porch and watched the scrawny cats eat their fill.

The phone rang. Nathan tried to ignore it, until he heard the answering machine pick up and heard Missykes's high, scratchy voice on the other end. Nathan smiled at the sound of her voice, knowing more or less what she was saying without actually hearing it. He decided he'd go over to her house later to thank her for looking after things. He'd ask if she wanted him to carry her to the store tomorrow or the next day, she would answer that that would be very nice, and she would tell him all about Buster's doings over the last few days.

Fortified with a few cups of coffee, Nathan went about unloading his van. The long nap he'd had helped him make quick work of getting all his wares into the house. As it was August, the chore of unloading the van left Nathan sweaty and dirty, so he drew a bath and had a nice long soak, listening to Marianne Faithfull singing Kurt Weill songs.

After he got cleaned up, Nathan walked over to Missykes's house with a bouquet of flowers he'd cut from his garden. He knocked on the door and waited. After a few minutes, he heard a high voice screech from behind the closed door, saying "Who is it?" Nathan recognized the ritual as part of Missykes's savoring the prospect of having company. Of course she knew it was Nathan at her door; Nathan knew she'd been watching him from inside her house ever since she noticed his van was back in the front yard. She had probably been bending Buster's ear all afternoon wondering when Nathan was going to come over and try to act like a gentleman for once and say thank you and offer to do her a good turn for once in his life.

"It's Nathan Greenwood, Missykes," Nathan answered loudly, knowing she could hear perfectly well, but knowing she would fain deafness if he didn't speak up loudly enough, announcing himself by his full name.

One after another, a brace of locks was disengaged and the door to the small white cottage was cracked open. Inside the house it was very dark. From the darkness there appeared the head of a little white-haired old lady. As she opened the door further it you could see she was not much more than five feet tall, but nearly as wide, dressed in a white blouse and powder blue polyester pants, athletic shoes, carrying a cane. She looked suspiciously out and up at Nathan from behind the screen door, which remained closed. She squinted as she looked up at him. She asked, "that you, Nathan? Whatchyou doin' a-comin' over here this time 'o day? Land sakes. I's just fixin' to set down to supper. I reckon it'll all get cold now." Nathan was instantly horrified at his mistake. He knew Missykes was inviting him—in code—to eat supper with her, and as she opened the screened door to let him in, he wasn't sure he was prepared either to spend the evening with her or to make an escape. Missykes didn't wait to hear his answer, but turned back into the house, after he'd taken hold of the screen door. The tiny old lady tottered back into the gloom of her house. Nathan knew that if he didn't follow there'd be no end of feuding to face with Missykes. He had to take his medicine. Lesson to self: never go see Missykes between four and eight in the evening. Never never never.

The problem was two-fold: first, Missykes didn't believe in air conditioning; unfortunately, she also didn't believe in opening the windows unless there was an emergency. As a result, her house was hot beyond belief. How she didn't die of heatstroke was a mystery to Nathan. Second, she was so feeble and forgetful that her cooking was always suspect. She cooked constantly, too, making Nathan wonder how, just as a matter of the law of averages, she never managed to cook anything worth eating. She even cooked for Buster, who was the one fan of her kitchen skills. Nathan had the distinct impression, having forced himself to eat her food a few times, that she had used canned cat food to prepare one of the many casseroles she was fond of making and serving both to her human guests and to her beloved Buster.

"I'm sorry to barge in on you, Missykes," said Nathan, "I just wanted to come over and say thanks for taking care of Widdybug and the wild kitties. I brought you some flowers from my garden." By now Missykes had set up two tv trays in front of the couch. When she turned on a lamp, Nathan knew he was in real trouble.

"You want iced tea with your supper?" asked Missykes. "I only got sweet tea; I run out 'o cokes on Saturday. Them flowers'll have to go in the trash, on account o' my allergies 'n whatnot. I reckon I'll have to remember to take the trash out 'fore I go to bed, if I don't fall down daid first," she added. This was a warning that Nathan was not to try to leave without passing time with her, lest he end up burning in hell for the rest of eternity for having left a poor old woman to die alone after doing nothing more than toil over his dinner. Nathan shuddered at the mention of Missykes's sweet tea. It was brown like tea, but that was where the similarity to tea ended. Nathan didn't see any way out. She was alone and desperately lonely, and she'd done him a favor. She'd probably been waiting for him to get back all weekend, just so she could savor the aggravation of having to fuss over his dinner and clean up after him. At this point Buster waddled into the living room. Missykes lit up like a movie marquee when she saw her cat. In a high falsetto voice that would pulverize igneous rock, she said, "Well, look-ee there, it's my Mister Buster! Come to say hey to Nathan? You gonna let Nathan have some o' your supper, pretty boy? Pretty boy? Come here and say hey to Nathan. Nathan, fetch me them kitty treats on the coffee table! Pretty boy? Pretty boy? Say hey to Nathan? Say hey!" The morbidly obese grey-striped tabbycat flopped down, raised one leg and tried to lick his ass but couldn't reach it. Finally he gave up and lolled there, tail twitching slightly. "Pretty boy!" said Missykes, disappearing into the shadows to fetch dinner. Nathan resigned himself to his fate and followed Missykes into the kitchen.

"I wish you wouldn't fuss, Missykes," he said loudly, so as not to startle her. He knew it was entirely possible she would forget he was there. He was hoping he would be able to fake his way through a quick dinner without actually having to eat, then make a quick retreat, having done his duty to his neighbor who had done him a kindness.

"I reckon I done fussed all I'm a-gonter for one day," said Missykes. "You'll have to get your own plate." Nathan noticed she had two plates stacked up on the counter to the left of the stove, where there was a frying pan full of greasy fried catfish, a pot of what smelled and looked horribly a lot like rutabagas, and some creamed corn. Nathan couldn't stand catfish or rutabagas no matter who cooked them and no matter how drunk he was when he ate either. He was as Southern as anyone he knew, but for the life of him, he could not understand how any creature other than a coprophage could regard either catfish or rutabagas as food. Well, he thought, reeling from the heat, at least I can look busy with the corn. Maybe she won't notice me not eating the catfish. He felt like running out the door, without any explanation at all, but he knew there'd be hell to pay if he did. So he took his medicine. Besides, it was so hot in that house, he couldn't have run if the place had caught on fire.

So Nathan sat with Missykes in silence in her living room, picking at his plate, pushing the bit of fish around, trying to avoid the small dollop of rutabagas, trying to make the large helping of creamed corn take up his time. The corn was, luckily, right out of the can, so it was not as bad as he'd feared. He knew the drill with Missykes. She would watch the news on tv, silently, while they both ate, and then she would sit back and let Nathan clear the food away after they declared themselves finished. Nathan knew that he wouldn't be expected to stay much longer, as Missykes generally went to bed shortly after nightfall. Out of politeness and affection for the old lady he played his role, throwing out the leavings on his plate, washing the dishes by hand and putting away the leftovers. Per the ritual Missykes had established, she tottered in about the time Nathan finished drying the dishes, feigning surprise he had cleaned up.

"I don't reckon you remembered to rinse them plates," she said. "You use too much soap on them dishes, it don't rinse off good." She opened the refrigerator door and looked for the containers of food Nathan had put inside. She bent over feebly and rearranged the entire shelf on which he'd placed the containers, scowling as she did so. "They ain't 'nough left over to be puttin' in a box this big," she said, rather too loudly. Missykes called plastic containers boxes, because "containers" sounded too "nice-nasty," too fastidious, to suit her, and she would have none of being nice-nasty. The last comment was her way of saying she thought Nathan had eaten enough to give the impression her cooking was up to her standards of excellence and that, hence, there was relatively little food left over; in short, the evening meal had been a success. Nathan read the code and remembered to say, "That sure was good dinner, Missykes, thank you."

"Well at least it's over and done with," said Missykes. "I like to have died from the pain in my hip when I was a-cookin' all this afternoon, but I reckon I'll make it, Lord willin'." Nathan smiled at her veiled admission she'd planned the evening meal and spent her afternoon attending to it, giving the lie to her initial assertion that Nathan had caught her by surprise when he appeared at her door.

Nathan realized the evening was now coming to a close. It would end back in the living room. If Missykes sat down on her recliner and titled it back, it would mean that she had news to tell of the neighborhood during Nathan's absence. If she came in and turned off the tv, it would mean that she was tired and ready for Nathan to leave. Nathan followed her into the living room and saw she was headed for the recliner. He made a bet with himself that the story she would tell would be either about something Buster had done that weekend or about some outrage committed by Ben Suggs, the ne'er-do-well neighbor three doors down and a thorn in Missykes's side.

Nathan sat on the couch looking at Vana White smile on the tv. He waited for Missykes to tell her tale. She looked at the TV and asked, "You reckon that girl's as dumb as she looks? What kind of fool thing is that, just a-standin' there and a-pointin'? She ain't purty, neither. Look-a them horse teeth, will ya?"

"I bet she makes more money than you or I will ever see, Missykes," said Nathan.

"Land sakes!" said Missykes. "I reckon them that pays her is dumber than she is, then. If all you gotta do to get rich is be skinny white traish, I reckon I sure was born the wrong time." Then there was a short space of silence, but Nathan could tell Missykes wasn't through talking. Then she spoke up again:

"Well I reckon you ain't heard about ole Ben Suggs," said Missykes.

Nathan smiled at the mention of Ben's name. "No, ma'am, I haven't. What'd he do this time?"

"Well, he done got him another DUI," said Missykes. "In jail right this minute, praise the Lord! Got hisself all likkered up and ran right into a police car, right out yonder on the Savannah Highway. It was on the TV news last night! He right-smart like to have killed hisself, daggum fool." She looked at Nathan with a scandalized expression, which was different from her other expressions only in the severity of the scowl she applied to it. Ben's drinking had gotten him into trouble before, and was, in fact, the source of the enmity between Missykes and him. Some time back Ben had driven, drunk, right into Missykes's front yard, thinking he had arrived in his own yard. Falling out of the car, he puked onto her front lawn and passed out. She was so deaf she didn't hear the commotion, so when she woke up the following morning to find her neighbor passed out and covered in his own vomit on her badly torn-up lawn, she was understandably angry and disgusted. Ever since then she swore she thought Ben, an unemployed truck driver, would come to no good. She was too much a Christian to wish him ill outright, but you could tell when she reported to Nathan that Ben had shown up on the evening news, that she felt vindicated in her dislike for the man.

"Well," said Nathan, "maybe if the judge really gives him a harsh sentence, he'll mend his ways."

Missykes shook her head. "Naw," she said, "that boy's a-headin' fer the 'lectric chair. Anythin' gets between him and a hangman's noose is a accident." Now that Nathan had received the big neighborhood news from the weekend, he knew he was about to be set free. He was covered with sweat and had a headache, but he was glad he'd endured. He looked for a minute at Missykes, trying not to let her notice he was looking. How does it feel to get that old, he asked himself. Do you still think of yourself the way you always did? Does the world seem completely fucked up and unreal? I wonder what it feels like to be her?

Chapter Fifteen

When Nathan got home from Missykes's house, he realized he was slightly sick from having been in the overheated house for a couple of hours. His own house wasn't cool, either, as he hadn't turned on the air conditioning before he'd gone over to Missykes's house. The first order of business was to turn on the air conditioning in his bedroom and close the door so it would cool down quicker. Next he went into the kitchen and poked around in the refrigerator to find something to drink. He thought about making some iced tea, but that would involve boiling water, and that would heat up the kitchen, and that would make him feel sicker than he already did. He settled on mixing up some Gatorade using water he'd chilled.

He got his glass of iced Gatorade and walked into the living room, trying to decide whether to take a bath or just go to back to bed. He looked around the living room: what a mess it was. The whole house was crammed full of things he'd collected over the past God-knew-how-many years, but the nucleus of the cramming was definitely the living room. It was not so much a room as an assemblage, an installation only someone with bad OCD would put together. He looked around and thought about all he had dragged into that house. Every object had a place, and among all the arrangements of objects, there were themes of organization. The basic theme of the living room was excess. There was the giant 50s lamp with an astonishing shade that suggested a drag queen's hat influenced by Napoleonic military uniform styling. The base of the lamp looked like a collection of leafy sphincters cast in brightly painted porcelain. It was the sort of lamp that, if you looked at it long enough, it began to trouble you. It sat on top of a two-tiered boomerang end table, and on the lower tier of the same table was a Roseville bowl full of teeth. The teeth had been given to Nathan as a gift when a friend of his whose father was a dentist retired and closed his practice. Beside the Roseville bowl full of teeth there was a graphic novel Nathan had assembled from scribbles, newspaper items mentioning people with improbable names, crime scene photos, and pornography catalog cuttings. Behind the homemade graphic novel was a stack of books on erotic art: George Platt Lynes, Bruce of Los Angeles, Tom of Finland, and Bruce Weber. Arranged in a neat pattern in front of the graphic novel was a set of eight plastic nipples, very realistic in their coloring and texture—Nathan had found them at the dirty bookstore and thought they were irresistible. The end table was next to the window, which was draped with floor-length 50s drapes adorned with a very busy tropical floral pattern. Hanging in the window was a large, heavy stained glass window, late Victorian in style. Next to the end table was an S-shaped couch covered in a zebra-patterened naugahyde. The couch had black metal legs with round brass feet. In front of the couch was a Heywood Wakefield coffee maple coffee table on which was a group of Howard Finster statues. There was also a stack of old *Fortune* magazines from the 1930s. On the floor was a cheap knotted rug from Target that managed to fit into the setting. Below the coffee table was a group of crystal balls of various sizes, arranged like eggs in some odd creature's nest. Across from the couch was a massive 1950s chair that looked like a Mayan throne. It was upholstered in red mohair, and it was appointed with faux leopard skin throw pillows. Beside it was a mica floor lamp from early 20th century Vienna, and to one side of the chair was a black metal magazine rack full of old shoe fetish magazines Nathan had found in a trunk somewhere. On the other side of the chair was a small end table outfitted with an atomic reading lamp, a porcelain bed pan that served as an ashtray, and a stack of books on art: Francis Bacon, Paul Cadmus, Egon Schiele, Pierre et Gilles, and Jeff Koons.

Across the room was an old department store display case that was full of 1939 World's Fair artifacts. On top of the display case was a series of large World's Fair artifacts, and on the walls on all sides were paint by numbers paintings, religious icons and paintings done by penitentiary prisoners.

Nathan was no fool, mind you. He understood that his choices in decorating were out of the ordinary in many respects. He called his style "radioactive Victorian" on account of the clutter and the overwhelming sense of dangerous energy it imparted. It was his aspiration to create the impression in each room of a fabulous tomb that had just been opened for the first time in centuries. He understood that the array of objects he'd gathered around him gave an indication of the state of his mind, a state no one would regard as normal. What occurred to him more than anything else as he surveyed his living space at that moment was that he'd created a room full of invitations to conversation—if not to heated argument—and yet he'd ended up living there in almost complete isolation. Almost no one came to visit except Missykes, and she didn't notice anything she saw—this almost certainly on purpose. On those rare occasions when Nathan did let people into his house, unless it was someone who had been there a good many times before, much of the conversation centered around the objects in the room—especially the living room, which was the most finished room in the house.

Once in awhile neighborhood kids would appear on his front porch, peering into the windows or, if he was home, looking through the screen door at the sights inside. The fact that his house had become a source of fascination made Nathan think of the Radley house in *To Kill a Mockingbird.* Do these kids think of me as Boo Radley?, he asked himself. He could think of worse things.

As he looked at his living room now, standing there in the sweltering August evening, Nathan thought to himself that, for the first time, he felt surprised at what he'd created for himself in his house. Surprise didn't quite catch it: it was as if, looking at all he'd done to fill the space up, all the choices he'd made to gather things into a tableau, he'd created a space that now, for the first time, looked odd to him. He thought it was odd, all of a sudden, that he lived in a house that looked like this. It was baffling, all of a sudden, to think how much time he'd passed putting all of this stuff together. Suddenly it seemed to him that he'd built this strange environment during some long episode of something like sleepwalking. He knew he'd done it—he'd gone out and found all this stuff, he'd dragged it all home, he'd arranged it—but all of a sudden, he couldn't think how it had all happened. This is who I am, he thought. How did I turn into this person?

He decided to take another bath before going to bed. He chose to listen to some early Billie Holiday music while he was bathing. Billie as a girl, singing for Teddy Wilson. Her voice sounded plump, the voice a of a teenager, still unharmed, he thought. He soaked for a long time, listening to Billie's sweet voice. He soaked long enough so the water got a bit cool and his hands and feet turned into prunes. He got out, toweled off, got into bed naked, lying on the towel he'd used in the bath. The bath made him feel cool, and he laid there, enjoying the feeling of the ceiling fan blowing on him as he listened to Billie Holiday before the junk got to her. He dozed off to sleep.

Some time later he woke up when he heard Widdybug making strange sounds. He went to investigate, and saw that he'd left the front door open, so the cat was able to look out onto the front porch. On the porch was a baby possum sniffing and tottering around the potted plants, looking for left-over cat food. Nathan thought the possum was cute—it was a baby, so it hadn't yet grown into full possum ugliness. Nathan went into the kitchen and got a bowl of dried cat food. He brought it back to the front of the house, unlatched the screen door and went out onto the front porch, still naked, standing in the moonlight. The possum had scampered away, but he set the bowl of food down anyway, thinking the possum would come back as soon as he went back inside. He knew by now Missykes was already in bed. As he had no other neighbors who could see him standing naked on his front porch, and seeing the moon had set, he thought it must very late, and so it was safe to be standing naked on his front porch, if only for a minute. He looked up at the stars and saw the Milky Way, and he remembered why he lived where he lived. He stood there for a minute taking in the stars. When he felt a mosquito buzzing around his head, he knew it was time to go back in—by now he'd been bitten probably ten or twenty times but hadn't noticed it. So he went back in, listened to Widdybug talk to him, felt the cat weave between his legs as he closed and locked the front door, turned off the music, turned out the lights, and went back into his bedroom in the back of the house, doing his best not to stumble over the cat.

Nathan realized he would be better able to sleep if he turned on the air conditioning. HE got out of bed, went into the living room and turned on the window unit to cool down the front of the house. He went back into his bedroom, turned on the other window unit, and got back into bed. The he got back into bed, listening to the air conditioners and the ceiling fan, trying to empty his mind. He was already thinking about what he would be doing for the next few days: going to his booth at the antique market in Charleston, moving things around, setting out things he'd bought in Centralia, and beginning to plan his next set of buying trips to prepare for the next month's weekend show. He knew he had little time to spare. He had to look in all the places he knew to look to find the schedules for the shows that would be happening in and around Charleston for the next few weeks, especially the shows and auctions around Labor Day. He had to find out what the auction schedule for Roumillat's would be, so he could plan to work around it. Some of the best large pieces he found anywhere came from the auctions at Roumillat's, and luckily, he was on good terms with the auction house owners.

Chapter Sixteen

After dropping Nathan off, Grant went back home, showered and got ready to go into the shop. He didn't open up until eleven, which was one of the things he loved about working for himself. No one worth knowing shops for art before eleven in the morning. Only people like Mrs. Tuttle go about early in the morning grasping and clutching at beautiful things. So Grant always had his mornings, at least his early mornings, to himself, and this made him feel rich. He couldn't imagine working under any other circumstances.

The night before with Nathan had been a very pleasant experience. Nathan had taught Grant a few very surprising things, not the least of which was how good it feels to have someone run his mouth up and down your spine while applying a judicious amount of suction. The sensation had made Grant hyperventilate. So they played, in the usual ways that men together played, and they talked in the dark, and fell asleep and woke back up, and then taught each other a little more about one another. All in all, a very pleasant night.

Okay, then, now what? That, Grant knew, was the question to be answered. Grant liked Nathan a good deal, and he thought Nathan liked him. They got along well in bed. Very well. But then, getting along well the first time is no great accomplishment. Anyone can get laid. Anyone. And if it takes more than a few hours from first thinking about it to feeling the earth tremble, then one isn't trying very hard. So Grant thought that now was the hard part, now was the figuring out what could come next. And what did he want to come next? He didn't say to himself, he didn't elaborate in pictures or extensive fantasies, but he did keep thinking about Nathan, and he did continue to see Nathan, remember what Nathan had said as they'd laid in bed together, he did remember that Nathan felt warm and that they'd fallen asleep in each others' arms. And then there was that business card. Maybe we're cut from the same cloth, Grant thought to himself. It looks like we actually speak the same language.

The day went by quickly. Grant worked in his shop, spent time organizing papers from the previous weekend's sales, and went over the task list he kept to help him remember what framing work was due when. He went about his business pretty matter-of-factly, finding in the work an effortless release from thinking. Before he knew it, the sun was low in the sky, and when he finally looked up and noticed the time, he found he'd forgotten to close the shop at six and had worked until almost seven. He locked the front door, turned on the front window lights, and quickly got himself out of the shop.

Almost as soon as Grant got home, the phone rang. He picked up the phone and heard the voice of Darren, the man he'd been dating for a few months. He blushed at hearing Darren's voice. Darren sold computer software; he had been out of town all weekend on a business trip. Having gotten back into town Wednesday night, the same day Nathan and Grant had said goodbye, Darren made it clear he now wanted to see Grant. Grant felt nervous talking to Darren. He felt guilty. Darren was Grant's age. Darren was cute; he was successful; he knew lots of people; he drove a new Mercedes convertible. Darren wanted to have sex with Grant, as soon as possible.

Grant felt horrified at the prospect of doing such a thing. Less than twelve hours earlier he'd been having sex for the second time that night with Nathan. He'd already had sex with Darren, a number of times, in fact, but remembering how things had gone with Nathan, Grant found the prospect of a coupling with Darren to be intolerable. He simply couldn't allow it.

Grant listened to Darren talk. Darren was fond of talking at length about himself, giving minute details about where he went to eat and who he talked to and where he stayed in a city out west that Grant had never been to and probably would never see. Darren had a habit that Grant initially found entertaining but that, lately, had become annoying: namely, his habit of talking about people he knew Grant didn't know and referring to them only by their first name, never giving any information about how they came to know each other. It was always "Deborah and I did this," or "So Ken told me he thought I shouldn't let Sam get away with that kind of thing." Who was Deborah? Ken? Sam? Grant didn't have a clue about most of the people who co-starred in Darren's many monologues about the adventures of his daily life. Darren talked about himself as if the subject were worthy of its own newspaper, complete with multiple sections and an index.

This time it was about all the wonderful things Darren had done in Billings, Montana. At the end of his report, Darren suggested that he come over to Grant's house, maybe spend the night. Grant felt a knot in his stomach.

"I don't think you can see this place right now," said Grant.

"Why not?" asked Darren.

"It's a mess. I just got done doing a show," said Grant.

"So?" asked Darren. "I wasn't thinking about coming over to look at your furniture. It's not as if I don't know you're a slob. What's the big deal?"

"Well, I'm, I'm just embarrassed to have you see the place looking like this," said Grant. "You know I worked all weekend at the Centralia Antique Market, so it's just really a mess here. I mean, I haven't been here to put even a little order in this mess." His apartment was actually pretty clean, so he started walking around as he was talking on the phone, messing up some newspapers and throwing pillows out of place, in case Darren ended up coming over.

"What are you talking about?" asked Darren. "What's *wrong* with you, do you have *company* already?"

"What do you mean?" asked Grant.

"I mean, am I disturbing you?" asked Darren. The tone in his voice had more schoolteacher than bedmate in it.

Grant understood the insinuation, and at first he was mad that Darren would imply he was getting blown or something while talking on the phone to the man he'd been dating the past four months. Then he remembered that, in fact, he'd just spent the night with another man. And *then* he thought, maybe this is a good thing. Grant thought, *You know, maybe Nathan fucked some sense into me last night.* Grant said, "I wouldn't say you're disturbing me, actually, but now that you mention it, I really am kind of busy."

There was a moment of silence at the other end of the phone. Grant flopped on the couch and held the phone in his shoulder while he fluffed some pillows to put behind his head. He said, "I'm glad you had a nice trip, glad you got back in town." As if that was all that needed to be said—meaning that the conversation was nearly over and it was time to say goodbye, not I'll see you in twenty minutes. Continued silence at the other end. "You there, Darren?" asked Grant.

"Ye-e-e-s," Darren said in a drawn-out way, sounding exasperated. "But I guess I'm not going to be *there*. Not tonight, anyway." Then silence.

Grant let the silence just sit there. It was enjoyable listening to the silence. Finally he spoke up: "Yeah," said Grant. "Well, I'm glad you got back okay. Billings sounds very nice. So, I'm going to go now, tie up a few loose ends and hit the sack early. So, thanks for calling, talk to you later. Bye!" And with that Grant hung up the phone, feeling relieved. He wondered immediately if he'd handled the conversation the right way. Did I just blow him off? He asked himself. Did I just kiss that relationship goodbye? What did I just do? Did I really just do what I just did?

A few minutes later Grant was annoyed to hear the phone ring again. He thought about answering it, but then decided to let the machine pick it up. It couldn't be, he thought to himself. He sat in the living room, waiting to hear if whoever was calling would leave a message. He heard his own voice, then the beep, then he heard Darren: "Hello, Grant, this is Darren." Very exasperated, very admonitory. "I just called to say I'm sorry you're so *tied up*, and I hope you get *things* under control. I was really hoping to see you tonight, but I guess you're just not in the mood, which is *fine*. I am, um, disappointed, but I'll get over it, and so, um, I just wanted to say I'm sorry I didn't get to see you tonight, and I guess I'll, uh, I'll wait to hear from you, um, to let me know when you feel like getting together. I hope everything's okay, but, um, I guess I'll just have to rely on you to let me know what's really going on, so I'll just wait and let you tell me in your own time. So, I miss seeing you, I have to confess I could use a little contact, if you know what I mean, and, um, I'll hope we talk in the next day or so, um, and I guess that's all. So, this is goodnight, and I hope all's well, and I, um, um, hope you will, ah, I'll talk with you real soon. Oh—and I'm going to Philadelphia on Thursday, won't be back for another week or so. Actually, I might, might end up extending that trip. Grant, are you there? Are you listening to this? Grant, pick up the phone, please? Grant? Well, goodnight, and, and, goodnight!" Click.

Listening to Darren, Grant was a bit embarrassed. I never noticed what a girl he is, Grant thought to himself. Is he always that nelly? Then he thought, is it me, or does it sound like he's got somebody waiting for him in Philadelphia? First he does this whole I'm wounded you won't let me come over and fuck you thing, then he's all, and by the way, I got me a piece of ass waiting in Philadelphia? Class act! *Jesus, thought Grant, I took this whinging, mewling, manipulative queen to meet some of my closest friends. Wonder what they've been saying behind my back? How did I not notice what a loser he is?* Listening to himself think these thoughts, Grant then thought, *you're a bad person, you deserve to have your friends making fun of you and your nelly boyfriend, what makes you think you're any better, you asshole?*

After listening to Darren and then rehashing the whole conversation in his head, Grant puttered a bit, fidgeting, skimming through magazines, thinking about cooking something. He thought about going out, and then it occurred to him, hey, my luck, I'd probably run into Darren first place I went. That's no good, he thought. Maybe go for a drive? Just get out and clear my head? What time is

it, anyway? He looked at the clock. Eight-o-seven. Not so late,
maybe he could just cruise around a bit, just to get out. Anyway, he
was feeling too out of sorts not to do anything, so he finally decided
on a drive. It was just getting dark, and as it was the dinner hour for
most people and a Wednesday, the streets were pretty quiet.

Grant drove around in his truck, mapping out a path avoiding
red lights and stop signs as he went, driving through tree-lined
neighborhoods with long roads feeling himself calm down a bit as
he let the road stretch out in front of him. What had made him realize all of a sudden that Darren was not the person he wanted to
spend the evening with? Perhaps he hadn't noticed before that Darren only talked about himself. Was that possible? Or had something
changed in Darren? Had Grant misjudged him at the beginning of
their relationship, or was he misjudging him now? Why was he so
annoyed all of a sudden, annoyed with everything, it seemed? He
was having a good month money-wise, so what was the problem?

Grant stopped to get gas, using his debit card to pay at the
pump. When he pulled his debit card out of his wallet, he disar-
ranged some of the wad of papers he had stored in the wallet,
among them the business card that Nathan had given him. He took
the card out and looked at it. *What's going to happen, Nathan?*, he
thought to himself. *Anything?*

Grant finished pumping his gas, got back in his truck and continued driving. He tried to find a station to listen to on the radio, but
nothing sounded right. He turned the radio off and just drove in
silence, down the dark tree-lined streets of the lovely old neighborhoods of Centralia. After an hour or so, he decided he'd had
enough, so he headed back home. When he got home it was very
quiet. The apartment was dark, and it seemed the whole neighbor-

hood was asleep, though it couldn't have been that late. He sat for awhile in the dark in his apartment, just hearing the silence, just noticing that nothing was happening. He finally got up, took a shower, and went to bed.

The following day Grant decided he was going to try and contact Nathan. At first he thought he would just wait until the next Centralia antiques show, but that didn't feel right, and so he began to think how he might contact Nathan sooner. For what? What did he want to accomplish? He wasn't sure, not at all. He didn't like it that this person who liked quick snacks hairstyles would just show up and then disappear with nothing else there. It was just that simple. They shared that one thing, and it was enough, at least for Grant, to try and see to it that they established a friendship. Grant didn't meet people he could or even would want to talk with all that often, after all. Working in the shop and at the weekend shows, he met lots of people—hundreds, certainly, every month. Most did nothing for him. He saw lots of cute guys, that was for certain, lots of very good-looking men, but most of them were just not interesting, either. He had stopped noticing whether guys were flirting with him long ago, for one thing because he'd been seeing Darren, for another, he just didn't find most men interesting. Not that he was doubting being gay—if anything, he was more sure than ever that being gay was at the very center of who he was. What kind of sense to make of all this? He simply had not found anyone who interested him in a long, long time. Interest on any level at all: not the pretty gym rats, not the Abercrombie and Fitch crowd, not the many varieties of men who flitted about town. Was he beginning to develop a taste for older men, he wondered? Was it that Nathan was significantly older than his usual boyfriend/trick, and that was what was making him more interesting? Grant didn't think so. Nathan didn't look or act like any kind of fantasy character—he wasn't big and beefy, he recognizable as a type at all except that you could look at him and pretty easily figure out that he was almost certainly gay. Beyond that Nathan was interesting at the most superficial level because he didn't seem to fit into a type category. He was interesting, youthful-looking but clearly had a few miles on him, but more than that there was this very clear sense you had when you were around him that he was unusually intelligent, unusually perceptive in a way that most men wouldn't even want to be, matter less imagine being. All you had to do to figure out what an extraordinary mind he had was sit and talk with him for a few minutes. And what came out was not just that he knew a great deal about an astonishing variety of topics; what came out was that he really knew how to hold a conversation, he really was interested in listening as well as in talking. Most people Grant met bored him because they couldn't converse; trying to talk with them was like getting caught with a gaggle of drag queens, each one trying to outperform the other, no one ever really listening to one another, no one ever really interested in hearing each other, all just interested in performing, in making the noise s/he wanted to make. What it comes down to is that most people just seem to need each other for applause, but it seemed to Grant that Nathan really was genuinely interested in people and ideas, and it was also clear that he was able, very naturally, to do something selfless for the sake of doing a good thing, a right thing. There aren't many people like that, Grant thought, there aren't many people who really are civilized in that way.

So Grant was resolved to see if he could make some kind of contact with Nathan. He wasn't thinking about sex, he was thinking about contact. It wasn't that he ruled out sex; to be honest, he hadn't really thought about it. What he saw was that Nathan could give him something he couldn't easily get from most people, and he didn't want to let it go.

The next issue to be addressed was how he would contact Nathan. He knew Nathan's name, knew generally where he lived. Maybe he could call directory assistance in Charleston and get his phone number. What would Nathan think about his calling out of the blue? Why would he be calling? To thank Nathan again for his help with the woodcut, and to apologize for trying to get Nathan to make his decision on whether or not to sell the woodcut. Then what? Ask how his show had gone. They hadn't seen each other at the end of the show, after all, so they hadn't really said goodbye. What if Nathan acted offended by his calling? He wouldn't be offended, he'd just act cool at best. There'd be no ugliness at the worst; at the worst, there'd just be polite silence. On the other hand maybe Nathan would be happy to hear from him. Who knew what was going through his head when Grant last saw him? The fact was, Nathan had been very nice to him, and they'd only spent a little time around each other over the course of one weekend, so it was anybody's guess what would happen next. Nothing ventured, nothing gained.

Grant called directory assistance and asked for the phone number for Nathan Greenwood on John's Island. Did he have a street address? No, he didn't. The directory didn't list by locations like John's Island.

Chapter Seventeen

Grant's business was doing very well. Almost too well, in fact. As August ended and September began, he found that business was brisk. Word of mouth got him a lot of work, and he was so talented at framing—and so quick to get work done—that he was all but overwhelmed with new commissions, to the point that he had to start warning customers he couldn't guarantee due dates until his staffing situation changed. What complicated matters for him was that his helper had found another job. This meant he had to look for someone to replace her. It also meant he had to work in the shop by himself. So far, after nearly three weeks of looking, he hadn't found someone he liked. Everyone who answered his ad was either too eager or not eager enough. No one seemed to have worked in a print shop before. Most were art school students; they all looked like confirmed slackers and potential thieves.

Not finding someone to replace his part-timer, Grant put in lots of hours in the shop. Seven days a week, eight hours a day, more like ten hours if you counted the time it took him to open up and do his accounts. After three full weeks, all that work was beginning to take its toll on him. Young as he was, as much as he liked his work, he still needed rest and relaxation, and he wasn't getting enough of either. There was one advantage to working all those hours, though: he had the perfect excuse to beg off when Darren called to bug him about going out.

In the weeks since his conversation with Darren right after the Centralia antiques festival, Grant hadn't dated anyone. He'd chatted up a few guys online and tricked with one of them, but that had been a disappointment. In his online profile, the trick looked like just the ticket: sinewy, masculine and probably dumb as a fence post, nice dick and a confirmed top. When they met, Grant was shocked to see a smallish man who looked more like a squirrel monkey than a Tom of Finland dream. He was also whiny and fussy, and his house was so faggy and decorated Grant had to work to avoid letting his amusement at the place register in his facial expression. Oh, well, at least it got that urge out of the way, and Grant thought that the fact that he tricked with a guy off of Guyline.com confirmed his having broken up with Darren. He even told Darren he'd tricked with the guy, but that hadn't stopped Darren from calling and, worse, from writing:

Grant—

I have to write this knowing that you probably won't read it, as you appear to have decided for some reason I cannot understand that we are no more. That may be true for you, but please remember there was, there is—are two of us, and I'm the other one. So let me just say that I respect your decision not to go out any more, but I can't help letting you know I miss you and wish you would see that we are really meant to be together. I hope you will wake up one day soon and realize that we belong together, but Grant, please don't wait too long, because I need to get on with my life, too. Please remember that I love you and that I would do anything in the world for you. All you need to do is ask.

Yours truly,

Darren McKnight

Why did he include his last name?, Grant wondered. As if I'm getting pathetic love-me mash notes from a string of Darrens? And what happened to the guy in Philadelphia? Better not to ask.

It wasn't like Grant to feel so little sympathy for someone asking, as Darren seemed to be asking, for a little consideration. What made Darren's entreaties so noxious was the always-present undercurrent of threat: love me or else. Grant wasn't having any of it, though he hadn't quite brought himself to telling Darren to go to hell. For one thing, Grant was busy much of the time, so Darren occupied little of his personal time. For another thing, Grant found himself thinking, when he had time to think, about other things. Often, he thought about Nathan.

When the opportunity permitted, Grant thought about calling Nathan or writing to him. Darren's letter stopped the writing part. He looked Alice and Becky up in the phone book. He'd remembered that Nathan had said that Becky's last name was Turner, but he couldn't remember Alice's last name. So he looked up Becky Turner on Adair Street, but he didn't find a listing. So either their number wasn't listed or it was listed under Alice's last name, a name he couldn't remember. The thought occurred to him, then, that the only way he might get in touch with Nathan was to go to Alice and Becky's house and ask for it, and that meant coming up with a story that would reasonably explain why he wanted to do what he wanted to do. This meant that he had to make up a story that would sound convincing. He came up with this: he'd sold the woodcut at a good price, and he'd offered Nathan a commission, because Nathan had made him aware of the value of the piece and had saved him from selling it for a stupidly low price. Nathan had refused his offer, but Grant just didn't feel comfortable not giving him a commission, so he really would like to talk with Nathan and get Nathan to accept the commission. He'd looked up Nathan's number in Charleston, but he couldn't find it, and directory assistance was no help, either. Surely Alice and Becky would want to help Nathan bring in a few hundred extra dollars, living as he did?

The story was, basically, true. It just wasn't the whole truth. The fact was that Grant felt the absence of Nathan's company. It wasn't so much about sex, really, though Grant had already had a number of imaginary conversations with Nathan that had ended with a search for a towel. Grant had, in fact, only spent a few hours with Nathan. There was the time they spent talking on Saturday at the show: that was when he met Nathan. The time they spent together was not more than an hour, certainly. Probably much less than that, but it seemed to Grant, as he thought back on the visit, that they had been together a good long while. And then there was the time they spent at Alice and Becky's house on Saturday evening. Three, maybe four hours or so. But again, it seemed to Grant that there was much more packed into that time than could be accounted for by the passage of just that much time. And then there was the conversation they'd had on Sunday—just a few minutes. Not all that much time together, certainly, but when Grant replayed the events of his encounters with Nathan, they seemed bigger than the time that had contained them; they seemed, in fact, with every re-remembering to become larger.

If Grant had told someone about his thoughts of Nathan, that someone would have told him he was in love. But Grant didn't tell anyone, because there really wasn't anyone for him to tell. He didn't have a set of lesbian friends from school to talk to about men, and he wasn't given to talking about his romances with his gay friends, because he knew they couldn't keep their mouths shut. The real reason he didn't talk with anyone about Nathan is that Nathan was the only one he wanted to talk with, so finding a substitute just didn't occur to him.

Grant realized that the September Centralia show was coming up the following weekend, and he panicked. He was alone in the shop, he hadn't had a day off since the week before the August show, and he was exhausted. He'd already paid for his booth at the Centralia show, as old Mr. Farmer required payment in advance for each show. Being at the show was the perfect opportunity for him to catch up with Nathan, and that was really the primary reason for doing it. Grant had done so much business in his shop during the weeks since the August show that he could easily afford not to do the one coming up. Having worked so much the last few weeks, getting very little rest, he had lost weight, enough so that a number of his older customers commented that he was beginning to look gaunt, while a few of the anorexic housewives who came in regularly remarked that he looked great. He was so tired from working all the time that he couldn't think very clearly about what he would pull from the shop to offer for sale at the Centralia show, assuming he could figure out how to cover the shop while he worked the show. He realized that he had enough business to keep him working around the clock even if he never left the shop during the monthly show, so he had to conclude that it made no sense for him to do the show, even though he'd paid the $200 booth fee.

Mulling this problem over several times, it finally dawned on Grant that he could blow off doing the show, but plan instead to visit. That way he could keep the shop open and continue working, yet still take the opportunity to see Nathan. Business was so good that he could afford to take off even for an afternoon, or maybe he could take Sunday morning off. This last plan made the most sense to him—keep the shop open and go to the show Sunday morning, which would be quiet, anyway, and a good time to try and see if he could make friends with Nathan.

That really is what he wanted, after all: to make friends. He wasn't thinking about getting naked, figuring out who would top and who would bottom. Well, he wasn't thinking about all that most of the time. He was hungry to talk with this person who had shown up with an offer of genuine kindness and who had a business card that read "quick snacks, hairstyles, and more!"

It was settled, then. Grant felt good about the prospect of seeing Nathan. It was the Wednesday before the September show. He had Thursday and Friday to work through all the pending projects, and that would make it easier to enjoy taking off Sunday morning. He might end up closing Sunday altogether. He hadn't had a day off in over a month. He needed the time, whether or not he was going to see Nathan. The thought of seeing Nathan would make it easier to get his work done. It would make the next few days fly by. The success he'd hoped for in his little shop no longer meant anything at all to him. It was a job to get through, another chore. Sunday morning was what he was looking forward to.

Grant went happily about his work in the shop. He barely stopped the whole afternoon, working contentedly, churning out beautifully framed pictures, wrapping them, labeling them, and setting them in bins reserved for work that was ready to be picked up. The afternoon went by quickly, indeed, and it didn't even bother him that people continued to come in, continued to place orders. He had his new speech down pat: on all orders, the shop calls the customer when the work is ready; no guarantee date orders until he got a helper in the shop and trained; two weeks minimum on all framing orders, special ordered framing and matting up to a month. None of this seemed to bother anyone who came in.

Wednesday evening Grant closed up the shop, as usual. He counted the money and saw, to his astonishment, that he'd brought in nearly three thousand dollars that day in sales. Luckily it was mostly plastic, so he didn't have to deal with that much cash. As tired as he was, he could only feel mildly amused, not giddy, at the thought of pulling in that much money in a day. It was a lot of money for one guy cutting mat board and picture framing, selling the occasional old print. It made him smile to think, as he closed the shop, that having arrived at that point in the ownership of his business, he no longer cared. What he cared about was Sunday morning.

Grant gathered together his belongings, got the bank deposit bag, put it in his shoulder bag, locked the door, turned off all the lights except the ones in the front windows, armed the alarm, and went out the back door. He went to get into his truck, parked right outside the back of the building. He was alone. It was still daylight. It was a pleasant September evening. The poplars were already turning yellow. He put his key in the lock of the truck door. He felt a sudden sharp pain in the left middle area of his back. He felt a sudden weight against the back of his neck. He passed out.

When Grant woke up, he was very unclear about everything. It took him awhile to realize that he was in a hospital bed. He had a bandage on his head and wrapping tightly around his body. It hurt to breathe deeply. It was uncomfortable in the bed. It was hard to move to get comfortable. There was an unbroken string of noise: people talking, bells ringing softly, phones, computers alerting, announcements over a PA system, people moving things up and down the hallway outside the room where Grant lay in a bed. He could look straight ahead and see a picture hanging on the wall in front of him. At first he couldn't make out the contents of the picture. He could look up and see a television hanging from the ceiling. Luckily, it was turned off. He could look to his right and see out the window: lots of trees and a slice of nondescript brick building. It hurt to move his head. It hurt even to move his eyes. It hurt to move; it hurt to lie still.

Grant was so puzzled by his current state and his surroundings that he could do little more than lie there for awhile, trying simply to be clear about something: be clear about just one thing. It didn't happen quickly. Slowly, though, he became aware that his vision was clearing a little, though it hurt to try and focus too much. At length he could make out the details of the picture on the wall in front of him: it was some kind of print showing a fantasy tropical scene, perfect palm trees arranged on either side of a perfectly rectangular pool, sort of art-deco-looking, the sun setting in the distance, a single bird winging across the orange of the sunset. Seeing the image clearly, Grant felt an odd sense of horror. He wasn't sure if it was because of the triteness of the image or the dissonance between its tone and his present state of suffering. He tried not to look at the picture, which meant he had to turn his head. He turned his head towards the hall. It occurred to him that he might get someone's attention to ask what had happened. He tried to speak, but found when he breathed in to try to articulate a sound, the pain in his left side was as sharp as if he were being stabbed. He wondered if he had had some kind of operation that would account for the intense pain in his side. He began to panic a bit. He couldn't understand what had happened.

Chapter Eighteen

October began as an unusually warm month. The dryness of the air made the sky remarkably clearer than it had been throughout the summer. Nathan found himself looking up at it from time to time, never ceasing to wonder and the purity of the autumn sky's blue. It was the second Wednesday in October, he had spent the day unloading his wares and setting up his booth at the Centralia show, and was now returning to spend the night at the home of his friends Alice and Becky.

Nathan was feeling good about his prospects for having a pretty good show. He'd spent the previous month diligently searching the auctions and the estate sales, and he'd turned up some pretty interesting finds: a hand-hammered Wiener Werkstätte silver tea set; a Tiffany men's silver and bronze desk set; a set of two Francoma bronze lamps in the shape of a pair of demonic-looking cherubs, both lamps with their original shades; a few dozen early prints of Bruce of Los Angeles photographs; and a set of Mexican folk art figures depicting a series of musicians, one of which was a clarinetist depicted as the devil (it looked much more interesting than it sounds). He had a few other objects, and had brought a selection of his old stand-bys to round out the offering and to fill up the booth. All in all, he was happier than usual with what he'd paid for his wares and what he had to show people.

As he had done more times over the past ten years than he could remember, Nathan parked his van on the street in front of his friends' house near the heart of Centralia. He went through the gate and walked up the steps. By the time he got up the steps to the front porch he could hear dogs barking inside the house. He knocked on the front door, even though he had a key, and then let himself inside the house. As soon as he got inside, he was surrounded by a brace of wagging, gently whining dogs, delirious with glee at seeing him. A few cats jumped on the sofa, walked on tiptoe and arched their backs towards him, and finally Becky appeared from the her and Alice's bedroom. She was obviously just waking up from a nap.

"Hey, booger," said Becky, voice husky with sleep. She met Nathan and half draped herself onto him in a sleepy hug. "It's that time of the month again, huh?"

"You mean for me or for you?" asked Nathan, seizing on the opportunity to be crude.

Becky ignored the question, lady that she was (for the moment). She said: "I think Alice is probably still at the grocery store scaring up dinner. You want a drink or some pot?"

"A little marijuana might be nice, thank you," said Nathan. "My back is talking to me after spending the day setting up. I really need to buy you all a bag to pay you back."

"Oh, one of these days, darlin, it all evens out," said Becky. "Why don't you put your stuff in your room and then come sit down and we'll have a nice little smoke 'til Mizz Alice brings home the bacon."

"Why, thank you very much," said Nathan, who did as he'd been told.

When he came back into the living room Becky, barefoot as always, was sitting on the couch with an LP album cover on her lap, a bag of pot and some rolling papers. "What would you do to roll a joint if you didn't have album covers?" asked Nathan.

Becky looked up at him. "I know. I couldn't do it. The record player doesn't even work anymore, but I can't do away with these LPs 'cause I need 'em for other things," she said, smiling as she looked up briefly at Nathan, then back down as she continued with her handiwork. Becky had an endearing way of sticking her tongue out the corner of her mouth and wiggling it slightly whenever she set herself to a task that required some dexterity, as did the proper rolling of a nice, tight joint. Nathan watched her silently, trying not to let it show how entertaining it was just to sit there and watch her roll a joint. The job completed, she lit the elegantly slim, neat cigarette, took a toke and passed it to Nathan. He took a long drag off the joint and passed it back to Becky. Exhaling, Nathan said, "shouldn't we be listening to something kinda loose, maybe some blues or some afternoon jazz?"

"Well, find a cd you want to hear and put it on, then," said Becky, taking a drag of the joint, then getting up as she passed it to Nathan. "You want something to drink? I'm going to get some water."

Taking the cigarette from Becky, Nathan smiled and shook his head. He said: "No, I'm fine," and went to the cd shelves and scanned the music. He found what he wanted and put it on: Little Jimmy Scott's *Holdin' Back the Years.* He sat back down and the music started. Becky came back in with two glasses of ice water. She sat down next to Nathan, who took up his glass and tilted his head in silent thanks. "If I weren't gay and you weren't married, you'd still be getting your pussy eaten every damn day that comes along."

Becky smiled with mock beauty queen enthusiasm. She said, "You're too kind, sir." She sipped her water. "Matter of fact, I *do* get my pussy eaten every damn day that comes along. Why Little Jimmy Scott?" she asked. "You got the blues?"

"No, not at all," said Nathan. "Actually I was just saying to myself a bit earlier I feel better about the show than I have in a long time. Have lots of new stuff, should do pretty well. I just really like this album. I like the soulfulness in his voice."

"That's nice," said Becky. Her *that's nice* conveyed something else.

Nathan shrugged and smiled at Becky. He was used to having her dig at him all the time. The issue with Becky was always this: when are you going to get over David, Nathan? When are you going to resume your life? David, thought Nathan. If ever I thought I *had* forgotten him, Becky would remind me. Oh well, he thought, who are you gonna get to torment you if not the friends you love the most?

Nathan thought a moment further, and then answered Becky: "Sweetheart, with David it's always going to be like a broken arm I got over. David is my badly broken arm. It was a very bad break, no doubt about it, and it has, indeed, taken a long time to heal. But it gets a little better all the time."

"Does it, honey?" asked Becky, looking very earnest, conveying with that earnestness that she didn't believe what Nathan was telling her.

"Yes, it does," said Nathan. "Believe it or not. But one thing I've had to learn to live with, and I wish you could, too: no matter what, I can't undo the fact that I had a very bad break. The fact of that break will always be there. The disaster that was David will always be the disaster that really did happen."

"So David left you crippled, is that what he did, Nathan?" Becky smiled slightly, with her mouth, not with her eyes, and toked on her joint, and spoke softly.

"He left a mark," said Nathan. "I get around pretty well, so I think crippled is too strong. But he did leave a mark."

Becky nodded, took her turn at the joint. A long silence passed between them. Then Becky asked, "You going to do the show next March?"

Nathan gave a look of surprise. It was October, and she was asking about next March. Sometimes he did skip the show during the early part of the year, in part because the winter weather was so brutal and unpredictable, in part because he just needed a break sometimes. He said, "I don't know yet," he said. "It's a bit early yet. It kind of depends on how Christmas goes. Are you all going somewhere then?"

Becky nodded. "She doesn't know it yet, but I'm taking Alice on a cruise. Don't tell her. Really. It's a surprise."

"Oh, that's great," said Nathan. He was genuinely pleased to hear this bit of news. "Where are you taking her?"

"Costa Rica, baby," said Becky, prodding Nathan with one of her feet. "Lesbian paradise."

"What's prompting this?" asked Nathan. A large cat jumped up onto his lap and proffered its hindquarters. He stoked the back of the cat and looked around it at Becky. Before long another cat insinuated itself onto his lap. "You all had a fight recently? Are you having an affair with someone?"

Becky listened stone-faced, waited until Nathan shut up, then said: "The occasion is Alice's fiftieth birthday, dumbass. February 27th, remember?"

"Of course I remember," said Nathan, who couldn't help but blush, as he would not, indeed, have been able to tell the exact date of Alice's birthday if he'd been cornered, despite the fact that he'd known her for almost thirty years. Not remembering birthdays was one of his unfortunate character traits.

Becky nodded, gave him a look that told him she knew he was lying. "Of course you do," she said, squinting. "And I know she'll miss you on your birthday, because she'll be getting drunk on board ship and getting *her* pussy eaten and her titties rubbed." Nathan's birthday was March 15th. Even though his birthday was only a few weeks after Alice's, the best he could ever do with Alice's birthday was to remember it was in late February. This lapse in his otherwise very good memory was a source of frequent mockery among his friends. ("I'm also not a good dancer," he'd say when cajoled by one of the women about his inability to remember this single fact. "Shoot me for that—not for remembering the anniversary of Alice's advance towards death.").

"That's lovely," said Nathan. "Don't look at me like that, I mean it, goddamit! I'm honestly glad you're going. And thanks for telling me so early. March is usually a bad show, to be honest, so I could easily sit it out."

"I wasn't telling you all this to get you not to come, Nathan," said Becky. "In fact, I was hoping you might be interested in maybe staying a little longer so you could housesit for us during the trip."

Nathan nodded. "So how long are you going to be gone?" he asked.

"Ten days," said Becky. "The cruise is seven days, and I added a few days on at a resort so we could see a little more."

"Well," said Nathan, "I think it's a great idea, and I'm glad you're doing it. Man, I'm glad we smoked—I didn't realize how bad my back was hurting until it stopped. No, but of course, I'll be glad to housesit for y'all, if you want me to. All I have to do is let Missykes know to feed the wild cats, and I'm free to roam."

Becky blew Nathan a kiss. "Thanks, Nathan. If I could afford it I'd pay for you to go with us."

Nathan blushed at this last comment, smiled and looked down at the floor. The mention of expenses among close friends always made him bashful. He was poor and always had been poor; he figured he'd always be poor, living, as one friend said, off the birdseed left on windowsills. That was the lot of the peddler. At least it was the lot of the kind of peddler that Nathan was—honest, a little too lazy, and not very ambitious. He didn't mind not being able to go with his two friends, really, and he loved them so much that he could really and truly feel happy knowing they'd be going together.

Alice comes in—she has news that Grant's store has closed.

Chapter Nineteen

Grant Barker woke up in his hospital bed. He didn't know it at the time, but he had been in that bed for nearly two days before waking up. He had slept the first day almost all the way through, never fully waking up, only occasionally emerging slightly from the haze of painkillers he'd been given. When he finally did wake up, he hurt too much to talk, and felt too weak to move. He had fleeting thoughts about the shop: there was no one there to run things, no one, really, to put up a sign and explain why he wasn't there. People would just come by and find the shop closed. That was assuming whoever had attacked him had not cleaned the place out or, far more likely, simply trashed the place. He couldn't think about all that too much, because he couldn't move, couldn't even breathe deeply, couldn't do anything except squirm a little in his bed. Oddly, the realization that he was more or less a prisoner in his hospital bed, with no one to come to his rescue and keep the business going, this realization was not a troublesome one for him. He could tell he was pretty doped-up, because he felt pretty happy—at least as long as he didn't move much. The fact that his life was falling apart just outside his field of vision felt like a huge wind washing over him, like the roar of jet engines in a plane he was on, far more powerful than he was, far beyond his power to do anything at all.

Gradually it became evident to Grant that he was not alone in his hospital room. He already understood there was he, himself, there was the unsettling tropical print on the wall, and there was the TV which, thankfully, remained turned off, though he didn't trust it, and found himself occasionally staring at it just to make sure it was still off and staying off. There were things on his bed and things behind him that periodically made sounds, and there was the pain. The pain was almost like someone else in the room with him, always nagging him like the equipment in his room and the endless noise in the hall, never leaving him alone as long as he was awake. Now, for the first time, he became aware that there was another person there with him. He wondered for a few moments whether the person was real or not. After considering the matter, it appeared whoever was there was a completely real person, actually sitting in the room with him, looking at him. He managed to turn his head in the direction of this person, to the right of his bed, by the window that looked out over the greenery outside. The chair was sort of a light purple, and it was upholstered, and it looked like the sort of chair that no one would ever have in his house. Thinking that last thought startled him, because it was another reminder that he really was in a hospital room. He thought for a moment that he was actually all right, but that he was the victim of a conspiracy on the part of all the objects that were working against his sense of composure and clarity. The purple chair conspired with the tropical print on the wall and the turned-off TV, and they all conspired with the noise in the hall that never let up, and all the gadgets strewn about the bed, and the things coming out of his arms, and the pain in his side, his left side, and the odd feeling in his mouth, as if there was something in it, like a cotton ball the size of a grapefruit, a very large, very dry cotton ball stuffed in his mouth for some reason, all of this conspiring quietly to not let him forget he was in a hospital bed for real, not knowing how he had gotten there or what was really wrong with him or, for that matter, who on earth it was sitting in the chair next to the window? Was it the leader of the conspiracy? Damn those trees are green, thought Grant, they really are a lot greener than they ought to be, he thought, that much green is really sickening, he thought, and then he started to be sick, and he could feel his head aching and his stomach convulsing as he started to vomit. He could feel his chest getting wet and his eyes roll back into his head as the person, was it a man or a woman? as the person who had been sitting by the window got up and started moving around quickly, talking loudly to someone, it seemed, and before long there was another person in the room and there was a lot of moving around and Grant felt someone undressing him, not asking or anything, and he protested being handled in that way, and all that movement only made him sicker than the sight of the too-green greenery outside, and before he knew it, he was passing out.

Much later that same day Grant woke up again, hurting a good deal more than he had earlier, but a bit clearer in the head. He looked around through foggy eyes, and noticed that indeed he was still in the same room, with the same tropical print and the same purple chair. He noticed he was wearing a hospital gown that was covering his front but not gathered at the back, so he felt the back of his body against the sheets, and he could tell there was a bandage about his midsection. He could also see there was still somebody in the room with him. Now he could see the somebody was Darren.

Grant tried to focus his eyes a little better, to make sure it was Darren. Actually, he tried to focus to make sure it *wasn't* Darren. In making this first effort he realized that part of his head was bandaged so that the left side of his head, including his left eye, was covered. Luckily his right eye was the stronger of the two anyway, but he still noticed what an effort it was to make the one eye work to see clearly, He moved his head a little to help his eye focus, and then he tried to speak, saying "Dawwen?" through the large cotton wad that really was in his mouth and, he soon discovered, the tube that was stuck down his throat. "Wha-ammah? Wha-oo doin heeuw?" It hurt like nothing he could remember hurting when he talked. He had to work on not choking on the tube in his throat, now he knew it was there.

Darren moved closer and began to speak in a soft whisper. Grant couldn't understand him, he spoke so softly. Grant asked, "Coo thpeak up, pweeth? Ah can't hewwu."

To this Darren responded by speaking a good deal louder. He said, "welcome back to the land of the living. I was beginning to think you were checking out for good."

"Whah ahm ah?" asked Grant.

"Where are you?" repeated Darren, shaking his head. "Is that what you're asking, where are you?"

"Yeth," said Grant. "Whah ahm ah, ng whah happuh me?" It was very difficult to talk. He had obstructions in his mouth and throat, and he couldn't move his jaw very well. When he talked he felt himself strangling, drowning. After managing to get out a few words, he coughed and snorted. He felt he needed to blow his nose and throw up, but couldn't do either.

"You're in Saint Joseph's Hospital, Grant, in the ICU. You nearly died. It's a miracle you're not a complete vegetable. You were attacked, stabbed, beaten, robbed, and left for dead—right outside your store. Stabbed twice, I think, and pretty badly beaten. You were really badly messed up when you got here. You have a broken jaw, in case you don't realize it. They put wires in your jaw somehow. You probably shouldn't talk too much. It's pretty awful right now, I guess, but I think you're going to be okay."

"Bwowkuh jah? Fuck! Cang moof mah mouf..." He tried to say 'like I normally would,' but nearly choked on the words. He took a few breaths and went on: "How long ah been lith plath? Copth find who thtab me?" He gasped between words, feeling oddly numb in his mouth as he tried to talk.

"I don't know I understand all you're asking me. You want to know how long you've been here?" repeated Darren. He sounded very apologetic as he asked to have his understanding confirmed. Grant was feeling impatient, though. The more able he felt to communicate, the more he wanted to know. "You've been here, well, it's been more than a week, ah, I think it's eight or nine days since they brought you in. Whoever did this got away, so nobody knows anything about him—or them, or whatever. The police are hoping you can give them something to go on, once you get to feeling a little better. Evidently a homeless man happened to wander onto the scene as you were being attacked. He got help from the people at the diner near your shop. He got their attention well enough to get you some help, but he didn't have much information about your attack. They knew him there, at the diner—I guess he's a neighborhood regular, so when he came to the back door at the diner with word that the fag in the picture store was being murdered—that's what the police said he said—the folks he approached took him seriously. The attacker—or attackers—got away with your bank bag, your wallet, your laptop and your keys. You may be able to figure out whether anything else is missing once you get back on your feet."

Grant felt annoyed at the way Darren kept mentioning the possibility that several people had attacked him. Did he have a whole gang of enemies stalking him? Was he so badly banged up only a group of people could have done this much to him? He had no way to assess how badly hurt he was, as he was too weak to get up and look at himself, too tied up with tubes and gadgets to move, and too covered in bandages to be able to see anything.

Aside from the upset of learning all that had happened to him, Grant was distressed to hear about a homeless man coming to his rescue. He wondered if he knew who it might be. He asked, "Wah it Bobo, guy who thave me?"

Darren couldn't make out what he was asking. He said, "I'm sorry, what are you asking?"

By now Grant was beginning to feel the effects of all the effort he'd expended at trying to talk. He was running out of steam fast. He had to know who had gone for help to keep him from being beaten to death. He had to know before he passed out again. With great effort, he asked again, "Oo know name of puhthen caw fah hewp foh ve?"

Darren listened carefully, and this time seemed to understand. "Oh, you want to know if I know who called for help. Do you mean the people at the diner or the name of the homeless man? No, I just know some homeless guy was what the police said. But don't worry about all that. Now, then, you've begun to come around, aren't you glad to see me?"

"Bet wuh Bobo," said Grant. "Thuv me wight." He began to cry, and before long passed out again, hearing the buzzing of Darren's voice receding into the background.

Bobo was a homeless man who lived in the woods in back of Grant's shop. He'd been living in a small stand of trees there for some time. Periodically the neighbors would get tired of Bobo and his makeshift lean-to and his foul-smelling, ragged clothes and his general haplessness. Bobo would get drunk and make a nuisance of himself, and someone would call the police, and Bobo would spend a while in jail. He always came back to the same place, though, always ended up gathering together a pile of trash in the stand of poplars and oaks that grew along the back of the property where Grant's shop was, on the edge of a nice, stately residential neighborhood in the middle of town. Grant ignored him mostly, made a point of never giving him money and tried not to notice him, never stopped to talk with him. Grant wasn't abusive towards Bobo, he simply ignored him. Bobo wasn't aggressive, wasn't a crackhead. He was just a torn-up, hapless drunk who couldn't figure out how to take care of himself any better than ending up living in a pile of trash in back of a small cluster of shops and a diner. Bobo wasn't even really his name. It was just what people called him, and no one knew why. No one knew his real name, and he answered to Bobo, so that was that.

Grant slept another day or so. The next time he woke up he was glad to find himself alone. He was ashamed to admit that he didn't want to see Darren still sitting there. How Darren had come to be in his hospital room the last time he'd awakened was a source of some puzzlement and alarm. The idea that Darren had begun to hold a vigil over him was nearly as alarming as the thought that he might come out of his predicament disfigured and crippled. Grant was ashamed of himself for thinking that it was a bad thing that Darren had been there. He couldn't help himself. He could thank Darren at the proper time for whatever service he'd rendered, but Grant was sure he didn't want Darren back in his life. He might burn in hell for thinking that way, but then, he didn't believe in hell. Good Samaritan or not, please, no more Darren, please, please!

As he lay in his bed, awash in floods of thought and dread, Grant began to wonder what he would do next. What was happening to the shop? Would he lose it? Had he already lost it? What had actually happened to him? He knew he must be very badly hurt, because he was in the ICU. Broken jaw. Stab wounds. Stab wounds! Good god, stab wounds? Wonder what else? Was he missing anything? He felt his legs by making them move. It hurt to move, but that was a good thing, considering. And his arms—they appeared to be intact, too. What about the bandage over his left eye? Did he still have a left eye? Jesus! All this at the end of working like a motherfucker for a month, more than that, really, more like six weeks, just being a good boy and working like crazy, minding his own business and just trying to make an honest living. Fuck! Fuck! Fuck! The receipts the thieves had gotten. Credit card numbers, personal information. All that was in his laptop. His whole fucking business was in that laptop. He hadn't backed up since forever. Everything was on the laptop. There was some stuff on paper in the shop, but he'd made a point of being a good modern business man and put everything on the computer. Now what? And—what had Darren said?—more than a week of being there? Who would have notified his customers, the people whose credit card receipts he had in his bank bag? The other folks whose personal information was in his laptop? There was no one to warn his customers that thieves had their personal information. No business partner, no one. Would he be crippled from all this? Just how badly messed up was he? What was his deductible on the hospitalization part of his medical insurance?

As he mused over all these matters, he noticed that a new person appeared at his side: an enormous woman with very dark hair and very pale skin. Her arms were bigger around than one of Grant's legs, and she had torpedo tits. She was wearing a uniform, and she smelled like cigarettes: he knew she must be a nurse. He could see her clearly, which made him feel better, as he knew it was an improvement to be able to say that. She had a faint mustache and very pink lipstick. She had very large blue eyes. She was chewing something; gum, he thought. Or tobacco, maybe? Had to be gum, he thought. He looked at her silently as she checked at the things in back of his bed and then stuck something in his ear. She pulled out the ear thing when it beeped, and then looked at him and said, "No fever. That's something. How you doing today, Mr. Barker?"

"Feew wike shit," said Grant, glad that he could say "shit" without sounding like Daffy Duck. The nurse smiled, fussed about him gently. There was something reassuring in the rustling sounds she made as she moved about him.

"Well, you're coming along pretty well, considering. You're a darn lucky guy, that's for sure and certain," said the nurse. She had a name tag, but Grant couldn't make it out.

"Wutthuh name?" he asked.

She looked down at him and seemed to translate the sounds he made quickly. Then she gave a half-smile and said, "Barbara. Barbara Lopez."

"Oo nurth?" asked Grant.

"Am I a nurth?" she repeated. "Yeth, I am."

Grant laughed at her imitating his lisp, then winced at the pain of laughing, then laughed again. Then he raised his left hand and extended his middle finger. Nurse Barbara laughed when she saw him giving her the finger. "Thum bedthide manner," said Grant. "Makin' fun o gimpth."

"Oh, you're no gimp," said nurse Barbara, "you're a short-timer here, I think. You'll be out of here soon, as long as you cooperate. Be back up to your old tricks before you know it. In fact, it looks as though you'll be leaving ICU before the day is over."

"Whuh ole twickth?" asked Grant. "Don't have any twickth. How you think I got heeuw?"

"Quiet now, and rest," said Barbara. "The doctor will be in soon, and we'll see what he has to say." Grant barely heard these last words as he passed out again.

Another week passed. Grant was transferred from the ICU to a regular unit. He grew a bit stronger each day. Other than the hired help, no one came to visit, and he was thankful for the solitude. As he had no family, he didn't expect to have any relatives visiting him. All he could do was surrender to the certainty that he was badly hurt and needed time to heal. From the doctors and nurses who looked in on him and examined him, he learned that he had been attacked from behind as he was leaving his store. As he got ready to get into his truck, the attacker (or attackers) stabbed him twice in the left side, puncturing his left lung but, happily, not hitting any other organs. He was kicked and beaten about the face. The brutality of the attack led the police to surmise that his attackers were motivated by something other than simple greed as they stole his belongings.

When his condition improved enough, his doctor allowed the police to talk to him. He remembered one visit from a police detective. He thought when he saw the detective the man looked very rough and weathered, like a functional alcoholic whose job was slowly killing him. The detective didn't ask him very much, and seemed most interested in finding out whether he knew his attacker, whether there was anyone who might be interested in settling a score for something. These questions puzzled Grant to no end; he couldn't imagine anyone having a grudge against him, as he had very good relations with his clients and his neighbors among the other shop owners. Having been asked if he might have any enemies, however, Grant began to worry about the prospect that there might, indeed, be someone out there who had an axe to grind with him. He couldn't think of who it could be, but the thought, once placed in his head, wouldn't leave.

As the days passed by and he began to feel better, he began to find it harder not to think about the shop. For all practical purposes, Grant was alone in the world. Well, that wasn't altogether true. He had friends, surely, people he went to movies with, to dinner, a few friendly customers, but none of them—except Darren—had been by to see him, as far as he could tell. And Darren's visit—what was it about? How had he learned about what had happened to Grant? This one detail really bothered Grant. He had nothing but time to think about all of it—the attack; the precariousness of his business; the near absolute certainty that the thief had parlayed his client information into an identity theft spree; the oddness of Darren's showing up—and so, as people are inclined to do, he began to think the worst. Maybe there *was* an enemy out there—what if it was someone he knew? What if it was someone who had been watching him for awhile? What if the person who'd done this to him was still watching him? One of the police even suggested that the robbery may have been a red herring, a distraction on the attacker's part, intended to confuse the police about the motive and hence the identity of the attacker. What if the real motive was not greed, or a desperate need for money, but simple, unalloyed hate?

Left alone with his thoughts, Grant kept coming back to this: that all along, without realizing it, he'd been living on the brink of disaster. It just took one push to move him from the dullness of an everyday routine into a state of utter helplessness and uncertainty. He had no one to turn to to protect his customers or his business. He had no choice but to lie in his bed and wait until he was strong enough to get back out there and begin to assess the real damage. What a thought: the real damage wasn't his body, it was his business. Thank goodness he had insurance, he thought. What would things have been like for him if he'd ended up in the county hospital? An even more grim picture than the one he was having to face now.

After a few more days passed, the bandage came off his head. His jaw, wired to repair the fracture he'd gotten during the attack, was healing up nicely. When he looked at himself in the mirror for the first time, however, it was quite a shock. The left side of his head had been shaved. He had a very swollen, badly blackened left eye. He had to take blood thinner to keep from having something go wrong with a blood clot from all the beating he'd sustained. He had had two surgeries on his head: one to address swelling of his brain arising from his beating, and the other to repair his broken jaw. It didn't appear he had any brain damage, but it was a bit early to tell. He'd also suffered a broken nose during the attack, but it healed up pretty well. By the time the swelling abated and his hair began to grow back, be became recognizably himself again. He ended up with a scar that started on his left eyebrow and went up the left side of his forehead. His nose was also a bit crooked from the break; crooked but not deformed. He was still a handsome man. If the attack did anything to him outwardly, it was to make him look more interesting.

After nearly a month in the hospital, he was released. He took a taxi home, where he found a huge pile of mail. He didn't bother to go through it right away. He spent some time on the phone, talking to the folks at the diner. They were nice and very helpful to him. They had made sure the shop was secure, and had put up a sign directing people to contact the diner for more information.

It was as bad as he had feared. It was worse. On top of a pile of bills, Grant had some nasty phone messages from a few customers. Being obliged to hear the most recent messages first, he already knew that Mrs. Johnson was turning the matter over to her attorney several ugly soliloquies before he got her breathless message that she hoped he was all right, having heard of his misfortune. There were, indeed, a host of messages from people pledging no end of support and help, and that was heartening if a little overwhelming to hear. But there were enough angry people telling him to solve his own problems on his own time and get them their merchandise or their supplies paid for or he needed to place this or that order or contact the bank about this or that account that was overdrawn— there were enough of those sorts of messages to make him think about just going back to bed.

He was broke. After nearly a month in the hospital, he had come home, a rented home, to find his business was in freefall, he owed everybody money, didn't have enough to cover all of it, and was in danger of losing everything. He didn't know what to do.

After sorting through the mail, Grant decided to go to the shop. It was late in the day, but he needed to go there, anyway, just to see what shape things were in. He felt pretty woozy, having spent the better part of the previous four weeks on his back in bed, and he still smarted somewhat from his stab wounds. But he needed to face the store and see for himself how things were there. He told himself that if the store was intact, it would make things bearable. If it were trashed, he didn't know what he would do.

It was about four in the afternoon when he got to the store. He parked the truck out front. He noted to himself that he felt scared of parking in back. No wonder. But that wasn't going to work. He would have to get over that in a hurry. He'd worry about that later. From the front the store looked fine, no obvious indication the place had been destroyed. Then it occurred to him that to get into the store he was going to have to go around to the back, because his security system was located too far from the front entrance for him to get to in time without setting it off. He panicked at the thought of going to the back of the store. He looked at the store and thought about it, and sat in his truck for awhile, thinking about what would happen next. It seemed he couldn't decide what to do next. He had to go in, but he couldn't make himself go in the front, and he couldn't go around to the back.

And so it went.

Grant eventually drove back home and said he'd wait until the following morning to go to the store. It wouldn't matter that much if he went in that evening. Things would be more or less the same the following day.

The following day he did come back to the store at around eight-thirty. He drove around to the back, and looked around to make sure there was no one lurking about before getting out of his truck. Then he dashed to the back door, unlocked it, and disarmed the security system. He went through the store room into the front of the shop. Everything was fine. It smelled musty and stale, because the place hadn't been opened up in a month. But as far as he could see, nothing was messed up. He went about organizing the mail that had accumulated at the store, a much larger pile than he'd had to deal with at home. Sorting the garbage from the real stuff, he realized he had several days worth of work ahead of him, just going through all the good mail. Then he started to set up the cash drawer. Then he realized he didn't have any cash on hand. This meant he'd have to go to the bank before the store was to open, withdraw a few hundred dollars from the business account, and come back to the store. This meant leaving the store, which meant going out the back way again. It also meant coming back into the store through the rear entry another time, this time with a few hundred dollars in a cash bag. He started thinking about whether or not it would work to leave the store locked but with no alarm on while he went to the bank. That way he could park out front when he came back, and get into the store through the front. Then he thought about thinking this, and it occurred to him that he wasn't ready to be facing all of this, that being in the hospital for the past month had shielded him from having to think practically about how he would start facing all that he needed to face, and that because he hadn't done any of that, he wasn't the least bit ready to face it. He thought about what it would take for him to find someone to take over the store. Maybe he could find someone to work for him, and he'd just manage things from behind the scenes. That didn't make any sense. He couldn't afford that. He would insist on paying his worker a decent wage, and that would mean he would end up not making any money. The business was only marginally profitable. For all his hard work, for all the money he had been bringing in before the thing happened, he had just been treading water. Only in the past month, the month before he went into the hospital, only then had he really had a surge in business, and much of that was new business—business he'd contracted for but not completed. He really was never more than a month away from disaster, and disaster had dutifully shown up to illustrate the point. He was on the edge of losing everything.

Grant struggled over the next few weeks. He struggled with the fear that came from reliving what he'd been through. And the reliving was made all the odder, all the more fearful, because he could actually remember so little of it. His attack had been from behind, and he hadn't caught a glimpse of the attacker. He wasn't even aware there was anyone there until the attack began. He didn't hear his attacker, and he didn't see anything, either. The attacker didn't speak, just hit him from behind and then stabbed him in the side with something that felt rough—as if it wasn't really a knife. Not that he had any idea what it would feel like to be stabbed by a knife. After being hit and stabbed, he passed out, so he didn't remember anything beyond that point. It would have been better if he had seen his attacker, he thought. He would at least know who to be afraid of. Or who to want to hurt. He had no idea who it was he needed to be afraid of. What if it were someone from the diner? Couldn't be. The homeless guy who saw the attacker would have surely been able to identify him to the police it had been someone from the neighborhood. All he knew was that the homeless guy saw someone running away when he came along. It looked like a man, but nothing was certain. Race, age, physical type—nothing. It was just a man, running around the corner and off into the neighborhood with a stolen briefcase.

Grant tried his best to resuscitate his business. The people at the diner came down and fussed over him, as did a few of his other business neighbors. He was grateful for the kindness, but a bit embarrassed by it, as well. He guessed there was really no good way for people to handle this kind of situation, so he supposed he just had to endure what came with the attention. He worked at his framing, he got his books in order, he talked on the phone with irate customers and did his best to reassure them they would get their work, and he did his best not to tell the nasty and whiny ones not to go fuck themselves. It was draining work, dealing with the customers. That was what stood out the most. Here he'd just averted a nasty death, and he was finding he was having to mollify all these spoiled, overindulged consumer goods junkies because they had had to wait for their crummy pictures. He was not feeling good about making his living this way. Even the nice customers were getting on his nerves. Everything about them was beginning to bother him. He found it difficult to listen to their banter, to listen to them whinging and dealing and laboring over decisions that didn't seem to amount to anything—what difference does it make if you get cream matting or flat white matting, you stupid fat slag! He didn't say it, but he thought it.

In fact he found himself doing that a lot—thinking nasty conversations with people, telling people to drop dead or go screw themselves. He also found himself, particularly when driving, fantasizing about hurting someone physically—being challenged to a fight and then beating the crap out of them or, better yet, knifing them. Whenever he had such fantasies, he stopped himself, thought to himself how ridiculous he was, and felt guilty for thinking about hurting anyone.

Eventually Grant came to believe that what was wrong was that he was living in a violent city. Before he'd been attacked, he had been aware that the inner city was a violent place, fairly well controlled by drug dealers, hookers, derelicts and gangs, like most American cities. A big part of the problem was that Centralia was growing up, like a number of young cities, into the new kind of American citihood: lots of wealthy, mostly young, mostly white and Asian urban pioneers, on the one hand, and an underclass of poor, mostly brown or black, angry or desperate people on the other.

Grant began to think how little connected he was to the place he lived and worked in. He worked virtually every day, which he didn't mind, because he enjoyed what he did. Making frames and mats was good therapy. It allowed him to focus on something simple, and it allowed him to see the results of his labor. Because he had an artist's eye, he could choose framing materials that actually enhanced the beauty of a good many of the images he was brought. He also got exposed to a certain amount of really good art, both old and new, among the piles and piles of stupid, boring or just plain bad imagery that people chose, for some reason he never could figure out, to adorn their walls. Yes, the business was fine. What complicated things, of course, were the clients. A few of them were interesting people, but most were just grey nothings. After all, that's like life, isn't it? Among the crowds we see, how many people stand out at all? And among those who stand out, how many do we actually connect with? Grant wasn't the type to schmooze with his clients, either. He let his work speak for itself. He made very nice mats and frames, and he sold very good quality antique prints.

It did occur to Grant from time to time how odd it was that he'd chosen his path. A young man in his early thirties at the turn of the millennium, he'd chosen to collect and sell prints from the 16th through the mid-nineteenth century. High Romanticism was as modern as his tastes got. He understood this, and simply made a habit of not even really looking seriously at anything that began to hint at the self-consciousness that pervaded what he thought of as modernity. The Romantics could use myth with an earnestness that was, he thought, simply lost by the time the Pre-Raphaelites showed up. The latter were all gesture and performance, the former were pure feeling and at least the possibility of faith, if only in demons. If he tried to articulate what he found lacking in the images that came after the Romantics, he found himself talking in circles. He only knew for sure that anything more recent just left him cold.

So he had that: the art he framed and made to look pretty, and the art he collected. Who was there to talk with about it? The occasional customer, but most of them left him cold, too. The men he dated rarely shared his interests in art. In fact, it occurred to him that he seemed to meet the most artistically challenged gay men, almost none of whom had any real interest in the kinds of objects that fascinated him.

What, then, was there to his life in Centralia? Very little. A few people he'd gotten to know from here and there, a customer or two, a shop owner from the neighborhood or a client from the weekend shows. None of his former boyfriends stayed in the picture for very long. Which reminded him: what had happened to let Darren know he was in the hospital? Had the visit with Darren been some kind of nightmare? Grant thought once or twice about calling Darren, just to satisfy his curiosity, but decided against it. Maybe Darren had happened to drive by when the police were there, or maybe he'd come by the store and seen it was closed, then asked someone nearby what the story was. Any number of things might have happened. The important thing was not to encourage Darren to reappear. So, that meant Grant would just have to live with his wondering.

What about his life in Centralia, then? Did Grant really want to stay there? Did he feel he belonged there? He talked with any number of men around his age who were moving or had moved to Chicago or Austin, two big destinations for up-and-coming gay men. Chicago he'd never seen, but he thought, it's too cold there. I'd die if I tried to survive there. Austin: he couldn't stand Texas, and he'd been to Austin once, and concluded it was just a place for lots of young and mostly straight people to gather, get high and play what Grant called the belonging game: the immensely popular game of forming social cliques and thrilling at who could never belong to yours. Straight or gay, same game. Austin was riddled with it. No thanks, not Austin. Where else, then? San Francisco? Overrun with rich lawyers, like Centralia was beginning to be. Miami? Too sleazy, though the climate appealed to him. Seattle? Too rainy. Los Angeles? Who needs to live on the fields of Armageddon? New York? Too cold, too expensive, and too overrun with money chasers. That didn't leave many places left, and they quickly fell of his list of candidates: Boston, too expensive and cold, Portland, too cold, Las Vegas, too far from the ocean, New Orleans, too run-down and full of angry poor people. Thinking about where he might run off to if he wanted to get away from Centralia was almost as unnerving as thinking about how little there was to keep him there.

Maybe he should just sell the business, put his stuff in storage, and just road trip his way through the issue. It was a thought. How long could he survive without working a steady job, that was the issue? He was healthy, thank God, so he had that in his favor. His truck was paid for and only three years old, so that was another good thing. He didn't owe much money, and he rented his apartment, so debts weren't a big issue, either. What, after all, was he doing staying where he was?

Chapter Twenty

Grant was facing homelessness. It only took three months for him to get there. One month in the hospital; a month trying to piece his business back together; and then little more than a few months for him to A) get an eviction notice from his apartment; B) a letter from several clients who were informing him of their intention to sue him for negligence in connection with their identity being stolen by the person(s) who robbed him; and C) a letter from his principal supplier of frames indicating that as his accounts were not up to date, he could not make any more purchases until his accounts were made current. He couldn't bring his accounts up to date until he untangled the mess of the paperwork that surrounded his documenting what charge slips had been stolen, and the bank was not being much help to him on that account.

By the end of six months after the attack, Grant was living in his truck. He lost his business, his apartment, and he faced a number of lawsuits for negligence. His lawyer, at least, didn't abandon him, but things didn't look at all good for him. The bank was treating him like a dog, more or less holding him personally responsible for the thefts that were being committed—and still being committed even six months after he was attacked—and insisting he assume personal responsibility for all the bad charges that were being rung up by whoever stole the credit information off his sales records. Everything he'd heard about how quickly banks reverse false charges after an incident of identity theft—all of it proved wrong. The bank was acting as if Grant had stolen the sales slips and was using them to charge purchases. There was no mistaking that he, the person who had survived a nearly fatal attack at the end of a hard day of work—a hard day of work that had come at the end of a full month without a day off—he was being treated as the wrongdoer.

Grant moved himself out of his apartment just short of his eviction date, donating much of his furniture and clothes—anything he didn't feel he really needed--to a homeless shelter thrift shop nearby. He moved into the back of his shop, sleeping in his supply room on a futon he bought at a second-hand store. He had a boombox for music, no tv, a stack of books, and a hotplate he bought at Target to cook on. There was no heating in the supply room, so he rigged up a space heater with an extension cord. As it got colder outside, he began to think of more ways to tighten up the shop so he could make living there bearable through the winter. Other than going grocery or supply shopping, he rarely went out. He stopped shaving, and he was surprised when his beard began to come in with a stripe of white down his right cheek. Every once in a while he found himself replaying what he could remember from the attack. Sometimes he would embellish it in his imagination, turning to see the person before the attack began. He could never see the person's face. He could never see how many people there were, but he thought there must only be one person. He thought about buying a gun now and then. He decided against it, thinking he would only end up blowing his brains out if he did have a gun. He felt lonely, but he was afraid to go out at night. He worked all day in his shop, trying to focus on the simple matter of getting the work done. There was lots of work. Despite everything, people still brought him pictures to frame. He tried not to think too much about how people had reacted to his attack. Some of the old customers disappeared. Then there were the angry customers who were suing him over the identity theft thing. Then there were new customers who seemed not to know what had happened to him. And then there were people who came in, people who lived in the neighborhood, who wanted to hear what had happened to him. They talked about their own experiences with violence in the area. How bad the police were; how little they cared about anything. The people at 911? Forget about it, they couldn't care less. And other neighbors, too: you'd think more of them would get involved, would care about what was happening in the neighborhood, all the gangs, the derelicts, the hookers turning tricks in people's yards in the middle of the night. Grant listened to people's stories but blanked out, zoned out as he went about his business. He was keeping his head low. He didn't know what else to do. All he could do was work. He wasn't even sure if working, if keeping his head low would help him find his way out of all this. And if he did find his way out, if he did work his way out of the hole he'd fallen into, then what? He tried not to think about that, either.

Grant began to feel a growing sense of isolation. All he did was work and putter around the shop afterwards. He didn't go out much except to run errands. Once in a while he'd go out to a bookstore to look for something to read. He read the *New York Times*, the *New York Review of Books* and the London *Guardian* online to keep up with what was current in the arts and the news. Much of what he read about in the news puzzled him or made him angry. The world really isn't getting any better, he thought from time to time. No wonder the rest of the world hates us, he thought as he read the national news. Why do people put up with these creeps, he asked himself? He asked himself, Why aren't there mass demonstrations in every city against the war, against the idiots who've manufactured it? There wasn't much reason to go out, he thought himself.

But then again, he found not so much that he missed the company of other people, as that not having company was beginning to change him in some way he couldn't clearly articulate. True, he saw people at the shop every day. He spoke to people every day: in the shop, in restaurants, grocery stores, bookstores, and gas stations he had lots of short, two-line conversations. Maybe if he added them up at the end of the day they amounted to the same volume of speech that most other people produced on a daily basis, on average. He couldn't be sure about that. But something was happening. He knew the attack had changed him. He thought about it every day. He knew he was becoming someone different. He knew he felt differently about everything.

Chapter Twenty-One

It was December and time for Nathan to start thinking about packing for the show. There had been a cold snap the first week of the month, so the weather was really very pleasant. For once, no bugs. Clear blue skies. And the novelty of wearing long sleeves, sweaters. The warm clothes gave him the comfortable, pleasant sense of being touched by something. He didn't want to get ready for the show. He found, invariably, that all the hub-bub of Thanksgiving made him feel lazy, all the eating and sitting around, digesting huge lunches while watching crap tv, talking about nothing. This year he had opted not to go to Centralia to see his father and, more importantly, to see Becky and Alice. They were very disappointed Nathan didn't come for Thanksgiving, and he knew it was a sore point he'd have to discuss when he got into town for the December show. For him it was a matter of just feeling tired of doing the same six-hour drive month after month. No one ever suggested they all come to have Thanksgiving at Nathan's house, but they surely were pissed off that he wasn't ready to hop in the van, for the second time in a month, and then drive the three hundred miles to Centralia, knowing he'd have to do the same thing all over again in a few more weeks, then again at Christmas, then again in early January.

So this time around he'd stayed in Charleston, instead. Slept through the day on Thanksgiving, as it was a cool and rainy day, then sat up all night watching old movies on TV. His friends may be mad at him, but at least he wasn't ready to check into a clinic for physical therapy after another long, dangerous ride on the highway on an especially dangerous weekend. He thought to himself, it really is getting a lot more dangerous on the expressway. The kinds of stories you used to hear about I-95—bizarre wrecks involving drivers being impaled by flying construction debris, drive-by shootings in the middle of the day, truckloads of pigs overturning to disastrous results—those kinds of odd, grotesque unpleasantnesses were no longer restricted to I-95. The other day he'd read about a road-rage killing on I-16. It was because of all the riffraff moving south from the rust belt, Nathan was sure. First it was people leaving shopping carts in parking lots, on the side of the road, in ditches—anywhere the urge hit them. That had been the first sign of the epidemic of bad manners driven by the influx of Yankees, years ago. Now it was drive-bys and road rage killings, in the sticks, out in the middle of nowhere. Yankees were okay when you met them in their own element, Nathan mused. New Yorkers were lovely people, by and large. But bring them South—Nathan hated it when some outlander yahoo said *down* south—and they behaved like idiots, trashing everything they could get their grubby little hands on. Oh, what difference does it make? Nathan asked himself, sighing. The whole world is dying anyway, with the missing link in the White House, and religious fanatics of every imaginable stripe taking over the world stage. This is an age of little men, Nathan thought. Little men tearing apart everything of any value.

And so on that cheerful note Nathan finally found himself realizing that he was avoiding the matter at hand: What shall I take with me to Centralia this month? Why hadn't he begun to think about all this sooner? It was the December show, and surely that would be the one great show of the year: people buying for the holidays, surely it commanded some kind of planning. Not for Nathan. He'd found the December show to be a crap shoot. Some years it was a great show, other years it was absolutely the show of the living dead, no matter what he did to try to sniff out buying trends, focus on product themes, all that marketing crap. He did much better, he believed, when he bought purely on instinct: here's something *I* like, and that's why I'm going to buy it. If the public doesn't like it, well, *fuck 'em and feed 'em beans*, as Esther Carr used to say. Whosoever questions my taste, thought Nathan, deserves what they get! And so, for Nathan, Christmas was just the last show of the calendar year, accompanied by a somewhat longer stay chez Becky and Alice than usual. Nathan was an accomplished cook, so one of the things he always had to do to earn his keep around the holidays was make a much-loved pork loin dish that Becky and Alice served at a dinner attended, among others, by a group of lapsed Jews who reveled in eating unclean (but very, very tasty) meat during the high holidays. Nathan's recipe was for twelve people, the number that Becky and Alice's dinner table was outfitted to accommodate. Word of mouth usually brought in an additional five to seven people, so that the table was made to seat upwards of twenty people for that one, rather scandalous meal.

When he gave it some thought, Nathan had to admit to himself that the whole prospect of staging an irreligious holiday dinner had lost its appeal after so many repetitions. In truth, he never looked forward to the Christmas season. Always too much money spent paying people back for the gifts they'd given him. A senseless ritual, no denying it. But one that he couldn't seem to free himself from. And of course there was the absolute promise of a fit of mel-

ancholy at some point along the way. During one of the many din-
ners it would occur to him, out of the blue, that yet again he was the
only person at the table without a mate present, and he would have
to swallow yet another realization that he'd just spent another year
alone except for the occasional trick.

That's really not fair, he would say to himself at such thoughts,
think of all the friends I have. Becky and Alice, foremost among
them. Cara and Dan, Lizz and Janet, Arthur and Howard, Sam and
Dennis, yes, lots of friends, once he started counting them up, it
really was impressive, and all of them as married as can be.

Which is why I don't spend much time getting ready for shows,
Nathan thought to himself, see where it gets me? Don't do much
planning, but I do, invariably, get all maudlin and weepy thinking
about the trainwreck of my emotional life and the vast wasteland
that separates me from anything resembling a normal adult human
relationship not based on dependency.

Are there, indeed, such relationships in the real world, wherever that is? He asked himself. No answer came.

So Nathan started thinking about what he had on hand in the
way of wares to take to the Centralia show—what was in the house,
what in the antique mall booth in North Charleston, and what in the
storage bin he'd rented. There was the set of mica reading lamps
he'd bought at the junior league sale: two very nice, hand-
hammered copper lamps with delicate mica shades. What else: the
three folk art paintings he'd bought at a folk art sale a few weeks
back: allegedly painted by prisoners in the state penitentiary, each
was very expressive and frankly disturbing. One depicted a grimac-
ing man in a suit sitting in an armchair; another an odd take on the
martyrdom of Saint Sebastian, with a beefcake man in blue jeans

lashed to a telephone pole, his body pierced with arrows in several places, and a galvanized bucket hung on his head; and the third painting, evidently copied from a photograph, depicting a little girl seen in close-up, casting a worried look over her shoulder. Is this the stuff for a Christmas show? Nathan asked himself, thinking of how the odd subject matter of the paintings might sit with some people. Well, he decided with a sigh, they'll fill up space, and they're bound to get people to stop and take a look, if nothing else. Then the thought occurred to him: since he'd stumbled upon a piece depicting martyrdom, and since it was Christmas, maybe he could organize a booth entirely around the theme of martyrdom. Did he have enough objects to make the theme evident, he wondered. Maybe he could do a little shopping, he thought, remembering how the Jesus and Mary nightlights had sold some time back. Maybe he could go to the dollar store and stock up on holy figurine night-lights, suggesting to shoppers what good stocking stuffers they made.

So, at last, Nathan had arrived for a plan for getting ready to do another show. Too bad he only bothered to think about all this in time to have not quite one week to organize things and get packed up. He decided to pick up the newspaper and look for estate sales, thinking he might find some nice crucifixes, paintings of the Madonna, that sort of thing. It also occurred to him he might even get a Savannah newspaper and see if there were any estate sales worth looking at. Savannah had lots of Catholics, so he might luck out.

Nathan decided that he would go to the BP station on the Savannah highway, because it had the best selection of newspapers. He went to the filling station, bought a large Snickers bar, the

Charleston *Post and Courier*, and the Savannah *Morning News*. He went back to the house, poured a cup of coffee, and went out on the front porch with his coffee, his newspapers and an ink pen, hastily looking for the classified ads sections. He found nothing of great interest in the way of estate sales in the Charleston paper, which disappointed him. Since he was looking at the Charleston paper, he couldn't resist looking at the obituary pages to scan and see if someone with a colorful name had passed away. Charleston being Charleston, there were all kinds of people—of all colors and backgrounds—who had peculiar names. They all passed through the obituary pages eventually, and whenever he thought about it, Nathan looked through the notices and saved the most interesting names for a collection he'd been amassing over the past several years. He didn't tell many people about this particular collection. Those of his friends who did know about it tended to think—and often to observe out loud—that it indicated his habit of collecting was in the nature of a sickness of some kind, maybe a form of obsession, even. On this particular day, Nathan did come across an interesting name in the obituaries, when he read that Boolebug Mitchell had passed away. In an astonishing second development, he read that LaVulva and LaVulgar Washington, twin sisters, were announcing their double engagement. The grooms, alas, had names of no great distinction, but Nathan was sure his day's work had been done just by finding Boolebug, LaVulva and LaVulgar.

This sublime discovery of unique musical names made Nathan lose track of his sense of purpose for awhile. He had to find his scissors, cut out the notices carefully, then find his rubber cement to attach the notices to some construction paper, which had to be cut to match the notices, and then figure out where to place them on the

wall in his bathroom that was devoted to displaying publicly docu-
mented remarkable names and extraordinary news notices. He decided at length that Mitchell and the Washington sisters needed to
be place in an array around the following newspaper story:

> Police were called to 1734 Dunfrey Terrace on Thanks-
> giving day when a domestic dispute broke out during a
> Thanksgiving Day meal. Erma Lee Singleton, 47, of
> North Charleston, was taken into police custody and
> charge with assault and battery for attacking Francetta
> Palmeroy, 38, of Aiken, with a turkey carcass. Witnesses
> reported that during the family gathering, which was held
> in the front yard of the Palmeroy residence, Palmeroy
> and Singleton engaged in a verbal altercation, though
> witnesses varied as to who started the fight. The dispute
> reportedly escalated until Mrs. Palmeroy told Mrs. Sin-
> gleton she was "a bitch and a bad cook," at which point
> Mrs. Singleton reportedly assaulted her with the remains
> of the bird. Mrs. Singleton later declined to press
> charges, according to Charleston police. No other people
> were arrested.

Once he had the new additions to his collection arranged on the
wall, Nathan paused a few minutes to admire the array. The thought
occurred to him that Mitchell and the Washington sisters had
achieved a kind of beatitude, and he felt satisfaction in the fact that
he had brought them together with Mrs. Singleton.

Eventually it occurred to Nathan that he was woolgathering and
that he really needed to get back to the newspapers and see if there
was a sale or two he could find to attend that weekend. Promising
himself not to get sidetracked again, he looked back through the
Post and Courier to see if he'd missed any interesting-sounding
estate sales. Nothing. Ho-hum, he thought, a bit vexed that his plan
to mount a true Christmas show was already running into a bit of a
snag. Another cup of coffee, and then he decided to forge on by
looking at the Savannah paper. To his considerable surprise, there

were four estate sales that looked interesting, including three in the historic district. He marked the ads, tore them out of the paper, then trimmed the ads to fit nicely in the portfolio he used for business notes and other documentation.

Nathan thought to himself that it would be nice to go to Savannah with someone else, if he could find someone willing to get up early enough to drive down early enough to make attending the sales worthwhile. He decided to call his friend the Empress.

"Mother-fucking cocksucker!" came the voice at the other end of the phone, amid hoarse cackles. "Girl, I thought you'd done died and dried up! How the fuck you been, monkey?" Mark sounded drunk, but Nathan knew that was just the way he sounded. He was glad Mark was glad to hear from him.

"Fine, Empress, just fine. Working my fingers to the bone trying to get ready to do the Centralia show," Nathan replied.

"Girl, you ain't already packed up yet?" asked Mark. He weighed over three hundred pounds and was, arguably, the nelliest bear east of the Mississippi River. Mark collected toys as a hobby. He worked as a freelance cook for catering companies to keep the wolf from the door. He had met Nathan years before at a volunteer orientation meeting for the Lowcountry AIDS Project, and they had been friends ever since.

"Oh, be serious," said Nathan. "You know me. I probably won't pack up until Tuesday night. I have been racking my brains for a theme for this month's show, and finally it dawned on me I might do a show full of Jesus things."

"Jesus things? What the fuck you talking about, Nathan?"

"You know, religious icons, crucifixes, Milagros, anything Christian-y," said Nathan.

Chapter Twenty-One

Mark laughed: "Chile, you gwine boin in *hayull*! So whatchu want me for?"

Nathan said, "Well, I got the Savannah *Morning News* and saw there are a number of estate sales this weekend, and thought I would drive down there and see if I can find anything worth hauling back here. Then I thought it would be nice to have some company, so I thought of you. You up for a roadtrip?"

Mark answered, "Hell, yeah, sweetness, I'll go with you, but on one condition."

"What's that?" asked Nathan.

"That you let me drive, and that we drive down Friday and stay in a real hotel rather than driving down like white trash before the crack of dawn on Saturday."

"That's not one condition," said Nathan. "I think that's three."

"Well, fuck, then," said Mark, "I tell you what: I'll pay for the room. I need to get out of town, anyway, so it'd be fun."

"Just what the doctor ordered," said Nathan. He was secretly glad Mark was willing to put them up in a hotel room. And so they agreed to go.

There were four sales that had caught Nathan's attention. Three were estate sales, and one was a bankruptcy sale. The bankruptcy sale was the least interesting to Nathan. Mark and he went to Savannah, stayed at the B&B Under the Rainbow, ate at the Crab Shack on Tybee Island, and got up the following morning. They set out, had fun gawking, and then at the end of the day decided just to pass by the bankruptcy sale. There Nathan finds the Kollwitz that Grant had sold. He takes his own money, also borrows money from Mark to buy it, getting it for $800.00. Having it makes him think about Grant.

That Friday afternoon Nathan sat on his porch waiting for Mark to show up. Mark had said he'd be at Nathan's house by four o'clock. The idea was to get on the road down to Savannah before the rush-hour traffic got bad, because if they were going all the way to Savannah, Mark wanted to go to the Crab Shack on Tybee Island. Nathan had nothing against going there, except he was sure if they went Mark would want to get the biggest platter for two on the menu, and that would mean Nathan would have to shell out about $25.00 for his portion of the dinner, which was about as much money as he would have spent for gas *and* food if he had gone by himself. Oh, well, it wasn't as if Nathan didn't know what to expect from Mark when he invited Mark to go with him, but he feared, now that he began to think about it, that the excursion might end up turning into Mark's trip to Savannah with Nathan tagging along as the resident stick-in-the-mud (as Mark might be inclined to tell about it later). Maybe it was a mistake. Maybe he should call Mark (it was already almost five o'clock and no word or sight of him) and tell him he changed his mind or something.

This was about the time Mark finally decided to show up, naturally, tearing down the road in his pea green Cadillac. He slammed on the breaks as soon as he got to Nathan's house, bringing the car to a lurching stop. Nathan thought he saw Missykes peering out the window from inside her darkened, no-doubt infernally hot house. Luckily she didn't come out of the house to yell at Mark for driving recklessly in front of her house. Mark got out of the car and walked up to the house carrying a Church's Fried Chicken bag, which he handed to Nathan. "Hey, sugar, you ready to go?"

"Yep," said Nathan, getting up to give Mark a kiss on the cheek, deciding against complaining about Mark's tardiness. "Come here and give me a kiss. How are you? What's that, late lunch?" he said, pointing to the fried chicken bag.

Mark wrapped his arms around Nathan, picked him up off the porch floor and kissed him on the mouth. "Hey, sugar," he said, putting Nathan down. "I just got hungry, thought I'd stop and get a snack before we got on the road," said Mark. "It is Friday, you know, and there might be a line at the Crab Shack, so I didn't want to take the chance."

"You want a diet Coke for the road?" asked Nathan, straightening his clothes after Mark's manhandling.

"Perfect," said Mark. "You know I need to watch my figure." He said, laughing. He went past Nathan into the house, and Nathan watched as Mark went into the kitchen, threw the bag away, then went to the refrigerator. Mark then bellowed from the back of the house: "You want a drink for the road, Nathan?"

"Bring me a diet Seven-Up," Nathan hollered back. He had his overnight bag on the porch next to him along with his bag of medicines, reading material (a book on the infamous Albert Fish), and writing materials for keeping track of what he might buy. He thought he was doing pretty well at foiling what he was sure were Mark's expectations about how he would behave. No scolding for Mark's lateness—very good move. Pretty much acting as though they'd just seen each other in the past few days, even though it had been more like a few months since they'd last set eyes on each other. Nathan thought it was a good thing he wasn't acting the way Mark would be expecting him to act. If he could keep it up, he might be able to keep Mark off-guard all the way there and back. As an impromptu plan for keeping some kind of control on someone with extra large appetites of all kinds, it wasn't all that bad a plan.

"Thanks," said Nathan, as Mark reappeared with the two drinks, sweating profusely. Then Nathan closed and locked the front door behind Mark, grabbed his bags, and the two men headed for the car. "How's the land yacht running these days?" Nathan asked, looking at the enormous car.

"Girl, I just put new shocks on 'er, so she's running pretty smooth. Drives like a motherfuckin' police car. Them goddamn shocks cost a fuckin' fortune, I tell you what!" Nathan loved the car, which Mark had inherited from his mother when she passed away a few years back. His mother had spent her last days in a condo in Boca Raton. She bought the Cadillac new in 1979 and drove it once or twice a week, to the grocery store or the doctor, so that by the time Mark got it, more than twenty years after she bought it, it had right at 31,000 miles on it.

Mark popped the trunk to let Nathan put his bag in. "Okay if I keep my medicine bag up front?" he asked. "It doesn't have any sharp edges." He smiled at Mark, knowing that Mark, who was more or less a slob in most respects, treated the car, inside and out, as if it were a newborn baby, with all the requisite care.

"You tear up th'inside o' my car, I'll snap your neck like a twig," Mark said in a faux-butch redneck voice. Nathan got into the front seat of the car with his bag, putting it on the spacious floor that stretched out in front of him. There was so much room in the front seat that he couldn't reach the windshield with his outstretched hand. He looked around briefly and smiled at the thought of Mark trolling the Battery late at night for hustlers to have sex with.

Mark got into the driver's seat, closed the door, strapped himself in, and started up the car. "So we're off," he said.

"How many hustlers have you blown this week in this car?" asked Nathan. "Whose pecker tracks am I sitting on?"

"Countin' right before I came here" asked Mark, smiling.

"So that's where you've been," said Nathan, smiling and putting on his sunglasses. "In broad daylight, Mark? The very idea! Let me guess: Folly Beach?"

Mark laughed. "Do I have sand in my beard?" he looked in the mirror as he asked.

"You smell like sex," said Nathan, knowing it would bother Mark to think he didn't smell pristine. Like many fat men, he had a horror of smelling nasty. Luckily, he didn't douse himself in cologne the way a lot of fat men do. He was, however, obsessive about appearing clean.

"I do not," said Mark. "I stopped off at the gas station and bought a bottle of Lavoris, and I used about a whole box of Handi-wipes."

Nathan arched his eyebrows, made a face and nodded silently. He knew Mark would take this to mean, *Yeah, right. You smell like cum, Mark. No two ways about it. Spooge, Mark, spooge.*

Mark looked at him and said, "I do *not*, you hateful faggot from a goddamn dingleberry in Satan's butthole! You fuck with me I'm gonna kick your ass out o' this car, then go have me a good time down in Savannah."

All of this vile talk was bluster, of course. Nathan ignored him and looked out the window. "So, what else have you been up to," he asked.

"Not a whole hell of a lot," said Mark. "Tired of catering, but okay otherwise."

"Oh," said Nathan, "I can't believe how stupid I am."

"What?" asked Mark.

"Did you give up a gig to drive me to Savannah this weekend?" asked Nathan, genuinely concerned.

Mark shrugged. "Fuck 'em," he said. "I've been cooking my fat ass off all summer, those motherfuckers don't give a good god-damn if I show up or drop dead. Business I'm in doesn't reward you for anything, 'cause they're too busy keepin' their eyes on you, makin' sure you don't steal the fuck out of 'em. Goddamn white trash bitches," he said, referring to the two sisters who ran the catering company he cooked for.

"You know you could open your own place and make a fortune" said Nathan. "And that's just if the only people who ever came to eat were your friends." Mark was, indeed, a spectacular cook. Brought up by great Southern cooks, he had studied at the Cordon Bleu in Paris. While a student in Paris he was courted by the Tour d'Argent. He never could explain exactly what went wrong with that opportunity. Nathan imagined he was just homesick for South Carolina and the boys on the Battery and Folly Beach.

"Yeah, and drop dead of a heart attack right about two weeks after opening," said Mark, shrugging. Nathan wondered at his underachieving, but tried his best to not make an issue out of it. How, after all, could he?

"So," said Nathan, "sounds like you're burned out. So the weekend off is something you can use?"

"Goddamn mutherfuckin' right it is, cocksucker," said Mark, blowing Nathan a kiss.

The drive to Savannah was uneventful enough. They pulled into town around six o'clock. Nathan didn't pay much attention to where they were going, noticing only when they exited from the highway that they were in a neighborhood he didn't know very well.

"Where are we headed?" he asked Mark.

"Little b&b I read about online," said Mark. "Pictures looked good, so I thought I'd give it a try. I think the two queens who run it used to live in Charleston," he said. "This is called the Victorian quarter," Mark continued. "I think it's something the chamber of commerce cooked up. It ain't the old part, and it ain't new, either. So that means it's Victorian, I guess."

The street they drove down was a beautiful divided street with large moss-covered trees forming a canopy over it from all sides. The houses looked to be late Queen Anne-style houses, here and there a fairly recent little brick bungalow or a ranch-style house shoe-horned in between the large, older houses. The houses weren't particularly pretty, just big. Some of them were being renovated, some looked as though they were about to fall down. There were very few business in the area, and a good many boarded up buildings. Nathan figured that the locals probably called this a "transitional" neighborhood, meaning it had been abandoned by whites long ago and was now being re-colonized by them as the poor blacks were slowly being eased out of the picture. The neighborhood reminded him of the area around the College of Charleston, which had recently been claimed for gentrification after decades of neglect.

They finally turned down 37th Street and there, on the right, was a bevy of rainbow flags, telling them where they were. It was a nicely redone double house that had been combined into a single dwelling. There was a sign hung from the front porch that read, "Under the Rainbow."

The house, which Nathan judged to have been built around 1900, was very nicely kept, furnished with a judicious array of antiques, and tastefully painted. The house had obviously been restored, as the heart of pine floors were newly finished, and the wall separating what had been the two separate dwellings had been removed to make the house one large residence. The house was long and narrow, with a central hallway running its full length, giving access to a series of rooms on either side, and at the back, a kitchen leading out onto a small terrace. The owners of the house were also the hosts. They were two very kind and friendly gay men in their early forties, John and Daniel, and they were very welcoming. Nathan realized, as he dealt with the house's proprietors, that the same kind of hospitality they were showing him was once commonplace back in Charleston, but had slowly begun to disappear under the influence of all the northerners invading the city to find great real estate bargains. Rich and eager to scoop up all the available mansions in the city, they had slowly turned Charleston into an outpost of Long Island and Cape Cod. With their money they brought a severe dumbing-down of the culture of gentility that had once ruled Charleston. Nathan had been told by a number of friends who regularly visited Savannah that it had managed to retain what Charleston had lost by becoming a rich Yankee's investment prospect. What Nathan saw in the great friendliness of his Savannah hosts seemed to bear out what his friends had said. In short, his hosts first showed the two men to their room, a lovely suite on the second floor of the front of the house with its own balcony. Once Nathan and Mark had gotten their belongings in their room, they were invited down to the front parlor where John and Daniel served them tea and cakes, which Mark eagerly scoffed up like a hungry animal. Nathan sipped his tea and nibbled on part of a scone while John and Daniel quizzed them on their travel plans and made suggestions about where to go and where not to go during their stay.

Nathan learned, to his great astonishment, that Mark had taken the room, which must be costing a couple of hundred dollars a night, for two nights rather than one. At first Nathan was a little peeved to hear this: he hadn't warned Missykes he'd be away for two nights, and that meant the wild cats under the house would go hungry for a day. Thinking this prospect through, Nathan was reasonably sure that Missykes, who spied on him virtually every hour of the day, since she had little else to do besides bill and coo over Buster, would clearly see he was away by Saturday afternoon. No doubt cursing and complaining at great length, she would certainly drag a large bag of generic cat food she kept on hand over to his house and sprinkle it around in the dishes he left for the cats. When he got back she would tell him how she threw her hip out tending to those poor *abandoned* kitties, he would thank her breathlessly, and that would be that. Once he worked this detail out in his mind, and realizing that he really had nothing compelling to keep him in Charleston that weekend, Nathan then shrugged and let himself be Mark's prisoner for the better part of the next two days. It was a very nice place he'd landed in as prisoner, so he couldn't really complain.

An hour later Mark, fresh from a shower, announced to Nathan that they were going to the Crab Shack on Tybee Island, and that was that.

Nathan was bone tired by three o'clock Saturday afternoon. He had been to three estate sales, had not stopped for lunch, and had waited for Mark to return from Kentucky Fried Chicken with one of his favorite lunch treats: dinner for two combo with a large diet Coke, intended to be eaten only by Mark himself. You're going to kill yourself eating that stuff, Nathan said to himself silently as Mark drove and ate. They had to find their way to the fourth sale—a bankruptcy sale—if they were going to go at all. Nathan wasn't sure about going, he had a headache, and he was jittery from not having eaten most of the day. He had a few trinkets from the previous three shows, but really not much, not enough to justify having driven all the way to Savannah for spectacular Christmas merchandise. Mark was chirpy, having the time of his life, even though he hadn't bought a thing. Nathan wasn't sure at all why Mark was in such a good mood, and found it all the more annoying, as there didn't seem to be anything to justify it. "I don't get it," Nathan finally said to Mark, "What has you so doggone happy? You haven't bought anything, and unless I've missed something, you haven't tricked today, so what has you so full of cheer?"

Mark munched on a chicken leg and drove, casting a quick glance at Nathan, then back at the road. He seemed to be thinking over what Nathan was asking him. "Well, until you asked me that," Mark said, "I really wasn't thinking about how I was feeling. Now you mention it, I do feel pretty good. So what's wrong with that? Am I bugging you, pumpkin?"

Nathan lied and said, "well, of course not! I just don't get how slugging along with me through all this crap, burning up the gas in your car, and I don't think I've seen you buy anything yet—so how does all that add up to you're having, it would seem, a pretty fun day? I'm about to drop in my tracks, and I have something really invested in finding something. You're not even shopping. You're being a tourist. How can you stand it? No normal person thinks this is fun."

Mark smiled and chewed, nodded and looked at Nathan quickly, then smiled and shook his head again. "Well, pumpkin, I guess I'm just happy 'cause I'm with you, and that just lifts me up."

Nathan blushed a little, trying to decide if Mark was stepping completely out of character and being subtle. Nathan didn't feel he could afford to push the issue any further, because if Mark were being subtle and Nathan showed himself up as an obtuse fool, he would never be able to forgive himself, and never be able to face Mark again. So he shut up about it, and just tried to figure out silently what could possibly be making Mark so happy.

Addled and tired, beyond hungry, he decided it was best to go ahead and go to the bankruptcy sale, which was being held at a gallery somewhere near Forsyth Square. He tried to help Mark navigate, but finally gave up. They found parking and then walked around the entire square before they found the art gallery where the bankruptcy sale was being held. Odd place for it, Nathan thought. When they got into the gallery they found out why the sale was being held there. Some rich lawyer from Centralia had moved to Savannah and set up her own practice, then evidently suffered a stroke and became completely disabled. Terrible thing, too-she was only forty-three years old. Her medical bills had eaten up her savings, and now she was reduced to having friends organize a sale of her personal belongings to defray the cost of her care. Hence the sale was not so much a bankruptcy sale as a distress sale, intended to help her liquidate her assets to pay her bills.

Learning all this from a flyer that was handed out at the gallery door, Nathan at first thought of leaving. He figured the items on sale would be too pricey for him. He started looking around, though, and liked what he saw. Evidently she collected a good deal of very nice print art. He decided to look around, just for the heck of it, and told himself he would leave after an hour or so at the most. What he saw in the gallery was a very nice collection of art by women artists. Paintings, photographs and print art by a good number of well-known and lesser-known women artists filled the walls of two rooms in the gallery. As Nathan looked around, he found himself drawn further into the exhibit, and found he was waking up a bit as he looked at the art on the walls. It was very good art.

When he entered the second room he was struck immediately by the sight of one piece on the far wall in the room: it was a piece by Käthe Kollwitz. Not just any piece, either. He walked over to the image, where several people were standing. He looked at the image. It was still in the same frame he'd seen it the first time, the previous August, when he met Grant. He felt his heart skip a beat as he looked at the image: a sad mother holding a small child. He found himself seeing Grant in flashes as he looked at the image. He recovered a bit after looking at the image. He inquired about the price: eight hundred dollars. He borrowed a credit card from Mark, and put half on Mark's card and the other half on his own. He had no idea why he was buying it, he had no idea what he was going to do with it, and he had no idea how he was going to pay for it. He was very certain, however, that he had to buy it.

Chapter Twenty-Two

The winter was warmer than usual, but very wet. You could usually count on January and February to be pretty dry in the South, but this year was an exception. No one except the newly transplanted Yankees noticed much when it rained, as it usually did, around Christmas. But the relentlessness of the rain in the months that followed began to wear on people, making Centralia a gloomy, quiet place.

None of this helped Grant's mood in the least. He had become a recluse. He worked hard to get his head above water, to recover the confidence his clients had lost. He worked hard to continue dealing with the bank, incredulous at every point when he had to deal with some idiotic functionary grilling him about some detail of the robbery's fallout—this or that stolen credit card number or client's signature showing up somewhere in some new incidence of fraud. Grant found it difficult to believe how easily it seemed that the thieves who stole his sales records were able to renegotiate the stolen information, despite the fact that it had already been reported and re-reported. He sympathized with his clients' frustration, and he didn't blame them anymore when they called him up and vented at him over the phone—always over the phone, never, of course, in person—because he, himself, could not believe how willing the bank and the credit card companies were to keep making the same mistakes and let the same information be used for illicit purposes. He received calls from the bank or this or that credit card company several times a week, essentially suggesting that he was somehow involved in the identity theft. It appeared to him the people in charge were spending much more time investigating him as a possible ringleader than they were trying to keep the crooks from doing any more harm.

In the meantime he kept cutting frames and mats, managing somehow to keep the little shop going. He read or listened to music at night, went out once in a while for a walk through the neighborhood, and once in a great long while he treated himself to a cheap meal out. His neighbors at the diner made attempts to befriend him, all the more so when it became evident that he had moved into the back of his own shop. Mike Kallos, the owner of the diner, was a good man, and he felt compassion for what Grant was going through. He did his best to strike a balance between being a friendly neighbor and a respectful one. It was hard for Grant to accept Kallos' kindness, but he did, from time to time, allow himself to be treated to a discount on the diner's food.

It occurred to Grant that he had never been in the diner prior to his recovery from the attack. This made him a little ashamed. Kallos was good to him, clearly kept an eye out for him, and he had never paid any attention to his neighbors before he almost got killed. It was easy to be ashamed of himself. Maybe the attacker had done him a favor by making him wake up to the world around him. He wasn't aware, before the attack, of being a bad person, a person who needed to mend his ways. He certainly didn't think he deserved the attack. But he could not deny that since he'd begun to get back on his feet, he was forced to see the world in a new way, that he was obliged to face the folly of the world around him and his own humility before the world's goodness.

On a cold, rainy Sunday morning in January morning Grant heard some rustling around the back of his store. He'd just woken up and was making breakfast of grits, per his usual routine, on a hotplate he'd bought at Target. He heard some odd noises outside the back of the building, and started to panic. At first he thought it was someone trying to break in the back of the store. He wasn't sure he could face an intruder, and he thought about calling the police. He listened intently, trying to hear for more sounds. He didn't catch anything and continued tending to his breakfast—real grits require being tended, adding butter and milk, stirring, making sure the heat isn't too high. He tried to convince himself it was nothing, or if it was anything, maybe it was a gust of wind knocking something over.

He heard another sound, as of something being riffled through. He started at the sound, not knowing what to do. There were no windows at the back of the store, so there was no way of his checking on what was happening short of going to the back, going out the back door, which was solid metal, and having a look around. Out back there was a small overhang, not quite a back porch, but a small area covered by a corrugated tin roof. He used it to store boxes when the back supply room filled up. At the time of the noise there were a few boxes out there, nothing more. The thought occurred to him that it might be a rat or a possum. Or it might be a homeless person rummaging around for something to use somehow.

Grant thought about it for awhile, trying to decide what to do: call the police or check for himself. He realized that the memory of his attack was affecting his behavior. He was scared, and he didn't know what to do. He decided at last that he needed to do something. If he called the police and it was nothing, and if the police came to check and found nothing, he'd look like an idiot or, worse, like a scared-y cat. He thought to himself that if he didn't go out there and check for himself, he would be giving up something else, he would be allowing the attack to take something else from him. So far it had claimed his apartment, some of his clients, virtually all of his social life, and certainly his peace of mind. He decided it was time to stop, time to not let the attack take any more from him.

He thought he might need a weapon, so he looked around for something he could use to defend himself. Nothing really presented itself immediately. He did not own a gun. The biggest knife he had was a butcher knife, so he took that, not being really sure it would help him in the event of an attack. He went back through the supply room, and he unbolted the back door, then turned the deadbolt lock, then opened the door. He looked outside. He could see it was raining. He could see the dumpster out in the rain. There was no one there. He waited a bit to see if anyone appeared. Maybe someone was in the dumpster. He waited. Nothing. Then he went out the back door. He was wearing jeans and a t-shirt, but no shoes. It was cold, and the rain was constant, light but relentless winter rain.

He looked around the little covered area right outside his back door, and saw nothing extraordinary. A few small boxes, piled together on the left side of the back door, up against a corrugated metal wall. The boxes were stacked, but they did appear to be not as neatly stacked as he had remembered. He didn't know why he remembered them as being any differently stacked than he now found them, but he did remember. He looked around the rest of the little enclosed area, and saw nothing. No mess, no indication a bum had crawled in there and used it as a shelter or riffled through anything, because there wasn't anything other than the boxes, all of them empty, to riffle through.

He went outside the little back porch area and looked around. Nothing. Just his truck, parked up next to the dumpster, which was very full. He thought to himself what a drag it would be for the garbage collectors to come and empty the dumpster after all the rain. He stopped a minute to listen to the rain. It actually felt good to be outside for a minute, listening to the rain but not standing in it. He thought to himself that he couldn't remember when it hadn't been raining most of the time. He stood there in the early morning wet, listening to the rain, and listened.

The diner was open, so maybe the noise he heard had something to do with food service. He usually didn't hear much noise coming from the diner, as it was far enough away from him so that there didn't tend to be a reason for him to hear what was going on there. Maybe someone had moved something, he thought. He was less nervous now. He was less scared he might have to deal with someone belligerent, someone who might want to attack him. He thought to himself, in the middle of this little bit of calm, what if the guy who attacked me decides to come back? What if he's watching me, waiting for another opportunity? He thought about stories he'd heard about stores being robbed more than once. Banks, convenience stores, liquor stores, those were the kinds of places that you heard about in the news. But a framing shop? He couldn't remember hearing about a framing shop that got repeatedly hit by robbers. But then again, he thought, maybe they don't tell you all about all that stuff, maybe the chamber of commerce or somebody gets to the news people and tells them, don't print this or that, it's okay to print that. Don't print stories that involve white people getting hurt, maybe that's the rule. You can say what you want about black people doing each other, but if someone gets hurt and he's white, or she's white, keep a lid on it, because it's bad for business. Everybody expects black people to be killing each other, so it's no shock, he thought, and you can't convince people there is no crime at all, so you have to report something. So, he thought, there could be all kinds of stories we never hear.

In this way he convinced himself he wasn't that calm any more, and felt himself getting nervous again, felt his stomach churning, felt the cold a bit more, found himself more aware how much he hated the rain. But still he stood there, in the rain, which seemed to be feeding from some really well-stocked source of water, relentless and constant, not bearing down, but coming down at a constant rate, as if it were fake rain, movie rain that worked a bit too well and wouldn't stop until someone turned it off somewhere right out of view.

Grant had no idea how long he'd been standing there, going through all these thoughts in his mind, when he saw the boxes next to the door begin to move a bit, rustle just a bit, and the hairs on the back of his neck stood up, and he lost his breath, and felt his heart begin to pound. He knew it couldn't be a person, because the pile of boxes was too small. He was scared anyway, because he'd just spent the past several minutes scaring himself. He didn't move because the thought didn't occur to him to move. He thought, It's a rat or something, I guess, and tried to make himself breathe.

Then he saw it: a small calico cat appeared from under the boxes, slinking out, looking around. It didn't seem to see him. It was a pretty cat, mostly dark brown tortoiseshell, patches of white, black and orange here and there. He thought, it's a stray kitten, that's what it is. Then it saw him, stood stock still as it found him, and then it growled at him. He was taken aback by the cat's growling, and a bit offended. "Who do you think you're growling at, you little freeloader?" he asked the cat, still aware his own hackles were up. He was relieved, though, to see it was only a cat. He stood and watched it for a minute. They seemed to be in a standoff. The cat didn't move and neither did he. He realized he was still holding the butcher knife, and he felt ridiculous. He tried to figure out whether it was a boy or a girl cat. He remembered that male calicos are very rare, usually dying before they get any size at all. He couldn't remember why that was supposed to be true, only that it was. So, he thought, it's probably a she. She, if that was what the cat was, looked to be fairly young, but probably a wild cat, probably lived on the street since her mother kicked her out. She looked very scared, too scared to move, scared enough to try to sound fierce.

After looking at the motionless, growling cat for awhile, Grant thought, this is stupid, I have to get ready to open the shop. He also thought, Shit! My grits! He hurried back inside, immediately smelling burning food. So, he'd ruined breakfast listening to the rain and looking at that stupid cat, and his mind filled with recriminations and a list of what was wrong with his life: living in the back room of his shop, eking out a living, huddled in this very small corner of the world, always scared, even when he wasn't aware he was scared, and seduced by a scared cat into burning his breakfast. Stupid life, stupid town, stupid robber, stupid cat, stupid grits, stupid Grant.

After he ate what he could from the burned grits, he sulked for awhile. He thought about not opening the shop. It was raining and it was a Sunday. Why bother to open up? He knew he would open, but he had to think about not opening. How long had it been since he'd taken the day off? He couldn't remember. How long would he keep on doing what he was doing? He had no idea. What was it doing to him to be working every day, staying inside that fucking shop, never going anywhere? He was becoming like the Unabomber, holed up, not having any normal contact with anyone, getting more and more peculiar every day. He didn't think he could continue like this much longer.

A bit later he decided to take out the trash. He hated to go outside, thinking about how cold and uncomfortable the rain would feel. Stop whining, he told himself. Just go ahead and get on with the day and stop crying about everything. He bagged up his trash and went out back again. It was still raining. He made a dash for the dumpster and threw the trash in, then raced back to the back entrance of the store. Just before he went through the door, he heard a sound: it was a mewling kitten. Great, he thought, I have a mother cat and her babies on my hands. Probably all sick eaten up with worms and ready to die. He went back in and tried to forget about it.

He found that he couldn't forget about it. It was cold outside, and it was raining. He thought more about the cat, as he was getting ready to open the store. He thought that maybe the cat's kitten, or kittens, were cold. He couldn't let go of the thought. It began to really bother him. He looked through the refrigerator. He found some sliced turkey. He put it in a bowl and put the bowl outside the back door. The cat probably won't get it, he thought. This is stupid. I'm probably attracting rats. Then he thought, well, maybe after the rat eats the turkey, the cat will kill the rat, so maybe it'll all work out. He went back inside. He still thought about the cat and its kittens. I guess the cat must really be a she, he thought. Like almost all the other calicos, he thought. He continued to think about the cat and her kitten. He couldn't stop. Finally he found a good, dry box, and took a couple of old wool sweaters, and put them in the box, and turned the box on its side. On its side it made a good nesting box, and it was thick, waxed cardboard, so it would hold up well outside. He went back outside, checking carefully before he did to make sure he didn't scare the mama cat, in case she was around. He didn't think she would be, in all likelihood. He thought she was probably either looking for food, if she hadn't discovered the turkey in the bowl, or she was with her kitten, or kittens, and keeping it/them warm. He went outside. He didn't see the cat. He looked for a place that was dry, out of the wind, to place the box. He found a place that was well-sheltered and placed the box, trying to make it seem as appealing as he could think a mama cat would want it to be. It was out of the wind, it had a good view of the back door, and a decent view of the area outside. He left the box and went back inside.

Grant went about his business, a little relieved, and opened the shop. Surprisingly a few people came in not long after he opened up. He felt tired of working, but he pushed past it. he had plenty of work to do, so he didn't have to be very attentive to the people who came in to browse. He looked at his paperwork, looked at the list of things he had to get done, the frames he needed to finish. He couldn't believe how much work he had. It made him panic a bit. There was no end to it. It was as if he was in some kind of dream that he couldn't wake up from. He was always working, always spending every day doing the same things over and over. He had wanted to own his own business, and he'd gotten it, and here he was, and it made him ache to think about it.

The day went by very much as he'd expected. He went out back a time or two, to check and see if the cat had eaten the food he'd left. The first time he went out, the food looked unchanged. The second time, the food was all gone. He thought about putting out some water. He knew it was bad to give cats cow's milk. He went through his day without thinking much about what he was doing. He thought more about the cat than about anything else. He wondered how many kittens there were. He wondered if the mother cat would like the box he'd fixed up. He wondered if there were other cats, or maybe dogs, in the area that might try to harm the cat and its—her kittens. Why did he think about the cat? He didn't know. It was better than thinking about anything else at the moment, he supposed.

He closed the store that evening and went to the grocery store. He got food for himself, and he got a few cans of food for the cat. He thought the cat will probably be gone tomorrow, she probably won't like it that I found her out, and that'll probably be that. But anyway, he got some food.

By the end of the week the cat was appearing when he opened the back door. The weather got drier and milder, and that helped. He didn't see the kittens or hear them. The cat wasn't friendly, but she did appear when he went through the door. A week later he saw the cat jumping out of the box he'd fixed up. He smiled at the thought that she was poking around the box. He thought about the things people say about curiosity and cats. It didn't occur to him at first to think she'd made her nest there, in the box. He just let things lie, and went on about his business. It got so that he looked for the cat when he went out the back door. He experimented with different kinds of food. She ate everything he put out there. He thought he might try dry food, because it was cheaper and kept better. He tried designer dry cat foods, but she didn't seem to care too much for them. He found she liked a certain brand of cheap dry food the best.

He didn't see a kitten until the beginning of the third week after he'd first seen the cat. It was late January, and it got cold again. He heard mewling one night out the back, and he went to look and see what the cat was mewling about. He went outside and looked around but couldn't see any cat. He thought to look down in the box, and saw three fuzzy little kittens: an orange tabby, a black and white, and a tortoiseshell. The mother cat didn't appear to be around at all. He wondered what he should do. He put his hands in the box to pet the cats, and they hissed and spat at him.

He stayed outside awhile and waited to see if the mother cat would show up. He had nothing better to do. He wondered why he was worrying about any of it. He thought, they're really not my cats, anyway, they're just strays, there must be a million or so of them all over this city alone, what makes me think I'm doing anything at all by worrying about these stupid kittens? Then he saw the mother. She was limping along, badly hurt. She'd gotten in some kind of trouble. He tried not to startle her as she limped back to her nest. He had no idea what could have happened to her, but she looked bad. She had a big wound on her back and hip. She managed to drag into the box he'd rigged up for her.

He was a nervous wreck. He didn't know what to do. He thought he had to get her to a veterinarian somehow, but he knew she was too wild to allow him to pick her up. He had no idea what to do.

He went back inside and looked for a phone book, found a vet clinic in the area that stayed open in the evenings. He took a towel and put it over the box opening, and carefully lifted the box up, slowly walking it to the truck. He heard mewling sounds inside, but nothing that sounded as though it was coming from the mama cat. He thought to himself, she's too badly wounded. If she were at all able, she'd be trying to get away. She must be about to die. He felt a bit dizzy from the stress of trying to keep the box from jiggling while he got it to the truck. He tried not to breathe too deeply. He didn't know why that was important, but it seemed to matter. He got the truck door open, carefully put the box inside, open side facing the seat. The kittens were mewling piteously. He thought the mama cat must be dead already. At least he would be able to get some help for the kittens.

He drove to the vet clinic. It took him about twenty minutes to find the place. It was in a part of town he didn't know all that well, near one of the universities. He got the box out of the truck and took it inside. It then occurred to him he should have called ahead and let the people at the clinic know he was coming. He hadn't done that. Instead he'd just gotten the address, and then gone. If he'd called ahead they might be waiting for him, ready to try to patch the mama cat back together, if she was still alive. It was a stupid mistake. Why was he so stupid? Working all the time, not knowing what else to do. The store had made him stupid. Doing nothing but cut frames and ring sales had made him stupid. Wonder if it's reversible, he asked himself. Am I permanently stupid or can I recover, he asked himself.

There were a few other people in the clinic. It looked like a clean enough place. It had obviously been around for awhile. The people behind the counter talked to the other customers as if they all knew each other very well. Hey, Mrs. Anderson, how's Dobbin? Thanks for waiting, Mr. Jones, Daisy will be right out. Leg's doing pretty well. Grant felt very out of place here. He didn't know why he'd bothered. The cats meant nothing to him. He blushed when he thought that to himself. The kittens were still mewling. He didn't look inside the box. He just told the folks at the counter why he was there. The other customers started asking him questions. He wished they would stop. He didn't feel comfortable talking with them. He wondered if he'd locked the shop. He was sure he hadn't turned on the burglar alarm. How could he go off like that and leave the alarm off? He'd never done that before. Well, he was here now, and he guessed there was just nothing he could do. He could leave the cats in the box and just say, Good luck!, but then there were all these people, really not that many, two behind the counter, three customers, but they'd know if he just left the box and ran. What if he saw one of them again? What if they came into the shop or saw him at the grocery store? Centralia turns into a small town when you don't want it to be, he thought, and tried to control his panic.

It seemed as though an hour passed before anyone came out to get the cats. A large young black guy with a sweet expression and a lisp came out and said, "Mr Barker?" and ushered him into a room. Grant was sure the mama cat was dead. The young black man was named Twan, or that's the way his name sounded, at least. He was very nice. He listened to what Grant told him about the mama cat and the kittens. The young man looked inside the box. "She's still breathing," the young black man said, "but she looks pretty bad." The young black man disappeared for only a few minutes, but it seemed like forever, seemed like way too long to be leaving a wounded cat like this, Grant thought they probably weren't too interested in this particular set of cats, because Grant wasn't a regular customer. He thought to himself, If I came here with my cat or my dog, they'd know me and they'd treat the poor cat like she mattered. Then he thought, I guess they probably get a lot of people dumping their animals here, since they're open late or whatever. Whatever: he thought to himself, I never say *whatever* to myself, like that, like some kid trying to sound hip. Why did I think that?

"You look pretty torn up yourself," said Twan or Toine or whatever his name was, *whatever*, thought Grant.

"Me?" he asked. "No, I'm okay." He lied. He was not okay. He felt very strange. He felt as though he was doing windowpane. Everything looked and seemed clear and vivid, and yet odd, strange, alien. Maybe it was the light. I hate overhead lighting, he said to himself. Makes everything look sick. How do they tell when something's sick here, with sick lighting like that, he thought to himself. He thought, am I saying these things out loud, or if I'm not, why is this guy looking at me so funny?

Eventually a veterinarian came in. A very small, very preppy-looking woman. She looks out of place, Grant thought to himself. She looks like a schoolteacher, first graders, not like a night-shift veterinarian. She was very nice. She looked that the cats in the box, and she said, "well, it was very nice of you to bring them in, I think we're going to have to see what we can do with the mother. She's breathing, but just barely. It would be a miracle for her to make it through."

Grant was surprised at how frankly pessimistic she was. She looked like the kind of person who chirped when she spoke, like one of those awful straight women who talk in high, whiny nasal voices like they're begging to be cut some slack. She didn't sound that way. She sounded hard-nosed, really. "What do you think happened to her?" asked Grant. "What about the kittens?"

"Hard to say," she answered. "Dogs, probably. It's pretty remarkable she made it back to her babies. And the kittens? We'll put them up for adoption, assuming they check out okay, and hope somebody takes them. Thanks again for bringing them in," she said. "Not everybody would have."

With that the vet and the young black guy took the box. And left the room. On the way out the vet asked Grant if he wanted the towels and the sweaters inside the box back. He said no. He watched them take the box with them. He felt oddly as if he should be going with it. He felt a pang of something, pain of some kind, throbbing in his head, sick stomach, as they left him alone. He didn't understand why he felt so bad. It was out of his hands. He'd done what he could. It was more than most other people would have done. More than some people would have done, at any rate. The vet said so herself. He felt a sense of panic, standing in the exam room by himself. There was nothing to panic, he thought. He was done.

After some time passed the nice young black man came back into the examination room, where Grant was still waiting. The young man sensed that Grant was upset, quietly fearing that he might also be one of the many types of wackos that tended to show up on the evening shift. For an instant it occurred to Toine, the young black man, that the mother cat might have been hurt by Grant himself. Maybe Grant had gotten frustrated with the cat for some reason, maybe just for having shown up with kittens. Maybe he, Grant, had tried to kill her. Failing to go through with it for any of a number of reasons, maybe he felt remorse and so brought her in.

Toine tried to see if he could ferret out some information, asking, "So how long have you had her?"

"Who?" asked Grant, not knowing why he couldn't leave the exam room. Knowing, however, that just at that moment, he couldn't.

"The mother cat," said Toine. Grant looked back at him dumbly, not understanding.

"She isn't my cat," said Grant. "She's a stray. I started feeding her a few weeks ago," he said. "Then she showed up hurt today. She crawled into the box I set up for her and her kittens, and I just took a chance and brought her in."

"You say she was a stray?" asked Toine. "And she let you pick up the box with her and her kittens in it?" Toine was growing more suspicious. What wild mother cat, even a hurt one, would let a human being pick her up in a box and take her somewhere? It was his cat, surely, or she wouldn't have let him do that. His story didn't add up.

"I don't know what to tell you," said Grant. "I didn't think she'd stand for it, either. Except she really looked hurt. You guys have any idea what got her?"

Toine was trying to evaluate this guy. Was he a monster or was he telling the truth? There are so many people who look perfectly normal and who torture animals, who could be sure? Toine said: "We don't know yet. Dr. Starnes is dealing with the mama cat, and we got somebody trying to look after the kittens."

It was helping Grant to talk with someone about all this. It was helping him to feel more settled, more connected. The room felt less weird to him now. He was glad to be talking to this guy. He could tell there was something bothering the young man. Grant said,

"You're looking at me like you think I'm crazy or something?" It was as much a declaration as a question.

Caught off-guard by such an honest question, Toine answered honestly: "It just doesn't make sense that a feral mother cat would allow you to get that near her, even if you had been feeding her a few weeks, and even if she was hurt. It doesn't usually happen that way," he said. He looked for something in Grant's reaction that would give him away. He saw someone who looked confused, tired. Someone who looked hurt.

"I don't know much about cats," said Grant, "I never had one. Like I said, this really isn't my cat. I found her sleeping in a pile of boxes behind my store, and it was cold, so I thought I'd leave her some food. She ate it, so I kept leaving it. She hasn't gotten really friendly, I mean, before she got hurt, but she got to where she didn't run away when she saw me putting out food."

"What about the kittens," asked Toine. "How did you know she had kittens?"

"One day I heard a little mew," said Grant. "I heard it and it didn't sound like it could be the sound she would make. Then I saw her come back to the pile of boxes from outside, like she was hurrying. Then I heard more mewing, and then it stopped. So I figured she had to have babies," he said.

"And that's when you put up the box with the warm things inside, for a nest?" asked Toine.

"That's right," said Grant. "I mean, it's cold outside, at least some days it is. I thought about trying to get her to bring her kittens into the store, but I didn't think she'd go for that. So I thought if I could at least get her a better warm place, she might put her babies there, and they'd all be better off. So I found a box that looked really sturdy, put some old clothes in it and set it in a place outside that was covered, out of the wind, and easy for her to get in and out of." Grant was finding that he had to struggle a bit to talk. He had to think hard about what he was going to say before he said it. Why is that?, he asked himself. Why is it such an effort to talk with someone like this?

Toine thought about what he was hearing. He was trying to decide whether or not to alert the veterinarian that they might be dealing with an animal abuser. He wasn't at all sure about this guy. Something isn't right with him, Toine thought. "So, when did you find the mama cat was hurt?" he asked. He was trying to be the best detective he could, trying to see if he could ask one really good question that would make Grant spill his guts and confess to trying to kill the mama cat and then realizing what he'd done.

"It was after I'd closed the shop," said Grant. "I was about to make some dinner, and I heard one of the kittens mewing," he said. "So I went outside and looked in the box, and saw the mama wasn't there. It was getting cold, the sun had already gone down, and I was afraid to leave the babies. After awhile the mama cat showed up, looked all beat up, dragged herself into the box. And I pretty much freaked out a few minutes, trying to decide what to do. So I looked you all up in the phone book, saw you were close, and then just put a towel over the front of the box, put her in my truck and got here as quick as I could."

Toine paused over one detail: Grant said he was in his shop, then closed it, then started cooking dinner. Why would he cook dinner in his shop? Why not go home and cook?

Toine asked: "Do you usually eat dinner at your store?"

Grant blushed, not knowing why he was blushing. He answered, "I live there." He felt a pang of shame. He didn't know why he should, but he did. The shame registered involuntarily on his face.

Toine was surprised again. He asked, "You *live* in your shop? Why do you do that?"

"Because," said Grant, "I lost my apartment. A few months back. I couldn't afford it, so I moved into my shop." He could read the disbelief in Toine's face. It dawned on Grant why the young man was taking time to talk with him. The thought made him smile, and at the same time he felt as though he might start crying at any moment.

Realizing what Toine thought, Grant had another realization: that everything about the cat, her kittens, and talking to this skeptical young man was urging him to see how badly wounded he was still from the attack. He'd tried to put his head down and deal with it, push through it and keep going, keep the business going, just keep on, but he hadn't faced it, hadn't really dealt with the fact that someone had nearly beaten him to death over a pile of crap. And that then, after that, he hadn't really dealt with the fact that the bank had begun treating him like the criminal, and that some— thankfully, only some—of his customers had blamed him and sought revenge, as well. It finally hit him, all of it. He saw the mama cat in his mind's eye, bloody and wet. He smelled her blood, heard her kittens mewling weakly, and he broke down and cried like a baby.

The mama cat pulled through. Two of her babies survived: the orange male and the calico. The little black kitten succumbed to ineuritis. Grant came back over the next week, each day, looking in on the mama cat. He got to know the folks in the vet clinic. He decided he would close the store one day a week, Mondays, so he could have a day off. The mama cat took to him, let him scratch her head through the cage. She was bandaged up with a broken hip. The vet surmised she'd either gotten hit by a car or maybe someone, a kid maybe, had tried to beat her to death. It was remarkable to see her respond to treatment. Grant decided he would keep her and her babies. He named her Hope. The orange tomcat he named Puff Daddy, for the way he puffed up and pranced. The little calico was Butterscotch, for the patches of color in her fur.

Chapter Twenty- Three

Nathan got home that Sunday thinking about getting ready for the show. He was so intent on being ready, he actually began to pack that very evening, even though he wasn't scheduled to leave until Tuesday. Ordinarily he would throw things together sometime during the day on Tuesday, then end up leaving sometime between late afternoon and midnight, or thereabouts. It was a ridiculous ritual he observed in getting ready to do the Centralia show, part passive resistance to the idea of the long drive and the often fruitless effort expended at setting up, part scatterbrained uncertainty about what to take with him to make the show a success. The public is so fickle, he often thought, I never will understand why the things that sell, sell.

The truth is, it wasn't the show he was focused on. It was seeing Grant. Finding the Kollwitz piece reminded him of Grant, and made him think, after not thinking about him at all, that it was, somehow, the most important thing he could think of to try and find a way to see him again, to talk with him again. Talk about what? He didn't know. And then what? He didn't know that, either. It was the oddest sensation he'd ever had, looking at the woodcut on the wall of the gallery in Savannah. He looked at the woodcut, and saw the image clearly, and in his mind's eye he saw Grant, as he'd first seen him, looking tall and palpation-inducingly handsome and then, on closer inspection, slightly nuts, which was even better. It was as if the time that had intervened between his first seeing Grant and his seeing him again in his mind's eye was no time at all, the time of a single breath. He knew only that he needed to see him again, that he needed to take the woodcut with him and then find Grant and then, then he'd find out what he next needed to do.

There had been so many times in Nathan's life when he felt he ought to do something but didn't, he couldn't count them. I don't mean the kind of ought that involves being beholden to someone or something. I mean the kind of ought that presents itself in a moment, a particular moment, and says, This is what needs doing now. In this little span of time, you could do X or you could not do it, and if you choose X, it will change your life. If you don't choose X, the life that comes afterwards will merely be the life that doesn't include the consequences, the harvest, that would come from X. And, like most people, I suppose, Nathan ignored most of those moments, rare as they were, regarding them as some kind of anomaly, some kind of false lead that didn't really amount to anything and that would never mean anything if he just went about his business and ignored them. Except, and maybe here again Nathan was like most people, he didn't really believe that ignoring the call that came at these critical moments was a good choice. He always thought it was a failure, a test that had been presented to him and that he had, once again, failed by not rising to the occasion. The occasion really consisted in heeding the voice to attend to the gravity of choosing, at a particular moment, something he intuitively knew was important to choose.

And so, the moment in the gallery when he saw the woodcut was yet another of those moments. He'd had perhaps his share of them, and had ignored almost all of them. And maybe it was the practice of ignoring all those moments before that had made him ready to choose, at this one single point, to answer the call to trust and choose something that didn't make much sense but that seemed, from some very obscure place, to be every bit as important as choosing the right way out of a burning building.

Nathan hadn't talked with Grant since that last Sunday at the show in August. It was now February. He hadn't seen Grant at the show since then, now that he thought about it.

Chapter Twenty- Four

Nathan pulled into the lot at the old Centralia exhibition center. He had driven all night to get there. Ever the procrastinator, he'd been packing the night before when Antonioni's "Blow-Up" came on TNT around midnight. He'd seen the movie any number of times, but he had to stop to watch it. He was glad he did, because he was impressed again with how fresh and new the movie seemed, how much a work of art that presented visually the point where modernism began to morph into postmodernism. Seeing the film made him want to go back and read Borges's story, but he knew after the movie ended he still needed to finish packing and drive to Centralia.

As a result of stopping to watch the movie, Nathan didn't get out of Charleston until almost three in the morning. Driving all night actually made the trip easier, as there was so little traffic and, luckily, a nearly full moon. Buoyed anew by the pleasant experience of seeing one of his favorite movies, he made the trip in a little under five hours. This meant he'd averaged over seventy miles an hour for the whole trip. He didn't feel at all worn out when he pulled into the Centralia fairgrounds. In fact, he felt pretty good. This was mostly because during the long car trip he'd amused himself by imagining himself as a gay version of David Hemmings' character from the movie—especially the parts about looking good in a pair of white slacks that never seemed to get dirty not matter what he did, being young, beautiful and bored with how beautiful everything was, and gadding about town in a sporty Rolls convertible.

About the time he got to Columbia, the sun started to come up. It was good to be awake at that time of day. It was a beautiful September morning, crystal clear and no humidity to speak of. Nathan knew he probably wouldn't make it through the morning without running out of energy, and when he did, he'd almost certainly regret staying up all night. He knew he would crash that evening as soon as he got to Alice and Becky's house, but that only made him look forward to the deliciousness of the sleep he would get that night. He had no great expectations from the show, but it didn't bother him. He was doing what he did, and that was all that mattered. By the time he got to the Centralia fairgrounds, the sun was high in the sky. The vendors were all crowding to get set up, already bickering with each other, trying to find bargains in each others' offerings, already complaining about how lousy the show was going to be. Like many of these people, Nathan was struggling to make ends meet. One small financial disaster, and his life would take months, maybe years, to recover. All it would take would be for his van to break down or his insurance premiums to go up a bit—just a bit—or one really bad show, and he'd be left fighting a long, long time just to get back to the position of uncertainty he'd occupied before the unfortunate event had struck. Nathan knew this. He also knew his fellow vendors knew it, of course; he knew the realization of their uncertainty was the thing that bound most of them together. This uncertainty made many of them greedy, irascible and generally unpleasant. None of this bothered Nathan—he had lived so long without a safety net, he had come to have a sort of pride in living that way. We're like the hobos in the thirties, he thought to himself, those of us who have abandoned any hope of making a straight living. He was glad for who he was and who he was with.

Nathan was glad to see one of his neighbors at the show this month: Shauntavius Washington, a woman who set up in the booth across from him. She was a wonderful woman of a certain age from Waycross, Georgia. She was also black, and this made her a rarity at the show. She became a dealer at the end of a long personal crisis that began with her bailing from life as an accountant for a big insurance company in Jacksonville and ending up as a porcelain dealer. What finally caused her to quit her stable, well-paying job was a single incident: one day she walked into her boss's office and found him, drunk in the middle of the day, urinating into the potted ficus tree in his office. She figured if she had to spend the rest of her life working for a man who peed in his own office, there was something seriously wrong with how life worked. After she was delivered the hateful vision of her boss killing a potted plant, Shauntavius spent some time thinking things over. Finally she decided she needed to take some time off to clear her head, and she ended up making an impromptu visit to Pasaquan, St. EOM's naïve masterpiece in Buena Vista, Georgia. Touring the odd collection of statues, thinking about what had driven the man who made them, Shauntavius decided the straight job world was not for her. Eventually, after looking at several possibilities, she decided to turn her hobby, buying and selling railroad porcelain, into a living. Under this new regime of self employment, Shauntavius made a modest income, she got to travel, she didn't have to endure inappropriate behavior from her supervisor, she met some interesting people, and she had fun.

The very first show she did at Centralia, Shauntavius set up opposite Nathan. As a new dealer, she was very lucky to get a booth
inside. Building Two was a preferred location, and being near—but
not right next to—the exit was even better. Very nervous about being a black woman vendor in a sea of very white faces, she didn't
know what to think at first when she saw Nathan's wares. The only
thing that helped her to connect with the oddity of Nathan's merchandise was the fact that, having lived most her life in a small
south Georgia town, she was used to people being peculiar—so
used to it, in fact, that she barely had a sense of the possibility of
people acting odd—especially white people. When she saw Nathan's booth for the first time, he had on display a child's baton
twirling outfit (complete with baton), a giant banner covered in
shiny spangles that read "Teen Lickers," some of the ugliest lamps
she'd ever seen in her life, a bunch of jewelry, small pieces of art
glass, a few very bad oil paintings and some silver—all of it very
old-fashioned and mostly very ugly. She had no idea how he could
make a living selling stuff like that. Upon reflection, she figured
that if he could make a living, so could she, and so she took heart
from the unattractiveness of his stock. She figured that, as ugly as
Nathan's stuff was, people would look at her stuff and think they'd
wandered into the Taj Mahal.

On the occasion of Shauntavius's first show, Nathan introduced
himself like a gentleman while she was getting settled in. He also
introduced her to other vendors close by whom he obviously knew
fairly well. He offered his services as a neighbor, and he generally
comported himself well. What cemented their connection was when
he began to play background music on a boombox. For one thing,
so far it had not occurred to Shauntavius to play music like that at a

show—just like you would in a real store. What really floored her was his choice of music: almost nothing but black music, and mostly the blues, the real article. When she first heard him play Big Mama Thornton's rendition of "Hound Dog," it brought back memories of her youth, and she had to ask him about his choice of music. From there they established that they were about the same age and had many shared and interestingly contrasted experiences of living in the American South. They became good friends, and even began a ritual of exchanging letters and postcards.

Shauntavius didn't do the Centralia show every month. Her mother, who had diabetes, had grown very ill, and so some months Shauntavius had to stay in Waycross and look after her. Knowing this, Nathan was glad to see Shauntavius at the September show, because it meant either that things had lightened up with her mother or that she had finally gotten one of her sisters to take on some of the responsibility of nursing. He didn't press the issue with Shauntavius, whom he nicknamed Pearl ("Shauntavius takes more breath than I go, lady, so from now on between us your name is Pearl. As in 'black Pearl, pretty little girl,' and so forth" he'd announced one day, and that had been that). Once he got settled in, and offered his greetings to Pearl, Nathan decided to do some window-shopping. He didn't have much money for buying anything, but he thought it was always a good idea to follow a hunch; since he'd thought about window-shopping, and since he felt in a surprisingly good mood, for a forty-something year-old crone who'd just stayed up all night, he thought it was a sign of some sort ("A message from the God I don't believe in," as he was wont to say) that he should go browsing. Indeed sometimes, he found, the morning of the show setup was a good time to look for bargains or unacknowledged treasures.

The kinds of *objets trouvés* that might make Mrs. Tuttle grit her teeth and ball her fists for having missed. So, having arranged his booth, Nathan set out and went browsing.

Note: what does he find? Dealers who are already dreading the show, even as they're setting up. People scarred by not making enough money for months on end, wondering what they're going to do to continue. A few books full of Lynd Ward woodcuts, which he will cut up and sell as individual images. Finding himself feeling guilty about cutting up old books, finding it makes him think about Grant.

Nathan decided to do what he rarely did when he went scavenging: he decided to start with the buildings farthest away from his own and work back towards Building Two. This occurred to him mostly for the sake of variety. So far he seemed to be proceeding based on some intuitive sense of what he needed to do, and that seemed to be the best course, one he felt comfortable with. His gut told him to start far away, so off he went to Building Six. He rarely made it that far when he came to the show,

Chapter Twenty- Five

There was finally a real cold snap in early February. It actually felt reassuring to get a bit of cold weather, though few real Southerners could truthfully say they enjoyed the cold. People from colder climates took pleasure in telling locals they didn't know what winter weather was, acting as though overnight lows in the twenties constituted something like a cool spring breeze. Locals, for their part, (sometimes) silently cursed the Yankees who had the bad manners to say such things. Nathan hated the cold; he had to dig out some sweaters from a box he kept on top of his chiffarobe, gloves and a woolen hat to dress himself for the change in weather. He knew it would be colder still in Centralia. Being inland, situated just about where the piedmont met the coastal plain, Centralia tended to get the worst of the weather from all directions, so whatever it was like in the wintertime on the coast, in Centralia it was generally gloomier and more bitter and more relentlessly uncomfortable. About the only good thing Nathan could say about the cold weather was that, as long as it didn't rain, sleet or snow, the roads were generally easier to drive on when it was cold, because there tended to be fewer people out joyriding.

As much as he disliked the cold, Nathan was nonetheless eager to get to Centralia. He had a truckload of religious artifacts he'd managed to scare up in just a few days' worth of hunting. It was amazing to him how, once he set his mind to it, he was able to go about Charleston and the surrounding area and locate a pretty respectable haul of iconographic booty. As was his wont, he found himself becoming attached to the articles he was collecting for his Christmas sale. Some of the better ones he kept leaning up against the living room clutter so he could see them as he passed back and forth on his numerous trips throughout the house. It struck him, as he looked at the paintings and prints he'd bought, how singularly frozen, how preserved they looked. He began to regard the images not as simple pictures but as pieces of taxidermy. Dolorous Madonnas looking downward in what was intended to be the utmost expressions of adoration and humility; lugubrious Jesuses looking imploringly toward heaven, really giving it their all as they asked with their eyes for everything, but everything, to change utterly; here or there a saint, a Sebastian or a Teresa or a Francis, caught in an image of the full flower of their beatitude; they all seemed to Nathan to be caught like insects in amber, rendered utterly incommensurate with everyday reality, frozen hideously in their freakish perfection. As he looked at the images, Nathan wondered more and more how people could stand to look at them routinely in public places. He wondered why people looking at these images didn't routinely get sick and vomit or run screaming in terror or, barring that, at least shake their heads and say, "That poor slob, what a bad gig s/he ended up with." He had to admit, though, that thinking to collect all these pictures of holy people and assemble them into his house gave him a new understanding for the enormity of the crimes committed in the name of Christianity. Such lofty, strangely abstract principle, he thought, and such ghastly, sanguinary practice. The entire religion, he concluded, is one long nightmare of blood-feasting.

Chapter Twenty- Six

Nathan decided to stretch his legs a bit, so he asked Shauntavius, his neighbor across the aisle, to keep an eye on his booth while he went for a stroll. She agreed to keep watch, so Nathan set out to look around. It had been awhile since he'd shopped the booths in the show, and it occurred to him that since it had been awhile, he might stand a chance of finding something new and interesting. He came upon a used book dealer who had some interesting items: a first edition of Lynd Ward's *God's Man*, woodcuts intact, binding in generally good condition. The book was priced at $100.00, and Nathan talked the dealer down to $80.00. The same dealer had an interesting and rare find: a book of designs for commemorative stamps by Jean Cocteau. Nathan, who was fond of Cocteau's art, had never seen the images before, and thought the book was worth buying just because none of the images in it had ever shown up in any other books he'd seen on Cocteau. The book wasn't cheap—$125.00. Nathan felt doubtful about the purchase, but finally decided the appeal of the images and the fact that they were otherwise not catalogued was enough to warrant buying the book.

Strolling further on, Nathan found his way to a vendor who dealt in Oaxacan arts and crafts. None of what the vendor was selling was antique, but Nathan found it appealing, especially the black glazed pottery and the yarn paintings of shamans dancing around peyote flowers. Nathan ended up buying a beaded jaguar head and a yarn painting, and suddenly found himself asking, What am I going to do with this shit? It was sometimes a problem for him to justify buying things—he had to buy things to make a living, and, like most gay men, he really loved to shop. Once he allowed himself to turn on shopping mode, he entered dangerous territory, as his short outing had just proven. Time to buy? Ok! Buy what? To do what with it? Well, that part gets muddier. Maybe this or that can be sold later, but if it can't, then there's nothing wrong with enjoying it until you find a buyer.

One of Nathan's most gratifying buying excursions involved the Dollar Store. The Dollar Store or Big Lots sold mostly crap, of course, but once in awhile you'd find something really tasty there, like the Virgin Mary and Jesus night lights: plastic statues of the Holy Family designed as covers for simple plug-in night lights. At the Dollar Store they cost—a dollar! Nathan could buy twenty of them easily, then take them back to his booth, mark them up to $5.00 apiece, and sell all twenty of them well before the show was over. In fact, the public never seemed to tire of Nathan's five-dollar Blessed Virgin nightlights. They helped pay for his shopping excursions.

There was a down-side to all this, of course. He had a Loetz vase, immaculate, excellent color, that showed up in catalogs for around $700.00. He had been schlepping it around for a couple of years, priced at $350.00. No one seemed interested in it. A similar story with the Secessionist bronze book ends he had underpriced by several hundred dollars. They were fine pieces, and pretty rare. But no one would buy them, or even make an offer on them.

Chapter Twenty- Seven

It was March and Nathan came to town early to do the show and to watch over the house while Becky and Alice went on vacation to Costa Rica. Becky had told Alice only that she needed her passport and summery clothes, keeping the destination a secret. Alice tried to cajole Nathan into telling her where they were going, but Nathan kept his mouth shut. He was glad they were going to go off on a nice jaunt through lesbian paradise, and he didn't want to spoil anything. So the women left, making Nathan promise to take care of the animals, which of course he was happy to do, and telling him to enjoy himself in their house while they were gone.

Nathan felt alone in the big house after the women left. As many animals as there were, he only barely noticed them as company. Besides, the animals and he were all so used to one another that there was hardly any excitement in their being left alone in the house. So Nathan settled in pretty quickly to a routine of reading, sleeping, occasionally walking some of the more tractable dogs through the neighborhood, and even more occasionally venturing out to do a little shopping in anticipation of the Centralia show. Since it was March the weather was very changeable; some days were beautiful, cool days, with exquisite blue skies; others were windy and stormy. Nathan was to be there for three weeks, including the weekend of the show, which meant that he had had to get Missykes to agree to look after the brood of feral cats living under his house. He dreaded his return trip, because he knew it meant spending an evening or two visiting with the cranky old lady. He liked her, he just couldn't stand to be around her for very long.

So Nathan ventured out once in awhile to do some shopping. He thought more than once that he needed to look up Grant, but didn't know how to begin with him.

Nathan found his way to Grant's shop: Quick Snacks, Hairstyles, and Picture Frames. Nathan wondered how Grant stayed in business. Did anyone complain about not being able to get a haircut? Or a sandwich? He felt very nervous as he got out of his van and approached the store. It appeared to be open, so he went in. there was no one inside the store, no customers, no one at the sales counter. So he wandered through the store a bit, looking around. It was a pretty large place, with bins full of prints, display shelves full of ready-made frames of all sizes, very nicely done, and then there was the large counter in the middle of the store where the custom framing was done. The building had a skylight, and there were lots of plants in the windows, giving the place a lived-in look that suggested the current occupant had been there for awhile.

At length Nathan heard some rustling from the back of the store. Grant appeared with an empty garbage can in one hand and a plastic bag in the other. He had an intent look on his face as he prepared to put the plastic bag into the garbage can. He looked up when he noticed there was someone in the store. Then he saw it was Nathan. He gave a look of astonishment.

"Never ends, does it? You empty the trash, and it starts showing up again right away," Nathan couldn't resist the temptation to make a joke. He wondered if he was wrong to start off that way. As he saw Grant, it felt so good to see him that it hurt to look at him.

"Nathan Greenwood?" said Grant, with a look of mock surprise on his face. "Well, well. You just get out of jail?"

Nathan felt a bit of gratitude that Grant shot back with a wee bit of a barb. He's missed me, thought Nathan. He wouldn't have just said that if he hadn't missed me.

"Who's to say?" asked Nathan. "Some prisons you carry around with you. Some you have to decide to just leave on your own."

Grant had put on weight. It looked good on him. It made him look a bit older, which Nathan found both reassuring and sexy. Nathan also noticed that Grant had a new scar over his left eyebrow. At least, he couldn't remember having seen it before. There was something different about his face, too. Not dissipation. Not sickness. Depth, thought Nathan. Why depth? He didn't know. That was just the word he saw in his mind's eye when he looked at Grant and noticed the something new in his face.

Grant nodded and made a thoughtful face. He went around to the inside of the counter and put the garbage can down. Then he leaned on the counter and looked Nathan in the eyes. He stood there for a minute, just looking. Nathan could tell he was pissed. Better pissed than just blank, thought Nathan, at least for the moment, it's better. Nathan looked at Grant and couldn't help but smile a little. He was so sad he'd run away from Grant, he could hardly bear it. And he was so glad to see Grant, he didn't know how to begin to say how glad he was. He had no idea where the change had come from within himself, but something had allowed him to look through his own stupidity, his own fearfulness, and realize that he needed to cultivate something with Grant. He didn't need to run anymore. He just needed to be with Grant.

"I hid from you," said Nathan. "I was afraid you'd be another David. I didn't trust you and I was too much of a coward to try and give it a chance. I'm sorry. I was an idiot not to want to thank my lucky stars for having met you, and I can't ask enough for you to forgive me. I don't have much self-confidence, and maybe it's my own fault that I don't, but the truth is, that's what makes me fuck up. I can't bear thinking that I hurt you in any way, and I have to make it right, if you'll let me. I know you could do much better, and I know I have no right to ask this, but I want to try again to be your friend, and I want us to make love again, if you'll allow it. I want us to be close to each other, and if you'll let me, I want to try to make you happy"

Grant stood and listened to Nathan. He felt pain as he listened: around his eyes, in his throat, and in his belly. His hands balled up into fists, and he found himself feeling a rising surge of anger. He listened to Nathan, watched him, and saw the sincerity in his face. He wondered if it was an act; he wondered if Nathan, having presented himself as a garden-variety psycopath's victim, was, in fact, the real psychopath, a much more clever version, one smart enough to bide his time, accomplished enough to cultivate a pigeon until it was the pigeon who offered himself up for the killing.

After Nathan finished speaking, Grant waited a bit, mulling all of this over. He asked himself how he really felt about Nathan. More than just time had passed since they'd last seen each other, since they'd last spoken. It seemed as though they hadn't seen each other for a year or so. It seemed as though they had known each other a long, long time, then lost touch, and then, here was Nathan, smiling, seeming to ask a lot. Grant tried to control himself as he began to respond. He said: "Well, I don't know where to begin with you. Why should I want to have anything to do with you?"

Nathan stood before him, smiling faintly. He looked into Grant's green eyes and knew he was looking at the love of his life. He knew nothing mattered more to him now than being the person he needed to be for the man who was standing in front of him. He said: "I guess the question is, *do* you want to have anything to do with me?"

Grant received the question like a slap in the face. Yes, he thought without thinking it, yes. He said: "I suppose that would depend on a few things."

Nathan felt stung by what he heard. He thought he understood what would come next. He said, "I'm sorry I didn't call you. I hid from you, I'll admit it. I was an idiot, and running from you was the stupidest thing I've ever done, in a long career of doing very stupid things. Please forgive me."

Grant needed to fight. He'd been beaten up for the past several months, and he needed to hit back. Nathan was asking for it. Grant said: "You know, what pisses me off more than your not showing up for the past several months, more than your not answering your phone, more than your not giving me any indication you were any different from any other man I've met who told a good story all the way to bed and, having gotten there, just paused long enough to have a little fun, blow his load and then just head out, more than all that? You know what pisses me off more than any of that? It's how easy it is for you to just show up all contrite and ready for us to ride off into the sunset and, hey, Grant, you ready to go? Come on, Grant, let's go! That's what really pisses me off!"

Nathan wasn't smiling now. He just stood there, listening to Grant. He said, "I'm sorry, Grant. Please forgive me. I was wrong, and I hurt you, and you didn't deserve it. I'm sorry."

Grant felt his whole body aching. He was trembling. He said, "Fuck you, Nathan! Fuck you! Fuck you fucking fuck you!"

Nathan stood there, looking straight at Grant. "I'm sorry, Grant," he said. "I'm so very sorry."

Grant felt himself panting. He was gasping for air. His face burned. His eyes stung. There was no one else in the store but them. Everything was quiet. The morning light, beautiful and silver, was bouncing off the trees outside. It was cold in the store. Shafts of light broke through the skylight. Dust motes danced silently in the light, the only motion in the store besides Grant's trembling.

Nathan waited a moment, then took a step towards Grant. Seeing Grant didn't move, Nathan moved closer, not saying a word. He just looked at Grant, looked him squarely in the eye. Being this close to Grant, he could see the details of the scar above Grant's eyebrow. "What happened here?" asked Nathan, pointing to the scar.

"I got mugged," Grant responded. "I almost fucking died, Nathan," he said, finally breaking down and sobbing. "I almost died." Nathan went to him, hugged him and held him. Grant bawled his eyes out, standing there, squeezing Nathan, crying and holding on for dear life.

A few hours later there was a banging on the door of the shop. Grant and Nathan roused from their slumber. They were lying naked on the futon in the storeroom that had been Grant's sleeping quarters for the past several months. They had drifted off to sleep for a bit, so the sound of the urgent door banging woke them up with a start. Nathan kissed Grant. Nathan said, "sounds like someone wants in."

Grant nodded. "It is a week day," he said. "It might be the folks from down the street. Since the attack, they've been kind of protective." He got up, pulled on some jeans and a t-shirt, some shoes, and dragged his hand through his hair. This gave Nathan a chance to see again how beautiful he was. The ass he'd been chewing on an hour earlier now still had a rosy glow from the morning's kisses. It was a very pretty ass.

"Grant?" called Nathan as Grant headed towards the front of the store.

"Yeah? What?" said Grant, looking down at Nathan.

"You've got a really nice ass," said Nathan. "Really nice."

The banging was continuing, and there were voices.

"Thanks," said Grant. "So do you."

Nathan lay on the futon, listening as Grant made his way to the front of the store, unlocked the door, and talked with the visitor. He heard several men's voices, a bit of laughing, and listened quietly as the low hum of the voices continued in the background. He took in the smell of Grant's body on him and on the sheets and pillows. He closed his eyes and saw Grant close to him, kissing him, caressing him, sucking his dick, fucking him, being fucked by him. He felt the smoothness of Grant's skin, he smelled Grant's hair and felt it against his face, and he saw, clearly in his mind's eye, the pure, pure green of Grant's eyes looking into his.

Within a few minutes Grant reappeared. He took off his clothes again and got back into bed. As he was getting into bed, Nathan noticed Grant was becoming aroused again. He smiled and felt himself respond. He closed his eyes and took in a long deep breath as

Grant snuggled close to him. He opened his eyes again as Grant was snaking his left am under Nathan's body, pulling him in close. They twined into each other, kissed and looked at each other. They smiled, kissed, and held onto each other. "So was that an angry customer?" asked Nathan.

"No," answered Grant. "The folks from the diner down the way a bit. They saw the place was closed up and they got nervous."

Nathan thought about what was behind that statement. Grant hadn't said very much about having been mugged, as he called it. Nathan got the impression that what Grant had called "being mugged" was actually more like attempted murder. Nathan felt a pang of guilt at the thought that he hadn't been there to help see Grant through what had happened. He thought to himself how strange it was, the fact that, so many years before, he'd been involved with David, with his story of being attacked, and now, all these years later, here he was with Grant, a very different kind of person, who had suffered something not all that unlike what David had suffered. Nathan wondered to himself if, maybe, he'd been unfair to David all those years ago. But how could he think about that now? Whatever else had happened, David had, in fact, stolen him nearly blind, and there was nothing that could justify that. Grant was not that kind of person. Nathan didn't know the details of his attack, but he sensed that it must have been nothing like what had happened to David. But still, how odd that one old fairy should hook up with two men who would turn out to be the victims of violent attacks. What were the chances of that kind of thing happening?

"They sound like very good neighbors," said Nathan. "I'm glad they've been looking after you," he said, kissing Grant on the fore-head. "I hope you can forgive me for not being there."

Grant squeezed him, kissed him back, snuggled again. It seemed to Nathan that Grant was doing everything he could to get and to stay as close as he could. It felt good to be that way. Grant said, "I wish you had been there." Nathan felt a horrible sting in his eyes, a pain in his face, as he heard those words. "But that's not what happened. It wasn't your fault I got attacked. It just hap-pened."

"I'm sorry, Grant," said Nathan, "I'm so, so sorry." They talked about the attack. Grant said he wasn't over it, but he'd begun to do a bit better. He still didn't go out much, but little by little he was taking risks. He explained that somehow, the cats showing up had helped. Maybe it was having something alive to have to look after, something that had creature needs as urgent as his own, maybe that was how the cats helped. As if on cue, a fat calico cat hopped up on the futon, back arched, tail erect, drooling, purring, and kneading the blanket. "Who's this?" asked Nathan.

"Butterscotch," said Grant. "She doesn't usually appear to other people—she's pretty shy. It's quite an honor for her to present herself to you." Grant lifted the covers so that the cat could peer down inside. She poked her nose into the lifted blanket, sniffed and stared at the darkness, and then waddled down into the space be-tween Grant and Nathan. "Careful with the claws, cat," said Grant.

"Amen to that, brother," said Nathan.

Around noontime Grant and Nathan had had enough of sex and cuddling so that they decided to take a break. Nathan was con-cerned that Grant was keeping the store closed, so he suggested that he leave and let Grant get on with his day. They could meet that evening. Though they hadn't discussed it, Nathan could see that Grant was living in the back of his own store. He wondered what had led to that turn of events, but didn't ask about it. He assumed that somehow the attack had made it necessary for Grant to give up his apartment. Every detail about the attack and what it implied about their separation made Nathan ache with regret and grief. He wondered how he could have been so stupid. He wondered if he could ever be sure that Grant would forgive him for it. He hoped he would never forgive himself for it. He needed Grant's forgiveness, but couldn't think about his own.

They agreed to meet that evening at Becky and Alice's house. Nathan was going to cook him dinner. They'd have the house to themselves, and they could continue sorting things out. Nathan hoped he could take the opportunity to begin to make plans. He was hoping that Grant would trust him enough to believe in the prospect of their building a life together. Nathan was ready to begin that process right now. He was ready to make it the primary business of his life. Knowing that Grant was recovering from a vicious attack put a slant on things he hadn't anticipated. He would just have to see how things went.

They met that evening at Becky and Alice's house, as planned. They surprised each other by delaying dinner for what was their third session of lovemaking for that day. By the time they got down to eating dinner, they were both very hungry.

"You know, for an old man, you sure have a lot of energy," said Grant, chewing on a pork chop.

Nathan was very glad that Grant felt sassy enough to risk hurting an old queen's vanity. It was a very good sign. Nathan responded: "I can't account for it, myself, to be honest. I couldn't tell you when I've been this frisky. I guess your youth is rubbing off on me."

Grant was immediately struck with the fear that he might have insulted Nathan. He blurted out, "I lied about my age that night."

"What?" asked Nathan, not remembering what night Grant meant.

"That first night we were here, after dinner," said Grant. "I told you I was twenty-five or something. I'm really thirty-four." Grant blushed as he said this, looking at Nathan. Nathan looked back at him with an expression of puzzlement.

"Well, I'm really fifty," said Nathan. "I must have figured you were talking in the same code as I was at the time. What gay man above the age of twenty tells the truth about his age these days, when a man of thirty is considered a 'daddy' in the porn industry, which is, after all, the gay world's beauty standard?" *Is this the worst secret we have to get beyond?*, asked Nathan to himself. *Is life going to be, for once, kind to us?* "Well," said Nathan, "as Joe E. Brown said in 'Some Like It Hot,' I forgive you." Again, the word *forgive*. It seemed to Nathan that there was something in his meeting with Grant that was urging him, Nathan, to look for forgiveness in a number of ways.

As they finished dinner, Nathan thought to give Grant the surprise he'd been preparing. They moved to the living room, along with a herd of happily panting dogs, who promptly fell asleep around them when they settled.

"You get enough to eat?" asked Nathan.

"Yes," said Grant, "I think so. Thanks for dinner. Thanks for having me here."

"Thanks for allowing yourself to be had," said Nathan, immediately uncertain as to whether Grant would take it the wrong way. He thought to change the subject quickly. "I have a little surprise for you," he said at last.

Grant arched his eyebrows. "That would be two in one day, then," he said, keeping a deadpan look. Nathan was somewhat taken aback by the remark, but decided to let it pass. Was it the attack that had made Grant a bit edgier?

"This one is wrapped in paper, not latex," said Nathan, getting up. "I hope you'll like it."

Grant was afraid he'd hurt Nathan's feelings. Actually, he liked Nathan's dick quite a lot. It was not the biggest dick in the world, but it was pretty, of a nice, serviceable size, and under Nathan's careful direction, it worked sufficient magic to keep Grant feeling interested to the point that he was already looking forward to noticing that his dinner had settled. Grant tried to think of a way to backtrack on his last comment, but wasn't coming up with anything. Meanwhile Nathan had disappeared into the back of the house. With Nathan gone, a constellation of dogs and cats moved in to take his place next to and around Grant. Grant petted a small, orange tabby that hopped up into his lap. One of the old dogs brought him a nasty, half-chewed up tennis ball. He did his best to avoid touching the ball, scratching the dog on the head. At length Nathan reappeared with a large rectangular package wrapped in brown paper. He was smiling with a great deal of self-satisfaction.

"Let's go into the dining room and finish what we started," he said, walking past Grant with the package. Grant had no idea what he meant. He got up carefully, goose-stepped over the pile of animals that had gathered around him, and followed Nathan into the dining room. There Nathan had carefully laid the parcel down onto the dining room table. Grant stood next to Nathan at one corner of the table, not understanding what was happening.

"Happy birthday," said Nathan, kissing Grant on the cheek.

"But it's not my birthday," said Grant. "Mine's in November."

"Well, I'm late, then," said Nathan. "Or early, if you prefer. Whatever. Open it."

Grant was pleased, but unable to comprehend what was happening. The whole day had been such a surprise he wasn't sure what to think. Now and then it occurred to him that it was entirely possible that Nathan would scare again and disappear. If that were to happen, Grant wasn't sure what he would do. He knew he couldn't face a world of Darrens any more than Nathan could face a world of Davids. The day had been so full, the day he'd just spent with Nathan, that he wasn't sure he could live in a world where Nathan wasn't around. And so as he looked at the parcel before him, he suddenly found himself hesitating. To open it meant to trust Nathan, to give himself up, and not mind taking the risk. He understood why Nathan had run away, but he wasn't sure he could survive its happening again. Grant felt fearful that somehow, by opening the parcel that lay before him, he was endorsing a risk like no other he had ever faced or would face again.

Nathan saw Grant's hesitation and understood it. He felt more deeply connected to Grant than he had ever felt to anyone, seeing in that moment how uncertain Grant was, how full of hope and how tenderly fearful he was that his hope would be disappointed. At that moment, seeing Grant teeter on the edge of a possibility, Nathan understood that his heart was open. He said, "I don't deserve to have you in my life, but I am very thankful that I do. I love you, and

I want to take care of you and go through life together with you. I know I hurt you by running away and hiding, and I'm not sure I even want you to forgive me for that so much as just give me the chance to make it up to you. I don't have a whole lot to offer, sweetheart, but I would be the happiest faggot on the face of the earth if you'd let me give myself to you. This thing here is just a token of that. It doesn't matter whether you open it or not, as long as you believe me when I tell you that I love you and I want to spend the rest of my life with you."

Grant looked at him. He knew Nathan was speaking the truth. He knew they were connected. He believed they had a chance at staying that way. He knew their life mattered.

And so, after another delay of an hour or so, Nathan and Grant puttered back into the dining room, Grant dressed in Becky's robe, Nathan in Alice's. they sat down at the dining table and Nathan watched while Grant opened the package. It delighted Nathan to see Grant's complete surprise at finding the contents of the package were a copy of the Kollwitz woodcut that had been the cause of their first meeting. Grant was completely dumbfounded. "Where on earth did you find a copy of the same woodcut?" asked Grant.

"It isn't another copy," said Nathan. "Look at the frame."

Grant couldn't believe what he was seeing. "How?" he asked.

"Fate," said Nathan. "I can't think of another explanation. I was in Savannah with my friend Mark, on a buying spree. I went to this estate auction, and there was your woodcut. I saw it and I realized what an asshole I'd been by hiding out, and I bought it, right then and there."

"But you must have had to spend some money," said Grant. "I mean, you shouldn't have, Nathan," he said. They both had a laugh over the honest triteness of Grant's response.

"It made me see what I needed to see," said Nathan. "What more could you ask of a work of art? Believe me, it was a bargain," he said. "And I think it's time we took it out of the frame and had a look at it. You game?"

"Sure," said Grant.

"Why don't you do the honors?" asked Nathan, handing Grant a utility knife.

"You don't think I'll fuck it up?" asked Grant.

"Just cut slowly, along one side of the frame," said Nathan. Together they turned the woodcut face down. "I think you'll do well to start at the top side of the frame," said Nathan. The entire back of the frame was covered in heavy paper that was tacked to the back of the frame. Nathan's idea was to take a utility knife and cut carefully along one side of the frame to free the paper from the frame. Once the paper had been cut free on all four sides, it would then be possible to remove the image from the frame, take it out and get a better idea of its overall condition. Nathan was also hoping there might be some writing on the part of the image that was obscured by the matting. Perhaps, he thought, there was something that would tell something about the image. It was all but a miracle that the people who had bought the woodcut from Grant hadn't taken it out of the frame. Nathan was glad the image was intact. He was hoping it would offer another discovery.

Grant cut very expertly along the paper. His experience as a picture framer helped him. When he got the paper free, he peeled it back to reveal the inside of the frame. He was, indeed, surprised to make a discovery, as was Nathan. Inside the frame was a small yellowed parcel of what looked like personal papers of some kind. Grant lifted the parcel out of the frame. It was made of fine, heavy paper, as were its contents. Barely able to breathe, Grant opened the parcel, which was simply folded together, and separated the papers. There were a couple of letters, and there was a single sheet of paper that looked much older than the others. The single sheet contained a musical score, handwritten, covered with notes and corrections.

"Well," said Grant, "you wanted to surprise me, you certainly did that. What do you think this is?" asked Grant, nodding at the papers.

"I'd have to say it has something to do with an early owner of the woodcut," said Nathan, his eyes as wide as they could be.

They began inspecting the documents. They had trouble deciphering them because the script was very old-fashioned, and because none of the documents was in English. Gradually they came to see that the letters were written in German, and the musical score had notations in Italian, French, and a language neither of them could make out. Little by little, Nathan was able to decipher the first few lines of one of the letters. It appeared to have been written by a man, judging by the weight and character of the handwriting. The letter was signed, at the end, "affectionately yours, Jan." Jan is a Slavic or Polish name, Nathan thought, a man's name. Nathan got a pen and paper and wrote down what he could make of the letter:

My dearest Klara:

I hope things are well with you, and hope your father is getting healthy again. I miss you very much, and hope I shall see you again soon. Things are not very happy here, and I am fearful of much that I see around me. Germany is not the place you left.

This monkey-government that has been placed in Berlin is now gathering all kinds of people, talking badly about them as the state's enemies, as poison....

From what he could read in the rest of the letter, Nathan came to see that the discovery they had made in the woodcut's frame went beyond anything he'd ever seen. They would need to find some help to figure out what they really had.

Nathan made some inquiries over the next few days. Eventually he found an appraiser who was interested in looking at the documents and the woodcut. What emerged became a front-page story in the Centralia *Beacon*.

Art World Rocked by One-of-a-Kind Discovery

Centralia: Local artist Greg Parker and his friend Nathan Greenward are living on easy street, having made one of the most surprising art finds of the century. The find, if authenticated, presents an unusual problem and, some say, an opportunity for the art world to attach a value to a work of art.

The work of art in question is actually a group of works, and therein lies the heart of this unusual find. While shopping at a junk sale, Parker, who buys and sells antique art prints, found a rare, limited edition woodcut, a kind of art print, by the German artist Kathy Kollwich. Having bought the artwork for pennies, he sold it quickly for a handsome profit. Some time later his partner, antique dealer and former Centralian Nathan Greenward, bought the print a second time at another estate sale.

The real surprise came when the two entrepreneurs decided to clean the woodcut. Because the picture had been in its frame for over two hundred years, it was time to take it out and examine it to see if it needed conservation. When this was done, the artwork revealed a hidden treasure more astonishing than the artwork itself.

What the two men found now has art historians, music experts, and even international diplomats talking. It appears the woodcut's frame was used to hide a copy of a previously unknown musical work by the French composer Frederick Chopin. In addition, a number of letters written by the woodcut's first owner were found in the frame.

These letters give details of a relationship between the owner, a woman named Klara Westover, and a European man. While the letters don't clearly state as much, it appears that the relationship between Miss Westover and the European man was a romantic one. It also seems likely that the gentleman connected to Miss Westover was lost during the events of Word War II.

Experts are now busy arguing over the implications of this rare find. At issue are a number of questions that experts are trying to answer. First, experts are trying to decide whether the musical score, reputed to have been written in Chopin's own hand, is genuine. Since the announcement of the existence of the musical score, the Polish government has shown some interest in the manuscript, and there has been some hint that pressure is being brought to return the score to Poland as a piece of war booty improperly removed by the Nazis. Conversely, the Kathy Kollwich Foundation in Berlin, Germany has expressed interest in acquiring the woodcut together with the love letters. If the Kollwich Foundation ends up with the artwork and the letters, it has announced it intends to display them together as a special homage to the Holocaust.

Still other art experts have said that the entire group of documents—artwork, letters and musical manuscript—should be regarded and valued as a single work of art. The argument is that the work of art is inseparable from its historical context, and since these three pieces have become linked to each other, they now belong together and for all time. The fact of this unusual connection between these objects, experts say, has created a remarkable, unique work of art that goes beyond the limits or the value of any one piece.

One thing is for certain: Greg Parker and Nathan Greenward have made a big find that is sure to lead to a big payday.

Grant and Nathan found out about the *Beacon* article from Alice, who called Nathan to read it aloud over the phone. Nathan's only comment was that he was glad to see the *Beacon* had made so much progress fact-checking stories before it went to print. Grant was dismayed by the articles errors, thinking first of all that it made him look like an ignoramus to have the *Beacon* appear to give such a wrong date on the woodcut. Grant worried that someone might think it was he who had told the *Beacon* reporter that Kollwitz had made the woodcut around fifty years or so before she had been born. Nathan properly pointed out that the *Beacon* had done an admirable job of protecting Grant from any censure by misnaming him in the article; Nathan concluded that any reader of the article would have little chance of tracing the story back to Grant without a lot of help, so there was nothing to be gained by worrying about the matter. All that remained was for Grant and Nathan to hear back from Sotheby's, where the whole lot had been shipped off to be sold at auction.

Chapter Twenty-Eight

"So what do you think we ought to do?" asked Nathan.

"About what?" asked Grant.

"About setting up house," said Nathan. "Together."

Six months had passed since the woodcut was sold at auction. The woodcut, the letters and the manuscript had been bought by an anonymous client. It was believed that the buyer was a wealthy Hong Kong businessman who had attended the auction by phone. The lot ended up being sold for two million, one hundred thousand dollars. Nathan had insisted that the proceeds be split evenly between Grant and him. After the auction, they had agreed to take things slowly, to not rush into anything. Grant stayed in his shop and outfitted the storeroom as a more comfortably appointed efficiency apartment. Nathan kept his rented house in Charleston, but ended up spending much of his time in Centralia with Grant, officially living with Becky and Alice. After six months of courtship, very successful, frequent lovemaking, and spending time together, Grant and Nathan found that, for all intents and purposes, they were living as a couple. Nathan had even imported a few of the less feral cats from Charleston and mixed them with Grant's gaggle of strays, so that Grant's store was beginning to look like a white trash petting zoo.

Business in Grant's shop was predictably brisk after the auction. News got out that Greg Parker was really Grant Barker, the owner of Quick Snacks, Hairstyles and Frames. People began frequenting the shop just to rub elbows with celebrity. A famous rock star who had taken up residence in Centralia came shopping with his entourage of clones, a curious group of men who all dressed and acted like him. The local morning news TV show orchestrated a segment shot from the store window of Grant's shop. Grant and Nathan had a great deal of fun watching the heavily made-up TV hosts chatter for the better part of an hour about absolutely nothing.

And so, at the end of a period of happiness punctuated by a few requisite tests of a budding relationship between two men with weighty histories, it became evident to both Grant and Nathan that the time was drawing near to decide how to cement their relationship with a more substantially blended household.

"So," said Nathan again, "What are you thinking?"

"About what?" asked Grant.

"About living together," said Nathan.

"Well, we're already pretty much doing that," said Grant. "I like it fine. You like it?"

"Of course I like it," said Nathan. "Never have been better. But we don't really formally live together. I have my stuff in Charleston and at Becky and Alice's, and this really is your space that I hang out a lot in. I don't think that really counts as a home." Nathan could see that though Grant was happy to be connected to Nathan, he was still, perhaps, a little bit skittish about whether or not to believe that they really were a couple. "Grant?" asked Nathan.

"Yeah?" answered Grant.

"You want to get married?"

"Sure," said Grant. "You did mean married to you, right?" he added.

"Yes," said Nathan. "I did. So if you want to get married, you think we might start looking for a real place to live together?"

"Wait a minute, wait a minute," said Grant. "Back up a little. Is that it?"

"What do you mean, is that it?" asked Nathan.

"Is that your idea of a proposal?" asked Grant.

"Honey, we're gay, we don't have to do it like straight people do it," said Nathan. "You know what you want, I know what I want, and that's that," said Nathan. Even as the words were coming out of his mouth, though, he knew he was making a mistake. "Should I start over?" Nathan asked.

"Depends on the outcome you're looking for," said Grant.

"Well, we're already pretty much married, except that we don't officially live together," said Nathan. He could tell by the look on Grant's face that his speech wasn't working particularly well.

"See?" asked Nathan. "I've already begun to take you for granted. Isn't that nice? Doesn't it prove how much I love you? Doesn't it prove I really do believe in you and trust you, and know that you won't leave and I won't leave and we'll keep on going? Honey, let's keep going, only let's take a few steps further and really become one man, together." Nathan wasn't sure where that last remark came from, nor was he all that sure what it meant, but he liked the way it sounded: becoming one man together. Like the myth of the androgyne. "We've already begun to act the same, and we've already—"

"Started finishing each other's sentences?" asked Grant. "one man together? Is that what you said?" said Grant. He wasn't sure he understood what it meant, either, but he also liked the sound of it.

Still, he didn't feel as though he'd been asked properly. "So, is that it?" asked Grant.

Nathan saw he wasn't going to get anywhere until he laid his cards on the table, completely, once and for all.

"Grant?" asked Nathan.

"Yes?" answered Grant.

"Grant, I love you more than I've ever loved anyone. When I look at you I can't believe you're here with me. You're so daggum handsome it takes my breath away. Every time I look at you I want to throw you down on the ground, chew off all your clothes and lick you 'til your own mama couldn't recognize you. I feel safer with you than I've ever felt with anyone I've ever met, I feel comfortable with you, and I want nothing more than to make you as happy as you make me, though I'm not sure I'm smart enough or special enough to accomplish that. But I'd love to try. Grant, will you please marry me and stay with me forever?"

That did it. Grant knew that Nathan loved him, and he knew he loved Nathan back. He knew he would never find a better match than he had before him now, and he knew he would never be as happy without Nathan as with him. Finally, Grant took a deep breath, and said:

"Sure," said Grant. "I have been waiting to hear those words for some time now. Yes, Nathan, I will marry you, and I will stay with you forever." Then it was Grant who added the part that Nathan was really looking for. "Nathan?" he asked.

"Yes?" answered Nathan.

"What would you think about looking around a bit for a place to build a nest?" asked Grant.

Nathan smiled. "I think that's a great idea," he said. They held onto each other for dear life. For both of them, a whole lot of crap fell away forever during that long, tender embrace.

Chapter Twenty-Nine

Alice woke up one Saturday morning and began going about her normal daily routine. She navigated her way through a crowd of large fat dogs with furiously wagging tails and plump mewling cats winding deftly around her feet. She made it all the way to the kitchen without stumbling or cursing or scolding a single beast. All the while she could hear Becky snoring loudly, never perturbed in the least by all the thumping, galloping and cavorting all the animals indulged in as they anticipated being fed their morning portion. Having quickly and efficiently fed the whole crowd, Alice ground the coffee, set it to perk, and toasted an English muffin. The coffee made, the muffin toasted, she slathered it with fake butter and real orange marmalade, set the muffin where she was fairly sure the cats wouldn't be likely to jump up and start sniffing at it, and then hurried to the front door to see if the paper and possibly the mail had arrived.

To her delight and surprise, both mail and paper were in. This would give her reading material for a good hour or so, which she would enjoy in silent solitude, not counting the ten or so animals always hanging about. She went back into the kitchen, poured her coffee, got her muffin, and sat down at the kitchen table. She flipped through the paper to find her favorite parts: the op/ed pieces by Maureen Dowd and Frank Rich, followed by the front page stories, then the arts section, then the magazine, reserving the rest of the reading material for later that day. Today she was especially interested in a piece on contractor fraud in Iraq, but she knew if she read it this early in the day, she'd end up staying mad the whole day, so she decided to hold off until later on reading that piece.

After reading the paper, she decided to look through the mail. She thought about going to wake up Becky, fearing that if the latter slept too long, she'd never get to sleep that night. After a little deliberation Alice decided to let Becky sleep a wee bit longer. Leafing through the mail, Alice found a letter with a foreign postmark. She wondered how she'd missed it when she picked up the mail. Sure it was from Nathan, she quickly grew excited at the prospect of hearing from her dear friend. She tore the envelope open and noticed, right from the start, that it wasn't Nathan's handwriting. Racing to the end of the letter to find a signature, she found it was from Grant:

> Dear Alice and Becky:
>
> Nathan has asked me to write to invite you all to come and visit. I'm glad he suggested this, as it gives me a chance to say hello, first of all, and because I agree with him that it would be wonderful to have Becky and you come and spend some time with us. I know you don't know me very well, of course, since we really haven't spent a whole lot of time together--at least not yet--but I hope that if you do come, as I hope you will, we will be able to get to know each other better. We've settled into our place pretty comfortably. It's large by French standards: two bedrooms, a nice-sized living room, a real kitchen, a real bathroom, and a balcony that overlooks the interior courtyard of the building we're in. We're on the fourth floor, and the building, which dates from the mid-eighteenth century, is typically Parisian, so that means lots of windows, for one thing.
>
> Given what we've undertaken to do, we're doing well and we've set ourselves up pretty comfortably. We've met our neighbors across the hall, who are also gay and very friendly. They're helping us both with our French, and they're also helping us to negotiate living in our new hometown. The French don't seem to be as interested in

getting things done as in making the most out of the
process of negotiating and arguing, so making the few
improvements we've wanted to make to our little space
(we are a couple of fags, after all, so accepting the place
as it is is, well, unacceptable) has been a learning experience. We're concentrating on looking around for a space
to open a business, if we can move our way through the
maze of complications that that entails, and given how
much of the time it seems that everyone in the city is on
strike, we're trying to learn to be patient. All in all, we're
in good shape. We're together, which is the most important thing, and we are doing what we are doing not because we have to but because it's what we want. Who
could ask for a better gig than that?

It's still hard to believe all that's happened in the past
several months. A year ago I was recovering from being
stabbed and robbed, thinking I was going to lose my
business, feeling pretty alone. Now I'm living in the
most beautiful city in the world with the man I love, and
we're having a wonderful time. None of this would be
possible without Nathan, and I can honestly tell you that
not a day goes by without my finding some way to thank
him for all he's made possible for me. I would have
loved him, of course, without all this happening—finding
the documents hidden in the frame of the woodcut, selling the whole lot at auction for all that money. Nathan
didn't have to share a bit of what he got off the woodcut
and the documents, but he made it clear over and over
that as far as he was concerned, it was all always ours
and not just his. I don't know if I can ever show him
properly how much I appreciate his generosity. I hope I
never fail to keep trying. I think I probably started falling
in love with Nathan the first time we met, so as I see it,
that's where my good luck really began.

So far, moving here seems to have been a good decision.
Being in Paris does have its downside, I'll admit. Like I
said before, it seems every week some group of workers
goes on strike, and often it's whoever is in charge of
running the trains. We're learning to cope with that kind
of disruption, but to tell the truth, this town's so easy to
get around in, the strikes don't—or at least haven't yet—
affect us all that much, except to provide a little street

theatre when the crowds come marching by, looking very chic and not the least bit distressed, for all their slogans about tyranny and liberty and all that French stuff. At the heart of things, we're finding that Paris is like a collection of villages, with the intimacy of village life, the comfort of good neighbors and the endless variety of new things and places to explore and come to love. The French are kind of tough and stony from the outside, and they can seem really forbidding. Once they let you in, however, it's wonderful. We know we're outsiders here, and even if we stay here a long time, we probably will always be outsiders, but I can't tell you how nice it is to be treated like neighbors by the people who are your neighbors. People here take time for each other, they don't put up with bullshit, and they don't hand it out, either. The honesty and the genuine friendship are a refreshing change from what I've found mostly back in America, with the exception of you two and a few others.

It's a shame that cities like Centralia are so lonely, that they do so little to take advantage of the potential for good that bringing large numbers of people to live in close proximity can offer, as it does here. I hope we can make a go of it, and I think Nathan is also very happy here, also very committed to staying. From time to time we miss some things about being in the South—all the things you might think we'd miss, like cicadas singing, warm summer evenings, soul food, that sort of thing. But aside from agreeing that neither of us likes what's happening to American cities: the Starbucking, what the French call the *disneyfication*, of everything, the shallowness and passivity of the people (a few folks like you all excepted, of course), the essential phoniness and blandness that seems to be overtaking the whole country under what has become the First Republic of Gilead— and the shoddy way the country has allowed gay people to be used as campaign fodder while the rest of the civilized world is behaving very differently, all that made it clear to us that we needed to leave, needed to find a more human place to try and make a living, to make an investment of ourselves. When the opportunity came, it didn't take much for us to decide. If we were going to move, it made sense to move to the best city on earth, and so, here we are.

If the French government will let us and if we can find a space to do it, we're going to open a business and operate it together. We hope that can happen somewhere in Paris. Right now we're looking in an area near the old Halles Centrales, in a neighborhood called Étienne Marcel. It's a little bit northwest of the center of town, and it's very French, and pretty gay-friendly. It feels and looks like a real French neighborhood that hasn't been messed up with cheesy tourist crap. We'd like to open a little place that offers coffee, art, gifts and collectibles. The French authorities are arguing over whether we can offer food and dry goods in the same place, so that's the hold-up. It also puzzles them that the name of the place suggests we offer hair care, when in fact we intend to do just about everything but that (may throw in fresh flowers, as well, but that's another trip down the licensing road, so we'll see). Anyway, if we can make it and find a niche here, we could end up turning into a pair of semi-real bourgeois Frenchies.

One dark cloud on the horizon: lately we're seeing a BUNCH of other Americans lurking around town, obviously stalking real estate deals. That makes us nervous. We hope the town doesn't get overrun by snotty yuppie lawyer couples and their ilk. Double prams and lots of conspicuous consumption and endless reserves of smugness: eeek! If things turn sour on account of the other expats, we may have to skeedaddle and find another un-American paradise to invade. In the meantime, we're doing all we can to learn to pass as a couple of Frenchies. Nathan looks pretty good in a beret, I think.

So this is your official invitation to come and see us and stay with us whenever you want. There is no better place on earth than where we are now, and we're lucky to be here. We have our life and our health, and we're in the most beautiful, most livable city in the world. The only way it could be better would be to have all our friends with us, so please come and join the fun when you can. Maybe when you come, we'll be able to walk through our new place, and maybe you'll be able to take home a souvenir from our little corner of heaven, our little Bistro Coiffures.

Yours truly, *GB*

www.ingramcontent.com/pod-product-compliance
Lightning Source LLC
Chambersburg PA
CBHW020653270326
41928CB00005B/100